Bring Your Own Devices (BYOD) Survival Guide

Bring Your Own Devices (BYOD) Survival Guide

Jessica Keyes

CRC Press
Taylor & Francis Group
Boca Raton London New York

CRC Press is an imprint of the
Taylor & Francis Group, an **informa** business
AN AUERBACH BOOK

CRC Press
Taylor & Francis Group
6000 Broken Sound Parkway NW, Suite 300
Boca Raton, FL 33487-2742

Printed on acid-free paper
Version Date: 20130204

International Standard Book Number-13: 978-1-4665-6503-6 (Hardback)

Library of Congress Cataloging-in-Publication Data

Keyes, Jessica, 1950-
Bring your own devices (BYOD) survival guide / author, Jessica Keyes.
pages cm
Summary: "This book explains and then helps readers live with the psycho-techno phenomenon that is bring your own technology (BYOT). Readers will learn how to understand these new end-users and their demands, as well as the strategic and tactical ramifications of these demands. Next, it covers the broad range of technical considerations such as selection, connectivity, training, support, and security. The text includes best practices and case studies of well-known companies, including IBM, Ford, and CarFax"--Provided by publisher.
Includes bibliographical references and index.
ISBN 978-1-4665-6503-6 (hardback)
1. Computer technical support. I. Title.

QA76.9.T43K49 2013
004.068'8--dc23 2012050919

Visit the Taylor & Francis Web site at
http://www.taylorandfrancis.com

and the CRC Press Web site at
http://www.crcpress.com

Contents

Preface

BRING YOUR OWN DEVICES (BYOD) SURVIVAL GUIDE

Where once end-users queued up to ask IT permission to buy a new computer or new version of software, they're now bypassing IT altogether and buying it on their own. From laptops to smartphones, from iPads to any number of software apps, end-users have tasted their freedom and love it. IT is just never going to be the same. *BYOD Survival Guide* explains and then helps you live with the psycho-techno phenomenon that is "bring your own devices."

The roots of BYOD can be traced back to the consumerization of all things tech, where technical wizardry is no longer purely the domain of the geek who works for the IT department. Geeks can now be found all over the organization. Many of them are Millennials, the first generation to grow up with computers from birth. These workers want to make their own technology choices, whether those choices are on the "approved" list or not. Whether the company pays for it or not.

BYOD Survival Guide provides the guidance necessary for living in this brave new world. You'll first learn how to understand these new end-users and their demands, as well as the strategic and tactical ramifications of these demands. We will then cover the broad range of technical considerations such as financial considerations, selection, connectivity, training, support, security, and integration with the cloud and social networking.

But BYOD cannot be considered apart from the rest of the enterprise. It must be properly integrated into the organization's IT infrastructure, including its information assets. Thus, we will spend some time in addressing topics such as content and data management, risk assessment, performance measurement and management, and even configuration management.

BYOD Survival Guide also comes with a set of Quick Start guides, which provide tips for such things as assessing costs, cloud integration, and even legal issues. There is also a full set of appendices that include information on everything from security settings for Apple iOS devices to a sample employee mobile device agreement.

This book is geared for the small- to medium-size enterprises (SME) that need to integrate BYOD into their environment. Since the typical SME does not have the formalized infrastructure that a larger organization might have, we do spend quite a bit of time going over the basics of typical controlling methodologies and discuss how BYOD fits into the picture. Larger organizations may benefit from this discussion as well.

I would especially like to thank those who assisted me in putting this book together. As always, my editor, John Wyzalek, was instrumental in getting my project approved and providing great encouragement. I would also like to thank Debra Nencel, who assisted in the compilation of the Quick Start guides.

About the Author

Jessica Keyes, PhD, is president of New Art Technologies, Inc., a high-technology and management consultancy and development firm started in New York in 1989.

Keyes has given seminars for such prestigious universities as Carnegie Mellon, Boston University, the University of Illinois, James Madison University, and San Francisco State University. She is a frequent keynote speaker on the topics of competitive strategy and productivity and quality. She is former advisor for DataPro, McGraw-Hill's computer research arm, as well as a member of the Sprint Business Council. Keyes is also a founding board of director member of the New York Software Industry Association. She completed a two-year term on the Mayor of New York City's Small Business Advisory Council. She currently facilitates doctoral and other courses for the University of Phoenix and is a member of the Faculty Council for the College of Information Systems & Technology. She has been the editor for WGL's *Handbook of eBusiness* and CRC Press's *Systems Development Management* and *Information Management*.

Prior to founding New Art, Keyes was managing director of R&D for the New York Stock Exchange and has been an officer with Swiss Bank Co. and Banker's Trust, both in New York City. She holds a master of business administration from New York University and a doctorate in management from Northcentral University.

A noted columnist and correspondent with over 200 articles published, Keyes is the author of the following books

The New Intelligence: AI in Financial Services, HarperBusiness, 1990
The Handbook of Expert Systems in Manufacturing, McGraw-Hill, 1991
Infotrends: The Competitive Use of Information, McGraw-Hill, 1992
The Software Engineering Productivity Handbook, McGraw-Hill, 1993
The Handbook of Multimedia, McGraw-Hill, 1994
The Productivity Paradox, McGraw-Hill, 1994
Technology Trendlines, Van Nostrand Reinhold, 1995
How to Be a Successful Internet Consultant, McGraw-Hill, 1997
Webcasting, McGraw-Hill, 1997
Datacasting, McGraw-Hill, 1997

The Handbook of Technology in Financial Services, Auerbach, 1998
The Handbook of Internet Management, Auerbach, 1999
The Handbook of eBusiness, Warren, Gorham & Lamont, 2000
The Ultimate Internet Sourcebook, Amacom, 2001
How to Be a Successful Internet Consultant, 2nd ed., Amacom, 2002
Software Engineering Handbook, Auerbach, 2002
Real World Configuration Management, Auerbach, 2003
Balanced Scorecard, Auerbach, 2005
Knowledge Management, Business Intelligence, and Content Management: The IT Practitioner's Guide, Auerbach, 2006
X Internet: The Executable and Extendable Internet, Auerbach, 2007
Leading IT Projects: The IT Manager's Guide, Auerbach, 2008
Marketing IT Products and Services, Auerbach, 2009
Implementing the Project Management Balanced Scorecard, Auerbach, 2010
Social Software Engineering: Development and Collaboration with Social Networking, Auerbach, 2011
Enterprise 2.0: Social Networking Tools to Transform Your Organization, Auerbach, 2012

1

The BYOD Revolution

It's not a question of if. It's not even a question of when. It's a question of, will you be ready? Employees have long been using mobile devices. First came laptops, then PDAs. When smarts were added to those PDAs, employees discovered that they could take their office on the road. BlackBerrys became so ubiquitous that the term *crackberry* was invented to describe the addictive properties of 24 × 7 connectivity. Then Steve Jobs made the smartphone even smarter.

At first, organizations carefully controlled the use of the mobile devices hanging off the corporate network. But employees soon became tired of lugging around multiple devices, one for personal and one for corporate use. Employees also didn't much like being forced to use a particular device in a particular configuration. Many started sneaking their personal devices onto their corporate networks. And a trend took off.

Let's look at some statistics. According to Cisco, three out of five workers say that they no longer need to be in the office to be productive. The same research predicts that knowledge workers will have an average 3.3 devices each by 2014. International Data Corporation (IDC) estimates that by 2015 there will be over 200 million mobile workers in the United States alone. Many of these workers are using smart devices such as the Apple iPhone or Android devices. Astonishingly, it is estimated that there are about 400,000 apps in the Apple App Store and over 200,000 apps in the Android Market—now Google Play. So, is it any wonder that over 70% of organizations have adopted Bring Your Own Devices (BYOD)? Further, Gartner predicts this number to increase to 90% by 2014. Most interestingly, a very high percentage of Gen Y workers think that it's a right rather than a privilege to use their own devices at work.

WHAT'S IN IT FOR THE ORGANIZATION?

The first thing companies think of is cost. BYOD generally shift some costs to the employee. Since employees are paying for their own devices and connectivity the organization can expect to save somewhere around $80 per month per user. This savings can quickly add up.

Another advantage is that most people tend to acquire the latest and greatest technology. Thus, it can be expected that many employees will always have the most recent models of the device and versions of software that runs on that device. Gone are the problems and costs associated with constant upgrading.

Perhaps the most significant benefit is employee satisfaction. Employees can use what makes them happy. In doing so, they'll be far more productive than if they are forced to standardize on a particular set of devices and software. Some even suggest that employees will work longer hours because they will be able to interact with their systems, using their tools of choice, at any time of day or night.

SO, WHAT CAN GO WRONG?

With the good usually comes the bad. Security is first and foremost. The number of Wi-Fi hotspots has grown exponentially, exposing more mobile devices to hackers who monitor traffic on open networks. In addition, losing a tiny smartphone is easy to do. McAfee, the security company, says that over 4% of smartphones are lost or stolen each year. Each unsecured stolen or lost phone opens the organization up to the chance of a breach of corporate systems and/or data.

Another major concern is how these mobile devices are actually being used. While corporate-owned devices usually come with an acceptable use policy, it's not all that straightforward to craft such a policy when the device is owned by the employee. Consider how a smartphone may be used. There is a proliferation of social networks and other websites that might be problematic. How should a BYOD acceptable use policy deal with this, if at all?

Costs might be an issue as well. Even though there is a cost saving to the organization as the employee picks up the bill for the device and the network, someone still has to man the help desk. There is some evidence that calls to help desks about devices not owned by the organization are three to four times more expensive than the equivalent calls for known technology.

Then, there's the data. Some organizations must deal with regulatory mandates that require very strict security measures. How shall this sort of security be architected when BYOD is the paradigm, or on any smart device? Trust is the underlying principle behind enterprise security. Which users to trust and when to trust them should be considered when the organization's security policy is being crafted. What to do about that high-level employee who is given access to proprietary financial data but somehow disables encryption?

Legal experts have weighed in on the subject and found that organizations might be vulnerable in several areas. BYOD necessarily blurs the line between work and play. This creates performance management challenges when trying to regulate on-the-job conduct. There is also a possibility of liability for disability discrimination if the employer finds out, for example, that the employee has downloaded an app for diabetes management and the employee is at some point terminated. Other legal concerns include harassment (e.g., untoward comments), overtime liability (e.g., unrecorded overtime), minimum wage problems (i.e., smartphone users often work long hours), privacy concerns (e.g., what can the employer delete), and workplace safety (e.g., texting-while-driving accidents).

MOBILE DEVICE MANAGEMENT

When personal computers became commonplace, organizations realized that they needed to somehow keep track of all of these assets. Thus, asset management was born. Essentially, asset management was a passive systematic process of operating, maintaining, upgrading, and disposing of assets cost-effectively.

With the advent of mobile, asset management needed a shot of adrenalin. This adrenalin is in the form of Mobile Device Management (MDM) systems. MDM secures, monitors, manages, and supports mobile devices deployed across mobile operators, service providers, and enterprises. MDM functionality typically includes over-the-air distribution of applications, data and configuration settings for all types of mobile devices, including mobile phones, smartphones, tablet computers, mobile computers, and mobile printers. This applies to both company-owned and employee-owned (BYOD) devices.

MDM gives IT the ability to control some aspects of device usage. For example, it can be determined if a jailbroken device is being used. Jailbreaking from the Apple perspective is the process of removing the limitations imposed by the company on devices running the iOS operating system. Jailbreaking allows iOS users to gain root access to the operating system, allowing them to download additional applications, extensions, and themes that are unavailable through the official Apple App Store. MDM also enables IT to forbid devices that aren't using PINs (personal identification numbers), if this is part of the security policy. MDM permits IT to disable remote e-mail, disconnect users from accessing the network, and even remotely wipe the device. A more complete list of functionality is listed in Table 1.1.

We'll cover MDM as it relates to mobile content management (MCM) in the chapter on content management.

TABLE 1.1

Typical MDM Functionality

Mobile Device Management Functionality
FOTA—Firmware over the air updates
Diagnostics
Remote Configuration and Provisioning
Security
Backup/Restore
Network Usage and Support
Server Deployment
Mobile Asset Tracking and Management
Remote Lock and Wipe
Device Provisioning
Software Installation
Troubleshooting and Diagnostic Tools
Policy Application
Logging and Reporting
Remote Control and Administration
GPS Tracking and "Breadcrumb" Mapping (last known location)

CONSUMERIZATION OF IT

Devices are just the leading edge of this revolution. The consumerization of IT, sometimes known as CoIT, also includes, among other technologies, open source software (think Google's Chrome browser) and cloud storage.

Apple, Google, and even Amazon have cloud offerings. The cloud provides the user with the ability to create, add, delete, and even share information not stored on corporate servers. The cloud is not really all that new. Back in the ancient days of computing, it was referred to as time sharing. However, this was pre-Internet and before there were the security concerns associated with the cloud you hear about today.

In the summer of 2012 these security problems became all too obvious as the press covered in depth the case of some hackers who used what is termed simple trickery to hack a prominent technology journalist's Amazon, Apple, Google, and Twitter accounts. Security analysts claim that these Internet-delivered services are not doing enough to properly authenticate users. These services require varying amounts of information to open and then access online accounts. Some ask for only a tiny amount of information to make changes. Mat Honan, the *Wired* journalist targeted, detailed how hackers tricked an Amazon rep into revealing the last four digits of his credit card number. They then used this information to persuade Apple to reset Honan's Apple ID password, which enabled the hackers to wipe Honan's iPhone, iPad, and MacBook, destroying all files in the process. A simple solution for this, one which most web services will not offer any time soon due to the inconvenience factor, is multifactor authentication. For example, if I want to change the password on my bank account, my bank will text me a one-time pin that I use to login. Not 100% secure, but far better than what many mobile cloud users are offered.

Aside from authentication, those assessing the use of cloud services for mobile users should closely question cloud services vendors about encryption of information. Questions companies would want answered include which encryption code is being used and information about device hardening methods. Some time ago the Cloud Security Alliance (https://cloudsecurityalliance.org/) created the Security, Trust, and Assurance Registry (STAR), the goal of which is to index the security features of cloud services vendors using a 170-point questionnaire. It's been a bit slow to catch on, but you can see the completed entries for Amazon, some Microsoft offerings, and Box.com, among others. If your prospective cloud services vendors are not on this list, then I suggest finding out why. You might also want to download the questionnaire yourself and require these vendors to respond to the points listed.

Still, there is a lot of value in moving to the cloud although cloud computing means different things to different people. In general terms, cloud computing is a convenient, on-demand model for network access to a shared pool of configurable computing resources (e.g., networks, servers, storage, applications, and services) that can be rapidly provisioned and released with minimal management effort or service provider interaction. The cloud element of cloud-computing derives from a metaphor used for the Internet, from the way it is often depicted in computer network diagrams. Conceptually it refers to a model of scalable, real-time, Internet-based information technology services and resources, satisfying the computing needs of users, without the users incurring the costs of maintaining the underlying infrastructure. Examples involve providing common business applications online, which are accessed from a web browser, with software and data stored on the "cloud" provider's servers, as shown in Table 1.2.

The list of cloud computing solutions and service providers continues to grow daily. The sample in Table 1.3 is illustrative and does not imply an endorsement.

Among internal sourcing approaches, the most relevant are the following:

- **Own**—Where the organization that uses the resource also owns or directly controls it. The resource may be totally insourced or totally outsourced, but the organization is its exclusive user.
- **Share**—Where several organizations share the resource, through joint governance arrangements and with one organization being

TABLE 1.2

What Is the Cloud?

Essential Characteristics	Delivery Models	Deployment Models
On-demand Self-service	Software as a Service (SaaS)	Private Cloud
Broad Network Access	Platform as a Service (PaaS)	Community Cloud
Resource Pooling	Infrastructure as a Service (IaaS)	Public Cloud
Rapid Elasticity		Hybrid Cloud
Measured Service		

TABLE 1.3

Sample Cloud Offerings

Software as a Service (SaaS)		**Platform as a Service**	
Google Apps	Oracle On Demand Apps	Amazon E2C	Coghead
Zoho Office	NetSuite ERP	Salesforce.com Force.com	Etelos
Workday	Salesforce.com SFA	Google App Engine	LongJump
Microsoft Office Live			Boomi
			Microsoft Azure
External IaaS		**Internal IaaS**	
HP/EDS (TBD)	Joyent	HP Adaptive Infrastructure as a Service	
IBM Blue Cloud	Rackspace		
Sun Grid	Jamcracker		
Utility Systems Management Tools+		**Utility Application Development**	
VMWare	Xen	Data Synapse	IBM WebSphere XD
IBM Tivoli	Zuora	Univa UD	BEA Weblogic Server VE
Cassatt	Aria Systems	Elastra Cloud Server	Mule
Parallels	eVapt	3tera App Logic	

responsible for either owning the resources or sourcing them as deemed fit.

- **Centralize**—Similar to the above, but without the joint governance component. That is, organizations are simply clients of whoever provides access to the resource.
- **Commoditizing**—Where the resource or the way to access it or both is completely commoditized, and it is managed outside the organization's boundaries without any control of where it is located.

Perhaps one of the most interesting cloud developments is the possibility for IT to provide cloud-based Windows desktop services, with shared resources. This is known as Desktop as a Service or DaaS or hosted virtual desktop (HVD), which works similarly to the client/server model with the server and services being in the cloud, as shown in Figure 1.1. Whether that BYOD user is lugging along his aging Windows XP laptop or a smart new iPhone, HVD enables that user to provide standard office functions

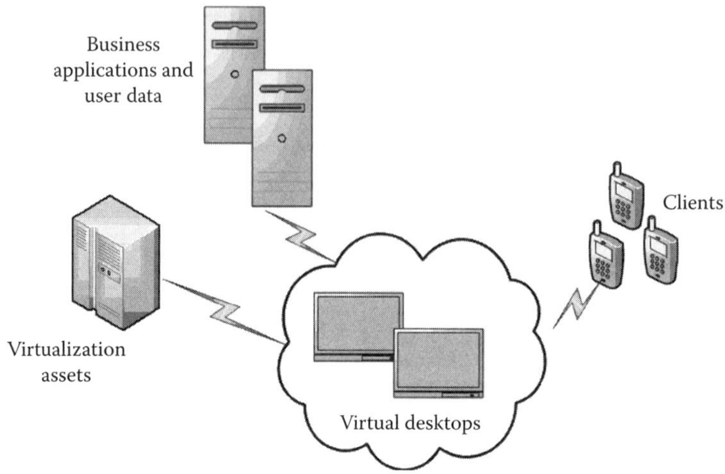

FIGURE 1.1
Hosted virtual desktop (HVD).

or application specific functionality. Quite a few vendors have jumped into this marketplace, such as Applications2U, Desktone, dinCloud, ICC Global Hosting, and Nivio, with a May 2012 test by networkworld.com finding that dinCloud was the best of the lot in terms of client options, management, compatibility, and speed.

One of the biggest benefits of cloud infrastructures such as Amazon's is the ability to store almost unlimited data without having to resort to purchasing new and more expensive servers. This has enabled organizations to amass what is known as big data, traditionally defined as exceeding the ability of commonly used software tools to capture, manage, and process the data within a tolerable elapsed time. It is now easier and cheaper to aggregate data from governmental, academic, in-house, and other sources. It's data warehousing and mining on steroids.

With big data comes the need to manipulate it. Apache's Hadoop (http://hadoop.apache.org/) is a framework that allows for the distributed processing of large data sets across clusters of computers using a simple programming model. It is designed to scale up from single servers to thousands of machines, each offering local computation and storage. MapR (http://www.mapr.com/) provides a commercial version of the open source Hadoop. The company provides some insight into how Hadoop can be used:

1. Customer insights—Large financial service providers have adopted Hadoop to improve customer profile analysis to help determine eligibility for equity capital, insurance, mortgage, or credit.
2. Fraud detection and analysis—Hadoop provides a scalable method to more easily detect many types of fraud or loss prevention, and perform effective risk management. Hadoop is also being used to develop models that predict future fraud events.
3. Micro targeting—Banks have numerous disparate data systems (e.g., loans, mortgages, investments) that need to be aggregated in order to provide an up-to-date view on customer profitability, consistent CRM, and customized product recommendations and offerings.
4. Risk mitigation—Hadoop is used to analyze potential market trends and understand future possibilities to mitigate the risk of financial positions, total portfolio assets, and capital returns.
5. Web-scale analysis—Hadoop is used to analyze what is being said on the web at large and on social networks in particular. Sentiment can apply to individual companies or products or reflect general customer satisfaction. This has potential to improve marketing to existing customers through better targeting.
6. Trade analysis—Financial service firms use Hadoop to analyze the daily streams of transaction data in conjunction with unstructured news or social media feeds, or to back-test their trading algorithms.

BUSINESS AS USUAL

Given all the brouhaha over BYOD, one would expect that the world has radically changed for IT. While it is quite true that there are some major management concerns with the control of these devices, one should not forget that it really is business as usual in terms of data coming into the organization, data leaving the organization, and data being transformed in the middle. Toward that end we're going to spend the rest of our time talking about how to integrate BYOD into the organization.

Before you embark on BYOD you will want to make a financial case for it. Although the big plus of moving to a BYOD model is that employees cover the costs, this is not the only model and variations really do need to be examined. In addition, there are some hidden costs such as training and support. Thus, performing ROI, cost benefit, and other financial analyses will give you a true cost picture for the organization and the employee.

Once a financial case for BYOD is made, the organization needs to develop its set of guidelines that will govern managing and securing BYOD as well as non-BYOD mobile devices. This includes use of the cloud, as we discussed above. A "free for all" or ad hoc approach to this is a sure recipe for disaster and presents a great deal of risk for the organization. A more detailed examination of assessment and mitigation of risks in a BYOD environment also needs to be performed.

The Capability Maturity Model (CMM) devised by the Software Engineering Institute of Carnegie Mellon (http://www.sei.cmu.edu/cmm/) has been used by a wide variety of organizations to increase the maturity level of their software engineering practices. A mature IT organization is one most able to align itself to meet the business process objectives of the organization.

The CMM model, as shown in Figure 1.2, consists of five levels of maturity that an IT department goes through on its way to becoming completely optimized and productive:

The initial level (level 1) of CMM is characterized by processes that are ad hoc where tools are informally applied. The repeatable level (level 2) of the CMM is characterized by the achievement of a stable process with a repeatable level of statistical control. The defined level (level 3) of CMM is characterized by the achievement of a solid foundation for major and continuing progress. The managed level (level 4) of CMM is characterized by substantial quality improvements and the use of comprehensive process

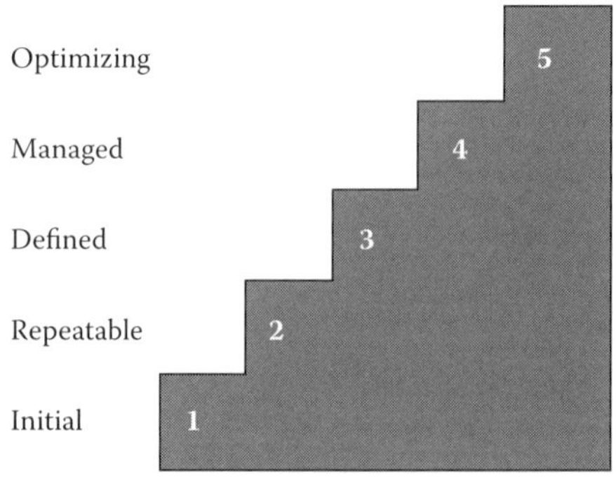

FIGURE 1.2
The Capability Maturity Model.

measurement. Finally, the managed level (level 5) of CMM provides evidence of major quality and productivity improvements.

Most organizations hover between levels 2 and 4, although all organizations should strive for level 5. To successfully integrate BYOD into the organization really does require an effort toward enhanced quality, controlled processes, and meticulous measurement. From an IT perspective this translates into tweaking standard processes to accommodate mobile usage. These processes include: resource management, which encompasses mobile device management (MDM); content management; configuration management; and performance measurement and management. All of these processes will be discussed later on in this book.

2

Making a Financial Case for BYOD

One would think that there is only a financial upside to employee BYOD. According to an Osterman Research Survey (http://www.osterman research.com/) of 117 mid to large enterprises, the annual IT labor cost per user was $294 in 2012, expected to rise to $339 in 2013. The survey also found that 41% of employees used a smartphone in 2012, expected to rise to 50% in 2013. Even if an employee uses his or her own devices, there are still costs associated with support, training, and service. Thus, a financial analysis needs to be done to justify BYOD just as you would any other technology. In this chapter, some typical financial analyses are presented that might be used toward this end.

SUPPORTING BYOD

BYOD is not an all or none proposition. While some organizations do pay the total cost for device and network, others pay for nothing at all. The vast majority fit somewhere in the middle. There are two financial models that organizations use should they want to financially support BYOD-enabled employees:

1. Stipends: Some organizations offer small stipends to employees on a monthly basis. The amount is typically between $40 and $70 per month. Some organizations offer a variable rate dependent upon job function. For the most part, the stipends are to be used to cover the data plan, although the voice plan is also sometimes covered.
2. Expense back: Some organizations have opted to permit employees to submit expense forms for the cost of services. Like stipends, most organizations will expense back just the data plan, with some opting

to also permit expense back of the voice plan. Often there is a cap on the amount that is permitted to be expensed back, with amounts exceeding the cap reimbursed with approval.

COST-BENEFIT ANALYSIS

There are many variables to be considered when performing financial analyses for BYOD, which can make analyses somewhat complicated. To make it easy to understand, I will provide very simplistic examples in this and the following sections.

In general, cost-benefit analysis is quite easy to understand. The process compares the costs of the system to the benefits of having that system. We all do this on a daily basis. For example, if I go out to buy a new $650 mobile device I weigh the cost of expending that $650 against the benefits of owning the mobile device. For example, these benefits might be the following:

1. Possible replacement of leased travel laptop. Cost savings $200/month.
2. Possible to reduce software maintenance costs due to replacement of laptop. Cost savings $450/year.

I summarize this in Table 2.1.

One-time capital costs such as computers are usually amortized over a certain period of time. For example, a device costing $650 can be amortized over five years, which means that instead of comparing one-time cost of $650 to the benefits of purchasing the device, I can compare a monthly cost instead. In the case of BYOD, I would not include the cost of the device, but I would need to include the cost of training and support.

TABLE 2.1

Cost-Benefit Analysis

Costs/One Time	Benefits/Year
$650	1. Rental computer savings: $200 × 12 = $2,400
	2. Maintenance savings: $450
$650/one time	$2,850/year
Potential Savings/Earnings	$2,200/year

Not all cost-benefit analyses are so clear-cut, however. In the example above, the benefits were both financially based. Not all benefits are so easily quantifiable. Benefits that can't be quantified are called intangible benefits. The following are examples:

1. Reduced turnaround time
2. Improved employee satisfaction
3. Compliance with mandates
4. Enhanced inter-company communication

Aside from having to deal with both tangible and intangible benefits, most cost-benefit analyses also need to deal with several alternatives. For example, you might want to compare the cost-benefit analysis of the employee purchasing the device versus the organization purchasing the device, or using a stipend or expense back option.

In each case a spreadsheet should be created that details one time as well as continuing costs. These should then be compared to the benefits of each alternative, both tangible as well as non-tangible.

An associated formula is the benefit-to-cost ratio (BCR). The computation of the financial benefit/cost ratio is done within the construct of the following formula: benefits/cost.

BREAK-EVEN ANALYSIS

All projects have associated costs. All projects will also have associated benefits. And make no mistake, BYOD is definitely a project. At the outset of a project, costs will usually exceed benefits. However, at some point the benefits will start outweighing the costs. This is called the *break-even point.* The analysis that is done to figure out when this break-even point will occur is called *break-even analysis.* In Table 2.2 the break-even point comes during the first year.

Calculating the break-even point in a project with multiple alternatives enables the manager to select the optimum solution. The project manager will generally select the alternative with the shortest break-even point.

TABLE 2.2

Break-even Analysis

Costs/One Time	Benefits/Year
$650	1. Rental computer savings: $200 × 12 = $2,400
	2. Maintenance savings: $450
$650/one time	$2,850/year
Potential Savings/Earnings	$2,200/year

ESTIMATING ROI FOR AN IT PROJECT

Most organizations want to select projects that have a positive return on investment. The return on investment, or ROI as it is most commonly known, is the additional amount earned after costs are earned back. In our "buy vs. not buy" decision discussed above we can see that the ROI is quite positive during the first, and especially during subsequent years of ownership.

IT and the finance department need to be joint owners of the ROI process. The basic formula for ROI is as follows:

$$\text{ROI} = \frac{\text{Benefit} - \text{Cost}}{\text{Cost}}$$

ROI calculations require the availability of large amounts of accurate data, which is sometimes unavailable to the manager. Many variables need to be considered and decisions made regarding which factors to calculate and which to ignore.

Before starting an ROI calculation, identify the following factors:

- Know what you're measuring: Successful ROI calculators isolate their true data from other factors, including the work environment and the level of management support.
- Don't saturate: Instead of analyzing every factor involved, pick a few. Start with the most obvious factors that can be identified immediately.
- Convert to money: Converting data into hard monetary values is essential in any successful ROI study. Translating intangible benefits into dollars is challenging and might require some assistance from the accounting or finance departments. The goal is to demonstrate the impact on the bottom line.

- Compare apples to apples: Measure the same factors before and after the project.

There are a variety of ROI techniques:

1. Treetop: Treetop metrics investigate the impact on profitability for the entire company. Profitability can take the form of cost reductions because of IT's potential to reduce workforce size for any given process.
2. Pure cost: There are several varieties of pure cost ROI techniques. Total Cost of Ownership (TCO) details the hidden support and maintenance costs over time that provide a more concise picture of the total cost. The Gartner Group's NOW, or Normalized Cost of Work Produced, index measures the cost of one's conducting a work task versus the cost to others doing similar work.
3. Holistic IT: This is the same as the IT scorecard, where the IT department tries to align itself with the traditional balanced scorecard performance perspective of financial, customer, internal operations, and employee learning and innovation.
4. Financial: Aside from ROI, Economic Value Added tries to optimize a company's shareholder wealth.

There are also a variety of ways of actually calculating ROI, but all should incorporate measures for the following:

1. Productivity: Output per unit of input
2. Processes: Systems, workflow
3. Human Resources: Costs and benefits for a specific initiative
4. Employee Factors: Retention, morale, commitment, and skills

The ROI calculation is not complete until the results are converted to dollars. This includes looking at combinations of hard and soft data. Hard data include such traditional measures as output, time, quality, and costs. In general, hard data are readily available and relatively easy to calculate. Soft data, hard to calculate, include morale, turnover rate, absenteeism, loyalty, conflicts avoided, new skills learned, new ideas, successful completion of projects, and so on.

After the hard and/or soft data have been determined, they need to be converted to monetary values:

Step 1: Focus on a single unit.
Step 2: Determine a value for each unit.
Step 3: Calculate the change in performance. Determine the performance change after factoring out other potential influences on the training results.
Step 4: Obtain an annual amount. The industry standard for an annual-performance change is equal to the total change in performance data during one year.
Step 5: Determine the annual value. The annual value of improvement equals the annual performance change, multiplied by the unit value. Compare the product of this equation to the cost of the program using this formula: ROI = net annual value of improvement – program

ROI calculations are based on valuations of improved work product, what is referred to as a cost-effectiveness strategy. BYOD ROI analysis should incorporate data such as the following:

Initial benefits worksheet
Calculation: hours/person average × cost/hour × # of people = total $ saved

1. Reduced time to learn system/job (worker hours)
2. Reduced supervision (supervision hours)
3. Reduced help from co-workers (worker hours)
4. Reduced calls to help line
5. Reduced down time (waiting for help, consulting manuals, etc.)
6. Fewer or no calls from help line to supervisor about overuse of help service

Continuing benefits worksheet
Calculation: hours/person average × cost/hour × # of people = total $ saved

1. Reduced time to perform operation (worker time)
2. Reduced overtime
3. Reduced supervision (supervisor hours)
4. Reduced help from co-workers (worker hours)
5. Reduced calls to help line
6. Reduced down time (waiting for help, consulting manuals, etc.)
7. Fewer or no calls from help line to supervisor about overuse of help service

8. Fewer mistakes (e.g., rejected transactions)
9. Fewer employees needed
10. Total savings in one year
11. Expected life of system in years

Quality benefits worksheet
Calculation: unit cost × # of units = total $ saved

1. Fewer mistakes
2. Speedier access to data
3. More responsive to customers
4. Faster decision making

Other benefits worksheet
Calculation: = $ saved per year

1. Reduced employee turnover
2. Reduced grievances
3. Reduced absenteeism/tardiness (morale improvements)

ROI spreadsheet calculation
Calculation: ROI = (Benefits – Costs)/Costs

1. Initial time saved total over life of system
2. Continuing worker hours saved total over life of system
3. Quality improvements with fixed costs total over life of system
4. Other possible benefits total over life of system
5. Total benefits
6. Total system costs (development, maintenance, and operation)

ROI evaluates an investment's potential by comparing the magnitude and timing of expected gains to the investment costs. For example, a new initiative costs $500,000 and will deliver an additional $700,000 in increased profits. Simple ROI = gains – investment costs/investment costs. ($700,000 – $500,000 = $200,000. $200,000/$500,000 = 40%.) This calculation works well in situations where benefits and costs are easily known, and is usually expressed as an annual percentage return.

However, technology investments frequently involve financial consequences that extend over several years. In this case, the metric has meaning only when the time period is clearly stated. Net present value (NPV) recognizes the time value of money by discounting costs and benefits over a period of time, and focuses either on the impact on cash flow rather than net profit, or savings.

A meaningful NPV requires sound estimates of the costs and benefits and use of the appropriate discount rate. An investment is acceptable if the NPV is positive. For example, an investment costing $1M has a NPV of savings of $1.5M. Therefore, ROI = the NPV of savings – initial investment cost/initial investment cost. ($1,500,000 – $1,000,000 = $500,000. $500,000/$1,000,000 = 50%.) This may also be expressed as ROI = $1.5M (NPV of savings)/$1M (initial investment) × 100 = 150%.

The internal rate of return (IRR) is the discount rate that sets the net present value of the program or project to zero. While the internal rate of return does not generally provide an acceptable decision criterion, it does provide useful information, particularly when budgets are constrained or there is uncertainty about the appropriate discount rate.

EARNED-VALUE MANAGEMENT

Most companies track the cost of a project or program using only two dimensions: planned costs versus actual costs. Using this particular metric, if managers spend all of the money that has been allocated to a particular project, they are right on target. If they spend less money, they have a cost under-run—a greater expenditure results in a cost overrun.

Earned-value management—or EVM—enables you to measure the true cost of performance of long-term capital projects.

The key tracking EVM metric is cost performance index or CPI, which has proven remarkably stable over the source of most projects. The CPI shows the relationship between the value of work accomplished ("earned value") and the actual costs. Fleming provides the following example to show how it works:

> If the project is budgeted to have a final value of $1 billion, but the CPI is running at 0.8 when the project is, say, one-fifth complete, the actual cost at completion can be expected to be around $1.25 billion ($1 billion/0.8). You're earning only 80 cents of value for every dollar you're spending.

Management can take advantage of this early warning by reducing costs while there's still time.

Several software tools, including Microsoft Project, have the capability of working with EVM.

RAPID ECONOMIC JUSTIFICATION

Microsoft developed the Rapid Economic Justification (REJ) framework as an assessment and justification process that helps organizations align IT solutions with business requirements and then quantify the direct financial benefits of the proposed solutions. This approach combines the Total Cost of Ownership (TCO) with project substantiation.

The REJ process consists of five steps:

1. Understand the business. IT managers should first evaluate the company's overall strategic direction and goals along with any tactical problems and opportunities. This is done to ensure that the initiatives being considered actually do fit with the organization's overall objectives.
2. Understand the solutions. Both technical and business leaders need to work together to design possible alternative solutions to the identified problems. From a BYOD perspective, this would include should the organization BYOD or not. If the answer is yes, then the model of reimbursement, if any, needs to be considered.
3. Understand the cost-benefit equation. This step calculates the summation of costs found under traditional TCO models. It incorporates hard financial benefits as well as intangible benefits (e.g., more productive employees).
4. Understand the risks. Standard risk analysis and development of risk mitigation strategies is performed.
5. Understand the financial metrics. Finally, the team projects the impact of the proposed IT investment in financial terms (e.g., payback, NPV) used by the specific company.

VALUE MEASURING METHODOLOGY

The purpose of the Value Measuring Methodology (VMM), developed by the U.S. Chief Information Officers Council (2002), is to define, capture, and measure value associated with electronic services unaccounted for in traditional return on investment (ROI) calculations, to fully account for costs, and to identify and consider risk. Developed in response to the changing definition of value brought on by the advent of the Internet and advanced software technology, VMM incorporates aspects of numerous traditional business analysis theories and methodologies, as well as newer hybrid approaches. It is really worthwhile considering doing this analysis as BYOD fits right into this rubric.

VMM was designed to be used by organizations to assist decision makers in choosing among investment alternatives, to provide the information required to manage effectively, and to maximize the benefit of an investment to the organization.

VMM is based on public and private sector business and economic analysis theories and best practices. It provides the structure, tools, and techniques for comprehensive quantitative analysis and comparison of value (benefits), cost, and risk at the appropriate level of detail.

What follows is an overview of the four steps that form the VMM framework:

Step 1: Develop a decision framework
Step 2: Alternatives analysis
Step 3: Pull together the information
Step 4: Communicate and document

Step 1: Develop a Decision Framework

A decision framework provides a structure for defining the objectives of an initiative, analyzing alternatives, and managing and evaluating ongoing performance. Just as an outline defines a paper's organization before it is written, a decision framework creates an outline for designing, analyzing, and selecting an initiative for investment, and then managing the investment. The framework can be a tool that management uses to communicate its priorities.

The framework facilitates establishing consistent measures for evaluating current and/or proposed initiatives. Program managers may use the

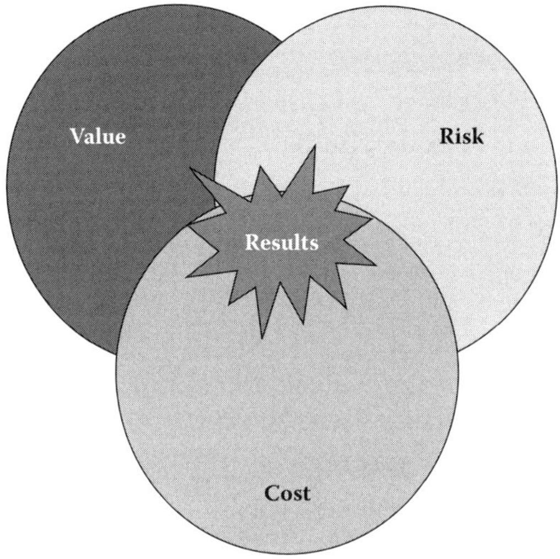

FIGURE 2.1
The decision framework.

decision framework as a tool to understand and prioritize the needs of customers and the organization's business goals. In addition, it encourages early consideration of risk and thorough planning practices.

The decision framework should be developed as early as possible in the development of a technology initiative. Employing the framework at the earliest phase of development makes it an effective tool for defining the benefits that an initiative will deliver, the risks that are likely to jeopardize its success, and the anticipated costs that must be secured and managed.

The decision framework is also helpful later in the development process as a tool to validate the direction of an initiative or to evaluate an initiative that has already been implemented.

The decision framework consists of value (benefits), cost, and risk structures, as shown in Figure 2.1. Each of these three elements must be understood to plan, justify, implement, evaluate, and manage an investment.

The tasks and outputs involved with creating a sound decision framework include the following:

Tasks:

1. Identify and Define Value Structure
2. Identify and Define Risk Structure
3. Identify and Define Cost Structure
4. Begin Documentation

Outputs:

- Prioritized Value Factors
- Defined and prioritized measures within each Value Factor
- Risk factor inventory (initial)
- Risk tolerance boundary
- Tailored Cost Structure
- Initial documentation of basis of estimate of cost, value, and risk

Task 1—Identify and Define Value Structure

The Value Structure describes and prioritizes benefits in two layers. The first considers an initiative's ability to deliver value within each of the five Value Factors (User Value, Social Value, Financial Value, Operational and Foundational Value, and Strategic Value). The second layer delineates the measures to define those values.

By defining the Value Structure, managers gain a prioritized understanding of the needs of stakeholders. This task also requires the definition of metrics and targets critical to the comparison of alternatives and performance evaluation.

The Value Factors consist of five separate, but related, perspectives on value. As defined in Figure 2.2, each Factor contributes to the full breadth and depth of the value offered by the initiative.

Because the Value Factors are usually not equal in importance, they must be "weighted" in accordance with their importance to executive management. You will note that each value factor presented in Figure 2.2 is appropriate for the BYOD analysis.

Identification, definition, and prioritization of measures of success must be performed within each Value Factor, as shown in Figure 2.3. Valid results depend on project staff working directly with representatives of user communities to define and array the measures in order of importance. These measures are used to define alternatives, and also serve as a basis for alternatives analysis, comparison, and selection, as well as ongoing performance evaluation.

In some instances, measures may be defined at a higher level to be applied across a related group of initiatives, such as organization-wide or across a focus-area portfolio. These standardized measures then facilitate "apples-to-apples" comparison across multiple initiatives.

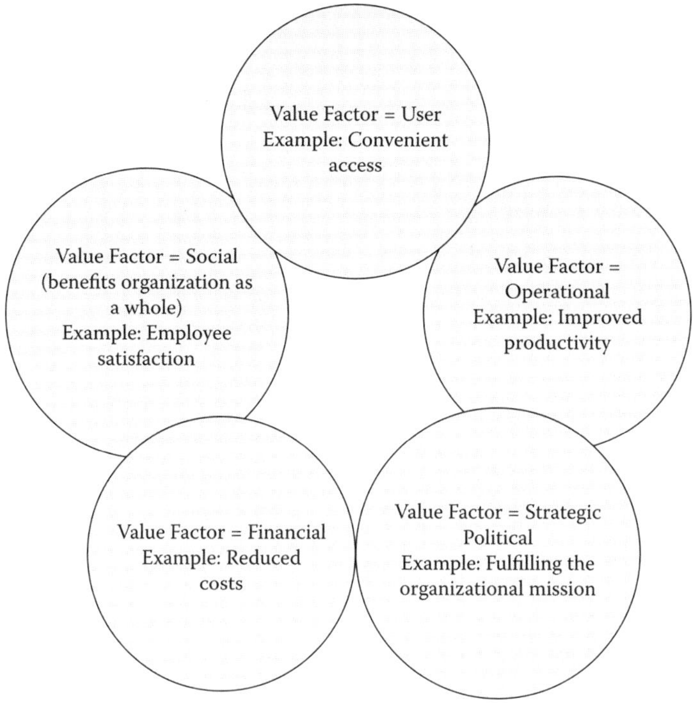

FIGURE 2.2
Value Factors.

This provides a standard management "yardstick" against which to judge investments.

Whether a measure has been defined by project staff or at a higher level of management, it must include the identification of a metric, a target, and a normalized scale. The normalized scale provides a method for integrating objective and subjective measures of value into a single decision metric. The scale used is not important; what is important is that the scale remains consistent.

The measures within the Value Factors are prioritized by representatives from the user and stakeholder communities during facilitated group sessions.

Task 2—Identify and Define Risk Structure

The risk associated with an investment in a technology initiative may degrade performance, impede implementation, and/or increase costs. Risk that is not identified cannot be mitigated or managed causing a project to fail either in the pursuit of funding or, more dramatically, during

Direct User Value Factor	
Concise, Illustrative Name	
24/7 Access to Real-Time Information & Services, Anytime & Anywhere	
Brief Description Are customers able to access real-time electronic travel services and policy information from any location 24 hours a day?	
Metrics and Scales	
% of remote access attempts that are successful (10 points for every 10%)	
% of travel services available electronically	
10 points = 25%	
90 points = 75% (threshold requirement)	
100 points = 100%	
Is data updated in the system in real time?	
No = 0	Yes = 100

FIGURE 2.3
A Value Factor with associated metrics.

implementation. The greater the attention paid to mitigating and managing risk, the greater the probability of success.

The Risk Structure serves a dual purpose. First, the structure provides the starting point for identifying and inventorying potential risks factors that may jeopardize an initiative's success and ensures that plans for mitigating their impact are developed and incorporated into each viable alternative solution.

Second, the structure provides management the information it needs to communicate their organization's tolerance for risk. Risk tolerance is expressed in terms of cost (what is the maximum acceptable cost "creep" beyond projected cost) and value (what is the maximum tolerable performance slippage).

Risks are identified and documented during working sessions with stakeholders. Issues raised during preliminary planning sessions are discovered, defined, and documented. The result is an initial risk inventory.

To map risk tolerance boundaries, selected knowledgeable staff are polled to identify at least five data points that will define the highest acceptable level of risk for cost and value.

Task 3—Identify and Define Cost Structure

A Cost Structure is a hierarchy of elements created specifically to accomplish the development of a cost estimate, and is also called a Cost Element Structure (CES).

The most significant objective in the development of a Cost Structure is to ensure a complete, comprehensive cost estimate and to reduce the risk of missing costs or double counting. An accurate and complete cost estimate is critical for an initiative's success. Incomplete or inaccurate estimates can result in exceeding the budget for implementation requiring justification for additional funding or a reduction in scope. The Cost Structure developed in this step will be used during Step 2 to estimate the cost for each alternative.

Ideally, a Cost Structure will be produced early in development, prior to defining alternatives. However, a Cost Structure can be developed after an alternative has been selected or, in some cases, in the early stage of implementation. Early structuring of costs guides refinement and improvement of the estimate during the progress of planning and implementation.

Task 4—Begin Documentation

Documentation of the elements leading to the selection of a particular alternative above all others is the "audit trail" for the decision. The documentation of assumptions, the analysis, the data, the decisions and the rationale behind them, are the foundation for the business case and the record of information required to defend a cost estimate or value analysis.

Early documentation will capture the conceptual solution, desired benefits, and attendant global assumptions (e.g., economic factors such as the discount and inflation rates). The documentation also includes project-specific drivers and assumptions, derived from tailoring the structures.

The basis for the estimate, including assumptions and business rules, should be organized in an easy-to-follow manner that links to all other analysis processes and requirements. This will provide easy access to information supporting the course of action, and will also ease the burden associated with preparing investment justification documents. As an initiative evolves through the life cycle, becoming better defined and more specific, the documentation will also mature in specificity and definition.

Step 2: Alternative Analysis—Estimate Value, Costs, and Risk

An alternatives analysis is an estimation and evaluation of all value, cost, and risk factors (Figure 2.4) leading to the selection of the most effective plan of action to address a specific business issue (e.g., service, policy, regulation, business process, or system). An alternative that must be considered is the "base case." The base case is the alternative where no change is made to current practices or systems. All other alternatives are compared against the base case, as well as to each other.

An alternatives analysis requires a disciplined process to consider the range of possible actions to achieve the desired benefits. The rigor of the process to develop the information on which to base the alternatives

Defining Risk

In the assessment of an e-Travel initiative, risks were bundled into five categories: cost, technical, schedule, operational, and legal.

The following sample table demonstrates how a single "risk factor" is likely to impact multiple risk categories. Note the level of detail provided in the description. Specificity is critical to distinguish among risks and avoid double counting.

Selected e-Travel Initiative Risk by Risk Category	Cost	Tech	Sch.	Op.	Legal
Different agencies have different levels of quality and security mechanisms, which may leave government data vulnerable. Web-enabled system will have increased points of entry for unauthorized internal or external users and pose greater security risks.	X	X			
The e-Travel concept relies heavily on technology. Although the private sector has reduced travel fees and operational costs by implementing e-Travel services, the commercial sector has not yet widely adopted/developed end-to-end solutions that meet the broad needs (single end-to-end electronic system) articulated by the e-Travel initiative. The technology and applications may not be mature enough to provide all of the functionality sought by the e-Travel initiative managers.	X	X	X	X	
Resistance to change may be partially due to fear of job loss, which may lead to challenges from unions.			X	X	X

FIGURE 2.4

Risk can be bundled across categories.

evaluation yields the data required to justify an investment or course of action. It also provides the information required to support the completion of the budget justification documents. The process also produces a baseline of anticipated value, costs, and risks to guide the management and ongoing evaluation of an investment.

An alternatives analysis must consistently assess the value, cost, and risk associated with more than one alternative for a specific initiative. Alternatives must include the base case and accommodate specific parameters of the decision framework. VMM, properly used, is designed to avoid "analysis paralysis."

The estimation of cost and projection of value uses ranges to define the individual elements of each structure. Those ranges are then subject to an uncertainty analysis. The result is a range of expected values and cost. Next, a sensitivity analysis identifies the variables that have a significant impact on this expected value and cost. The analyses will increase confidence in the accuracy of the cost and predicted performance estimates (Figure 2.5). However, a risk analysis is critical to determine the degree to which other factors may drive up expected costs or degrade predicted performance.

An alternatives analysis must be carried out periodically throughout the life cycle of an initiative. The following list provides an overview of how the business value resulting from an alternatives analysis changes depending on where in the life cycle the analysis is conducted.

1. Strategic Planning (pre-decisional)
   a. How well will each alternative perform against the defined value measures?
   b. What will each alternative cost?
   c. What is the risk associated with each alternative?
   d. What will happen if no investment is made at all (base case)?
   e. What assumptions were used to produce the cost estimates and value projections?
2. Business Modeling and Pilots
   a. What value is delivered by the initiative?
   b. What are the actual costs to date? Do estimated costs need to be reexamined?
   c. Have all risks been addressed and managed?
3. Implementation and Evaluation
   a. Is the initiative delivering the predicted value? What is the level of value delivered?

VMM In Action

Predicting Performance

Example 1: This measure was established for an e-Travel initiative in the direct user value factor.

Value	10	20	30	40	50	60	70	80	90	100
Average # hours from receipt of customer feedback message to response	48.00	44.67	41.33	38.00	34.67	31.33	28.00	24.67	21.33	18.00

Analysts projected the low, expected, and high performance for that measure.

	Low	Expected	High
Average # hours from receipt of customer feedback message to response	38	24	18

The model translated those projections onto the normalized scale.

Value	10	20	30	40	50	60	70	80	90	100
Average # hours from receipt of customer feedback message to response	48.00	44.67	41.33	38.00	34.67	31.33	28.00	24.67	21.33	18.00
				40				82		100

Low = 38.00
Expected = 24.00
High = 18.00

Example 2: This measure was established for alternative 2 in the direct user value factor. The normalized scale set for this measure was binary.

Normalized Value Scale

Value Points	0	10	20	30	40	50	60	70	80	90	
Duplicative Entry of Data	Yes										NO

FIGURE 2.5
Predicting performance.

b. What are the actual costs to date?
c. Which risks have been realized, how are they affecting costs and performance, and how are they being managed?

The tasks and outputs involved with conducting an alternatives analysis include the following:

Tasks:

1. Identify and Define Alternatives
2. Estimate Value and Cost
3. Conduct Risk Analysis
4. Ongoing Documentation

Outputs:

- Viable alternatives
- Cost and value analyses
- Risk analyses
- Tailored basis of estimate documenting value, cost, and risk economic factors and assumptions

Task 1—Identify and Define Alternatives

The challenge of this task is to identify viable alternatives that have the potential to deliver an optimum mix of both value and cost efficiency. Decision makers must be given, at a minimum, two alternatives plus the base case to make an informed investment decision.

The starting point for developing alternatives should be the information in the Value Structure and preliminary drivers identified in the initial basis of estimate (see Step 1).

Using this information will help to ensure that the alternatives and, ultimately, the solution chosen, accurately reflect a balance of performance, priorities, and business imperatives. Successfully identifying and defining alternatives requires cross-functional collaboration and discussion among the stakeholders.

The base case explores the impact of identified drivers on value and cost if an alternative solution is not implemented. That may mean that current processes and systems are kept in place or that organizations will build a patchwork of incompatible, disparate solutions. There should always be a base case included in the analysis of alternatives.

Task 2—Estimate Value and Cost

Comparison of alternatives, justification for funding, creation of a baseline against which ongoing performance may be compared, and development of a foundation for more detailed planning require an accurate estimate of an initiative's cost and value. The more reliable the estimated value and cost of the alternatives, the greater confidence one can have in the investment decision.

The first activity to pursue when estimating value and cost is the collection of data. Data sources and detail will vary based on an initiative's stage of development. Organizations should recognize that more detailed information may be available at a later stage in the process and should provide best estimates in the early stages rather than delaying the process by continuing to search for information that is likely not available.

To capture cost and performance data, and conduct the VMM analyses, a VMM model should be constructed. The model facilitates the normalization and aggregation of cost and value, as well as the performance of uncertainty, sensitivity, and risk analyses.

Analysts populate the model with the dollar amounts for each cost element and projected performance for each measure. These predicted values, or the underlying drivers, will be expressed in ranges (e.g., low, expected, or high). The range between the low and high values will be determined based on the amount of uncertainty associated with the projection.

Initial cost and value estimates are rarely accurate. Uncertainty and sensitivity analyses increase confidence that likely cost and value have been identified for each alternative.

Task 3—Conduct Risk Analysis

The only risks that can be managed are those that have been identified and assessed. A risk analysis considers the probability and potential negative impact of specific factors on an organization's ability to realize projected benefits or estimated cost, as shown in Figure 2.6.

Even after diligent and comprehensive risk mitigation during the planning stage, some level of residual risk will remain that may lead to increased costs and decreased performance. A rigorous risk analysis will help an organization better understand the probability that a risk will occur and the level of impact the occurrence of the risk will have on both cost and value. Additionally, risk analysis provides a foundation for building a comprehensive risk management plan.

Task 4—Ongoing Documentation

Inherent in these activities is the need to document the assumptions and research that compensate for gaps in information or understanding. For each alternative, the initial documentation of the high-level assumptions and risks will be expanded to include a general description of the alternative being analyzed, a comprehensive list of cost and value assumptions, and assumptions regarding the risks associated with a specific alternative. This often expands the initial risk inventory.

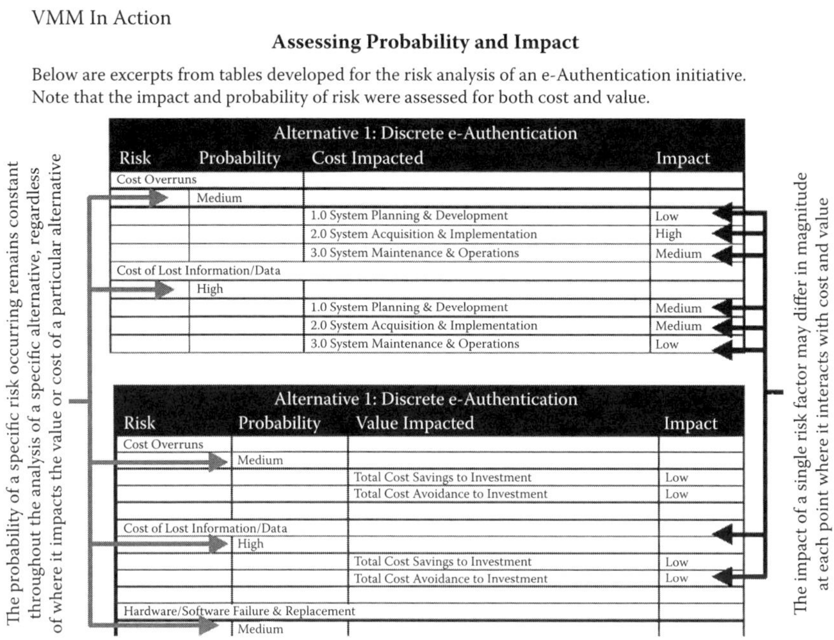

FIGURE 2.6
Assessing probability and impact.

Step 3: Pull Together the Information

As shown in Figure 2.7, the estimation of cost, value, and risk provide important data points for investment decision making. However, when analyzing an alternative and making an investment decision, it is critical to understand the relationships among them.

Tasks:

1. Aggregate the Cost Estimate
2. Calculate the Return on Investment
3. Calculate the Value Score
4. Calculate the Risk Scores (Cost and Value)
5. Compare Value, Cost, and Risk

Outputs:

- Cost estimate
- Return on investment metrics
- Value score
- Risk scores (cost and value)
- Comparison of cost, value, and risk

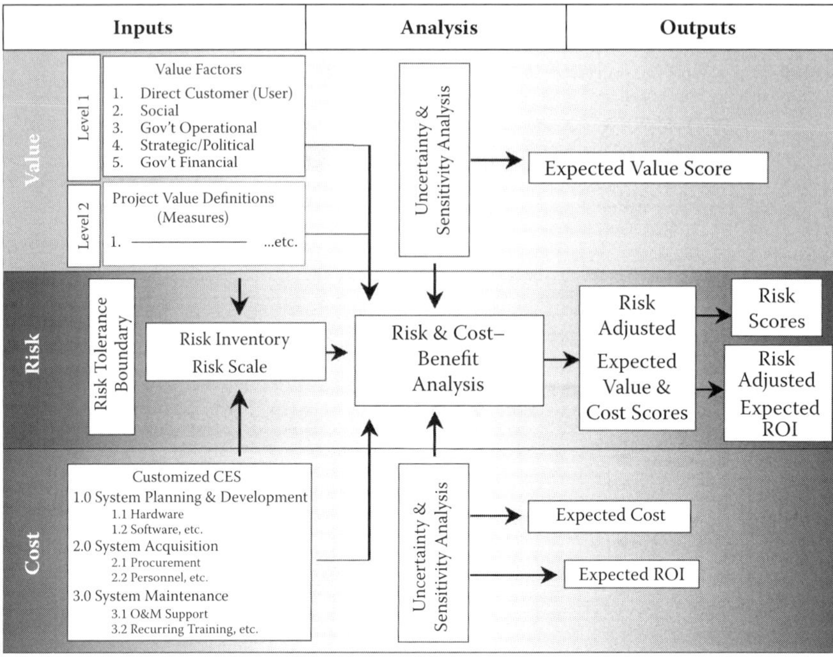

FIGURE 2.7
Risk and cost-benefit analysis.

Task 1—Aggregate the Cost Estimate

A complete and valid cost estimate is critical to determining whether a specific alternative should be selected. It also is used to assess how much funding must be requested. Understating cost estimates to gain approval, or not considering all costs, may create doubt as to the veracity of the entire analysis. An inaccurate cost estimate might lead to cost overruns, create the need to request additional funding, or reduce scope.

The total cost estimate is calculated by aggregating expected values for each cost element.

Task 2—Calculate the Return on Investment

Return on investment (ROI) metrics express the relationship between the funds invested in an initiative and the financial benefits the initiative will generate. Simply stated, it expresses the financial "bang for the buck." Although it is not considered the only measure upon which an investment decision should be made, ROI is, and will continue to be, a critical data point for decision making.

Task 3—Calculate the Value Score

The value score quantifies the full range of value that will be delivered across the five value factors as defined against the prioritized measures within the decision framework. The interpretation of a value score will vary based on the level from which it is being viewed. At the program level, the value score will be viewed as a representation of how alternatives performed against a specific set of measures. They will be used to make an "apples-to-apples" comparison of the value delivered by multiple alternatives for a single initiative.

For example, the alternative that has a value score of 80 will be preferred over the alternative with a value score of 20, if no other factors are considered. At the organizational or portfolio level, value scores are used as data points in the selection of initiatives to be included in an investment portfolio. Since the objectives and measures associated with each initiative will vary, decision makers at the senior level use value scores to determine what percentage of identified value an initiative will deliver. For example, an initiative with a value score of 75 is providing 75% of the possible value the initiative has the potential to deliver. In order to understand what exactly is being delivered, the decision maker will have to look at the measures of the Value Structure.

Consider the value score as a simple math problem. The scores projected for each of the measures within a value factor should be aggregated according to their established weights. The weighted sum of these scores is a factor's value score. The sum of the factors' value scores, aggregated according to their weights, is the total value score.

Task 4—Calculate the Risk Scores

After considering the probability and potential impact of risks, risk scores are calculated to represent a percentage of overall performance slippage or cost increase.

Risk scores provide decision makers with a mechanism to determine the degree to which value and cost will be negatively affected and whether that degree of risk is acceptable based on the risk tolerance boundaries defined by senior staff. If a selected alternative has a high cost and/or high value risk score, program management is alerted to the need for additional risk mitigation, project definition, or more detailed risk management planning. Actions to mitigate the risk may include establishment of a reserve fund, a reduction of scope, or refinement of the alternative's definition. Reactions to excessive risk may also include reconsideration of whether it is prudent to invest in the project at all, given the potential risks, the probability of their occurrence, and the actions required to mitigate them.

Task 5—Compare Value, Cost, and Risk

Tasks 1–4 of this step analyze and estimate the value, cost, and risk associated with an alternative. In isolation, each data point does not provide the depth of information required to ensure sound investment decisions.

Previous to the advent of VMM, only financial benefits could be compared to investment costs through the development of an ROI metric. When comparing alternatives, the consistency of the decision framework allows the determination of how much value will be received for the funds invested. Additionally, the use of risk scores provides insight into how all cost and value estimates are affected by risk.

By performing straightforward calculations, it is possible to model the relationships among value, cost, and risk:

1. The effect risk will have on estimated value and cost
2. The financial ROI
3. If comparing alternatives, the value "bang for the buck" (total value returned compared to total required investment)
4. If comparing initiatives to be included in the investment portfolio, senior managers can look deeper into the decision framework, moving beyond overall scores to determine the scope of benefits through an examination of the measures and their associated targets.

Step 4: Communicate and Document

Regardless of the projected merits of an initiative, its success will depend heavily on the ability of its proponents to generate internal support, to gain buy-in from targeted users, and to foster the development of active leadership supporters (champions). Success or failure may depend as much on the utility and efficacy of an initiative as it does on the ability to communicate its value in a manner that is meaningful to stakeholders with diverse definitions of value. The value of an initiative can be expressed to address the diverse definitions of stakeholder value in funding justification documents and in materials designed to inform and enlist support.

Using VMM, the value of a project is decomposed according to the different Value Factors. This gives project level managers the tools to customize their value proposition according to the perspective of their particular audience. Additionally, the structure provides the flexibility to respond accurately and quickly to project changes requiring analysis and justification.

The following are the tasks and outputs associated with Step 4:

Tasks:

1. Communicate Value to Customers and Stakeholders
2. Prepare Budget Justification Documents
3. Satisfy Ad Hoc Reporting Requirements
4. Use Lessons Learned to Improve Processes

Outputs:

- Documentation, insight, and support:
  - To develop results-based management controls
  - For Exhibit 300 data and analytical needs
  - For communicating initiatives value
  - For improving decision making and performance measurement through "Lessons Learned"
- Change and ad hoc reporting requirements

Task 1—Communicate Value to Customers and Stakeholders

Leveraging the results of VMM analysis can facilitate relations with customers and stakeholders. VMM makes communication to diverse audiences easier by incorporating the perspectives of all potential audience members from the outset of analysis. Since VMM calculates the potential value that an investment could realize for all stakeholders, it provides data pertinent to each of those stakeholder perspectives that can be used to bolster support for the project. It also fosters substantive discussion with customers regarding the priorities and detailed plans of the investment. These stronger relationships not only prove critical to the long-term success of the project, but can also lay the foundation for future improvements and innovation.

Task 2—Prepare Budget Justification Documents

Many organizations require comprehensive analysis and justification to support funding requests. IT initiatives that have not proven may not be funded:

1. Their applicability to executive missions
2. Sound planning
3. Significant benefits
4. Clear calculations and logic justifying the amount of funding requested
5. Adequate risk identification and mitigation efforts
6. A system for measuring effectiveness
7. Full consideration of alternatives

After completion of the VMM, one will have data required to complete or support completion of budget justification documents.

Task 3—Satisfy Ad Hoc Reporting Requirements

Once a VMM model is built to assimilate and analyze a set of investment alternatives, it can easily be tailored to support ad hoc requests for information or other reporting requirements. In the current, rapidly changing political and technological environment, there are many instances when project managers need to be able to perform rapid analysis. For example, funding authorities, partners, market pricing fluctuations, or portfolio managers might impose modifications on the details (e.g., the weighting factors) of a project investment plan; many of these parties are also likely to request additional investment-related information later in the project life cycle. VMM's customized decision framework makes such adjustments and reporting feasible under short time constraints.

Task 4—Use Lessons Learned to Improve Processes

Lessons learned through the use of VMM can be a powerful tool when used to improve overall organizational decision making and management processes. For example, in the process of identifying metrics, one might discover that adequate mechanisms are not in place to collect critical performance information. Using this lesson to improve measurement mechanisms would give an organization better capabilities for (1) gauging the project's success and mission-fulfillment, (2) demonstrating progress to stakeholders and funding authorities, and (3) identifying shortfalls in performance that could be remedied.

Uncertainty Analysis

Conducting an uncertainty analysis requires the following:

1. Identify the Variables: Develop a range of value for each variable. This range expresses the level of uncertainty about the projection. For example, an analyst may be unsure whether an Internet application will serve a population of 100 or 100,000. It is important to be aware of and express this uncertainty in developing the model in order to define the reliability of the model in predicting results accurately.
2. Identify the Probability Distribution for the Selected Variables: For each variable identified, assign a probability distribution. There are several types of probability distributions. A triangular probability distribution is frequently used for this type of analysis. In addition to establishing the probability distribution for each variable, the analyst must also determine whether the actual amount is likely to be high or low.
3. Run the Simulation: Once the variables' level of uncertainty is identified and each one has been assigned a probability distribution, run a Monte Carlo simulation. The simulation provides the analyst with the information required to determine the range (low to high) and "expected" results for both the value projection and cost estimate. As shown in Figure 2.8 the output of the Monte Carlo simulation produces a range of possible results and defines the "mean," the point at which there is an equal chance that the actual value or cost will be higher or lower. The analyst then surveys the range and selects the expected value.

Sensitivity Analysis

Sensitivity analysis is used to identify the business drivers that have the greatest impact on potential variations of an alternative's cost and its returned value. Many of the assumptions made at the beginning of a project's definition phase will be found inaccurate later in the analysis. Therefore, one must consider how sensitive a total cost estimate or value

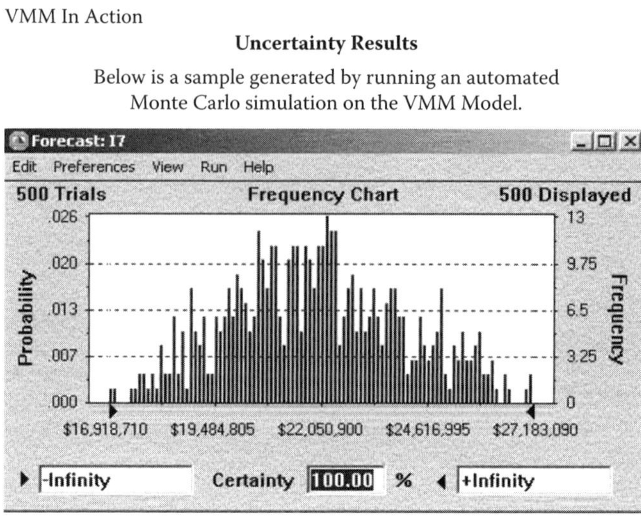

FIGURE 2.8
Output of Monte Carlo simulation.

projection is to changes in the data used to produce the result. Insight from this analysis allows stakeholders not only to identify variables that require additional research to reduce uncertainty, but also to justify the cost of that research.

The information required to conduct a sensitivity analysis is derived from the same Monte Carlo simulation used for the uncertainty analysis.

Figure 2.9 is a sample sensitivity chart. Based on this chart, it is clear that "Build 5/6 Schedule Slip" is the most sensitive variable.

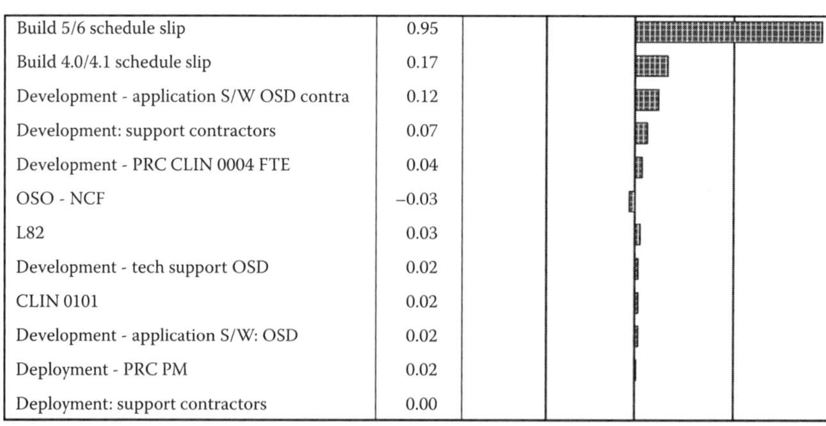

FIGURE 2.9
Sensitivity chart.

GLOSSARY

Analytic Hierarchy Process (AHP): AHP is a proven methodology that uses comparisons of paired elements (comparing one against the other) to determine the relative importance of criteria mathematically.

Benchmark: A measurement or standard that serves as a point of reference by which process performance is measured.

Benefit: A term used to indicate an advantage, profit, or gain attained by an individual or organization.

Benefit-to-Cost Ratio (BCR): The computation of the financial benefit/cost ratio is done within the construct of the following formula: Benefits ÷ Cost.

Cost Element Structure (CES): A hierarchical structure created to facilitate the development of a cost estimate. May include elements that are not strictly products to be developed or produced (e.g., Travel, Risk, Program Management Reserve, Life Cycle Phases). Samples include the following:

1. System Planning and Development
    - 1.1. Hardware
    - 1.2. Software
        - 1.2.1 Licensing fees
    - 1.3. Development support
        - 1.3.1 Program management oversight
        - 1.3.2 System engineering architecture design
        - 1.3.3 Change management and risk assessment
        - 1.3.4 Requirement definition and data architecture
        - 1.3.5 Test and evaluation
    - 1.4. Studies
        - 1.4.1 Security
        - 1.4.2 Accessibility
        - 1.4.3 Data architecture
        - 1.4.4 Network architecture
    - 1.5. Other
        - 1.5.1 Facilities
        - 1.5.2 Travel
2. System Acquisition and Implementation
    - 2.1. Procurement

- 2.1.1 Hardware
- 2.1.2 Software
- 2.1.3 Customized software

2.2. Personnel

2.3. Training

3. System Maintenance and Operations

3.1. Hardware

- 3.1.1 Maintenance
- 3.1.2 Upgrades
- 3.1.3 Life cycle replacement

3.2. Software

- 3.2.1 Maintenance
- 3.2.2 Upgrades
- 3.2.3 License fees

3.3. Support

- 3.3.1 Help desk
- 3.3.2 Security
- 3.3.3 Training

Cost Estimate: The estimation of a project's life cycle costs, time-phased by fiscal year, based on the description of a project or system's technical, programmatic, and operational parameters. A cost estimate may also include related analyses such as cost-risk analyses, cost-benefit analyses, schedule analyses, and trade studies.

Internal Rate of Return (IRR): The internal rate of return is the discount rate that sets the net present value of the program or project to zero. While the internal rate of return does not generally provide an acceptable decision criterion, it does provide useful information, particularly when budgets are constrained or there is uncertainty about the appropriate discount rate.

Life Cycle Costs: The overall estimated cost for a particular program alternative over the time period corresponding to the life of the program, including direct and indirect initial costs plus any periodic or continuing costs of operation and maintenance.

Monte Carlo Simulation: A simulation is any analytical method that is meant to imitate a real-life system, especially when other analyses are too mathematically complex or too difficult to reproduce. Spreadsheet risk analysis uses both a spreadsheet model and simulation to analyze the effect of varying inputs on outputs of the modeled system. One type of spreadsheet simulation is Monte Carlo simulation, which randomly generates values for uncertain variables over and over to simulate a model. (Monte Carlo simulation was named for Monte Carlo, Monaco, where the primary attractions are casinos containing games of chance.) Analysts identify all key assumptions for which the outcome was uncertain. For the life cycle, numerous inputs are each assigned one of several probability distributions. The type of distribution selected depended on the conditions surrounding the variable. During simulation, the value used in the cost model is selected randomly from the defined possibilities.

Net Present Value (NPV): NPV is defined as the difference between the present value of benefits and the present value of costs. The benefits referred to in this calculation must be quantified in cost or financial terms in order to be included.

Net Present Value = [PV(Internal Project Cost Savings, Operational) + PV (Mission Cost Savings)] – PV(Initial Investment)

Polling Tools:

Option Finder—A real-time polling device, which permits participants, using handheld remotes, to vote on questions and have the results displayed immediately with statistical information such as "degree of variance" and discussed.

Group Systems—A tool that allows participants to answer questions using individual laptops. The answers to these questions are then displayed to all participants anonymously, in order to spur discussion and the free flowing exchange of ideas. Group Systems also has a polling device.

Return on Investment (ROI): A financial management approach used to explain how well a project delivers benefits in relationship to its cost. Several methods are used to calculate a return on investment. Refer to Internal Rate of Return (IRR), Net Present Value (NPV), and Savings to Investment Ratio (SIR).

Risk: A term used to define the class of factors that (1) have a measurable probability of occurring during an investment's life cycle, (2) have an associated cost or affect on the investment's output or outcome (typically an adverse affect that jeopardizes the success of an investment), and (3) have alternatives from which the organization may chose.

Risk Analysis: A technique to identify and assess factors that may jeopardize the success of a project or achieving a goal. This technique also helps define preventive measures to reduce the probability of these factors from occurring and identify countermeasures to successfully deal with these constraints when they develop.

Risk Categories:

1. Project Resources/Financial: Risk associated with "cost creep," misestimation of life cycle costs, reliance on a small number of vendors without cost controls, and (poor) acquisition planning.
2. Technical/Technology: Risk associated with immaturity of commercially available technology; reliance on a small number of vendors; risk of technical problems/failures with applications and its ability to provide planned and desired technical functionality.
3. Business/Operational: Risk associated with business goals; risk that the proposed alternative fails to result in process efficiencies and streamlining; risk that business goals of the program or initiative will not be achieved; risk that the program effectiveness targeted by the project will not be achieved.
4. Organizational and Change Management: Risk associated with organization-wide cultural resistance to change and standardization; risk associated with bypassing, lack of use or improper use or adherence to new systems and processes due to organizational structure and culture; inadequate training planning.
5. Data/Information: Risk associated with the loss/misuse of data or information, risk of increased burdens on citizens and businesses due to data collection requirements if the associated business processes or the project requires access to data from other sources (fed, state, and/or local agencies).
6. Security: Risk associated with the security/vulnerability of systems, websites, information and networks; risk of intrusions and connectivity to other (vulnerable) systems; risk associated with the misuse (criminal/fraudulent) of information; must include level of risk (hi, med, basic) and what aspect of security determines the level of risk—for example, need for confidentiality of information associated with the project/system, availability of the information or system, or reliability of the information or system.

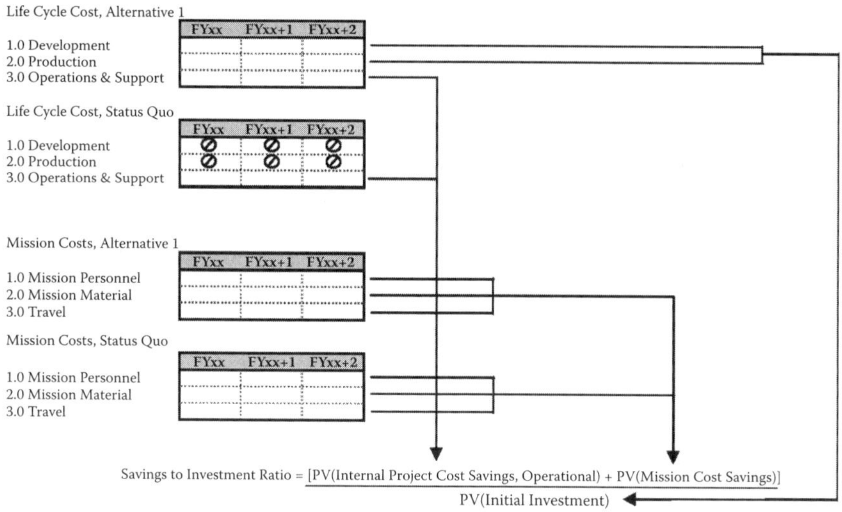

FIGURE 2.10
Savings-to-investment ratio.

7. Strategic: Risk that the proposed alternative fails to result in the achievement of those goals or in making contributions to them.
8. Privacy: Risk associated with the vulnerability of information collected on individuals, or risk of vulnerability of proprietary information on businesses.

Savings-to-Investment Ratio (SIR): SIR represents the ratio of savings to investment. The "savings" in the SIR computation are generated by Internal Operational Savings and Mission Cost Savings. The flow of costs and cost savings into the SIR formula is as shown in Figure 2.10.

Sensitivity Analysis: Analysis of how sensitive outcomes are to changes in the assumptions. The assumptions that deserve the most attention should depend largely on the dominant benefit and cost elements and the areas of greatest uncertainty of the program or process being analyzed.

Stakeholder: An individual or group with an interest in the success of an organization in delivering intended results and maintaining the viability of the organization's products and services. Stakeholders influence programs, products, and services.

REFERENCE

The U.S. Chief Information Officers Council. (2002). *Value measuring methodology—How-to guide.* http://www.fgdc.gov/policyandplanning/50states/valuemeasuring_methodology_howtoguide_oct_2002.pdf

3

Integrating BYOD into Performance Measurement and Management Systems

Whatever the organization size, it is important that BYOD be carefully measured for its impact on performance. To do this requires just a bit of tweaking to the organization's performance measurement and management systems. BYOD is definitely a strategy. What's interesting is that a study found that 70% of organizations do not link middle management incentives to strategy and that 60% of organizations do not link strategy to budgeting Balanced Scorecard Collaborative (2004). It would be worthwhile, then, to spend a bit of time discussing performance measurement and management systems and how the organization can integrate BYOD into these systems.

WHY MEASURE?

There are a wide range of definitions for performance objective, performance goal, performance measure, performance measurement, and performance management. To frame the dialogue and to move forward with a common baseline, certain key concepts need to be clearly defined and understood, such as the following:

1. *Performance objective*. This is a critical success factor in achieving the organization's mission, vision, and strategy, which if not achieved would likely result in a significant decrease in customer satisfaction, system performance, employee satisfaction or retention, or effective financial management.

2. *Performance goal.* A target level of activity expressed as a tangible measure, against which actual achievement can be compared.
3. *Performance measure.* A quantitative or qualitative characterization of performance.
4. *Performance measurement.* A process of assessing progress toward achieving predetermined goals, including information on the efficiency with which resources are transformed into goods and services (outputs), the quality of those outputs (how well they are delivered to clients and the extent to which clients are satisfied) and outcomes (the results of a program activity compared to its intended purpose), and the effectiveness of operations in terms of their specific contributions to program objectives.
5. *Performance management.* The use of performance measurement information to effect positive change in organizational culture, systems, and processes, by helping to set agreed-upon performance goals, allocating and prioritizing resources, informing managers to either confirm or change current policy or program directions to meet those goals, and sharing results of performance in pursuing those goals.
6. *Output measure.* A calculation or recording of activity or effort that can be expressed in a quantitative or qualitative manner.
7. *Outcome measure.* An assessment of the results of a program compared to its intended purpose.

A leading-edge organization seeks to create an efficient and effective performance management system to do the following:

1. Translate vision into clear measurable outcomes that define success, and that are shared throughout the organization and with customers and stakeholders.
2. Provide a tool for assessing, managing, and improving the overall health and success of business systems.
3. Continue to shift from prescriptive, audit-based, and compliance-based oversight to an ongoing, forward-looking strategic partnership involving agency headquarters and field components.
4. Include measures of quality, cost, speed, customer service, and employee alignment, motivation, and skills to provide an in-depth, predictive performance management system.

5. Replace existing assessment models with a consistent approach to performance management.

UNDERSTANDING PERFORMANCE MANAGEMENT

Several steps need to be undertaken to establish performance measures that make sense and are workable throughout the organization.

Define Organizational Vision, Mission, and Strategy

This ensures that the performance measures developed support accomplishment of the organization's strategic objectives. It also helps employees visualize and understand the links between the performance measures and successful accomplishment of strategic goals.

The key is to first identify where you want the organization to be in the near future and then set a vision that seems somewhat out of reach. In this way, managers have the instrumentation they need to navigate to future competitive success.

Use of BYOD needs to be aligned to the organization's strategy and the use of it needs to demonstrate that it will help accomplish stated goals.

Develop Performance Objectives, Measures, and Goals

Next, it is essential to identify what the organization must do well (i.e., the performance objectives) in order to attain the identified vision. For each objective that must be performed well, it is necessary to identify measures and set goals covering a reasonable period of time (e.g., three to five years). Although this sounds simple, many variables actually impact how long this exercise will take. The first, and most significant, variable is how many people are employed in the organization and the extent to which they will be involved in setting the vision, mission, measures, and goals.

The balanced scorecard, which we will discuss more in depth later in this chapter, translates an organization's vision into a set of performance objectives distributed among four perspectives: Financial, Customer, Internal Business Processes, and Learning and Growth. Some objectives are maintained to measure an organization's progress toward achieving its vision. Other objectives are maintained to measure the long-term drivers of success. Through the use of the balanced scorecard, an organization monitors both its current performance (financial, customer satisfaction, and business process results) and its efforts to improve processes, motivate and educate employees, and enhance information systems—its ability to learn and improve.

When creating performance measures, it is important to ensure that they link directly to the strategic vision of the organization. The measures must focus on the outcomes necessary to achieve the organizational vision and the objectives of the strategic plan. When drafting measures and setting goals, ask whether achievement of the identified goals will help achieve the organizational vision.

Each objective within a perspective should be supported by at least one measure that will indicate an organization's performance against that objective. Define measures precisely, including the population to be measured, the method of measurement, the data source, and the time period for the measurement. If a quantitative measure is feasible and realistic, then its use should be encouraged.

When developing measures, it is important to include a mix of quantitative and qualitative measures. Quantitative measures provide more objectivity than qualitative measures—for example, amount saved through use of BYOD. They may help to justify critical management decisions on resource allocation (e.g., budget and staffing) or systems improvement. The company should first identify any available quantitative data and consider how it can support the objectives and measures incorporated in the balanced scorecard. Qualitative measures involve matters of perception, and therefore of subjectivity—for example, employee satisfaction. Judgments based on the experience of customers, employees, managers, and contractors offer important insights into acquisition performance and results.

Give Measures Time to Evolve

Finally, it takes time to establish measures, but it is also important to recognize that they might not be perfect the first time. Performance management is an evolutionary process that requires adjustments as experience is gained in the use of performance measures.

ATTRIBUTES OF SUCCESSFUL PERFORMANCE MEASUREMENT SYSTEMS

There are certain attributes that set apart successful performance measurement and management systems, including the following:

1. *A conceptual framework is needed for the performance measurement and management system.* Every organization, regardless of type, needs a clear and cohesive performance measurement framework that is understood by all levels of the organization and that supports objectives and the collection of results. BYOD users must certainly understand that their use of these devices impacts the organization in some way.
2. *Effective internal and external communications are the keys to successful performance measurement.* Effective communication with employees, process owners, customers, and stakeholders is vital to the successful development and deployment of performance measurement and management systems.
3. *Accountability for results must be clearly assigned and well understood.* High-performance organizations clearly identify what it takes to determine success and make sure that all managers and employees understand what they are responsible for in achieving organizational goals.
4. *Performance measurement systems must provide intelligence for decision makers, not just compile data.* Performance measures should be limited to those that relate to strategic organizational goals and objectives, and that provide timely, relevant, and concise information for use by decision makers—at all levels—to assess progress toward achieving predetermined goals. These measures should produce information on the efficiency with which resources are transformed into goods and services, on how well results compare to a program's intended purpose, and on the effectiveness of organizational activities and operations in terms of their specific contribution to program objectives.
5. *Compensation, rewards, and recognition should be linked to performance measurements.* Performance evaluations and rewards need to be tied to specific measures of success, by linking financial and non-financial incentives directly to performance. Such

a linkage sends a clear and unambiguous message to the organization as to what's important.

6. *Performance measurement systems should be positive, not punitive.* The most successful performance measurement systems are not "gotcha" systems, but learning systems that help the organization identify what works—and what does not—so as to continue with and improve on what is working and repair or replace what is not working.
7. *Results and progress toward program commitments should be openly shared with employees, customers, and stakeholders.* Performance measurement system information should be openly and widely shared with an organization's employees, customers, stakeholders, vendors, and suppliers.

If used properly, the balanced scorecard approach provides a framework to accomplish these ends. Notice the emphasis on the word "properly." Balanced scorecard is not a panacea to all organizational problems. Just implementing it willy-nilly is not going to solve performance problems, nor will it enhance alignment between the business units and IT. For balanced scorecard to work it has to be carefully planned and executed.

DEVELOPING BENCHMARKS

The central component of any measurement system is benchmarking. The dictionary definition of benchmark is "a point of reference from which measurements may be made." It is something that serves as a standard by which others may be measured.

The purpose of benchmarking is to assist in the performance improvement process. Specifically, benchmarking can do the following:

1. Identify opportunities
2. Set realistic but aggressive goals
3. Challenge internal paradigms on what is possible
4. Understand methods for improved processes
5. Uncover strengths within your organization

TABLE 3.1

Benchmarking vs. Not Benchmarking

	Without Benchmarking	With Benchmarking
Defining Customer Requirements	Based on history/gut feel; acting on perception	Based on market reality; acting on objective evaluation
Establishing Effective Goals	Lack external focus; reactive; lagging industry	Credible, customer-focused; proactive; industry leadership
Developing True Measures of Productivity	Pursuing pet projects; strengths and weaknesses not understood	Solving real problems; performance outputs known, based on best in class
Becoming Competitive	Internally focused; evolutionary change; low commitment	Understand the competition; revolutionary ideas with proven performance; high commitment
Industry Practices	Not invented here; few solutions	Proactive search for change; many options; breakthroughs

6. Learn from the leaders' experiences
7. Better prioritize and allocate resources

Table 3.1 describes the ramifications of not using benchmarking.

Obviously, benchmarking is critical to your organization. However, benchmarking needs to be done with great care. There are actually times when you shouldn't benchmark:

1. You are targeting a process that is not critical to the organization.
2. You don't know what your customers require from your process.
3. Key stakeholders aren't involved in the benchmarking process.
4. Inadequate resources, including budgetary, have been committed.
5. There is strong resistance to change.
6. You are expecting results instantaneously.

Most organizations use a four-phase model to implement benchmarking:

1. Plan
2. Collect
3. Analyze
4. Adapt

Plan

When planning a benchmarking effort considerable thought should be given to who is on the benchmarking team. In some cases, team members will need to be trained in the different tools and techniques of the benchmarking process. Certainly, employees with a vested interest in BYOD should be represented on this team.

The creation of a benchmarking plan is similar to the creation of a project plan for a traditional systems development effort, with a few twists:

1. The scope of the benchmarking study needs to be established. All projects must have boundaries. In this case, you will need to determine which departmental units and/or processes will be studied. BYOD is actually a hybrid of technology and business, but it is probably more suitable to assign this to IT.
2. A purpose statement should be developed. This should state the mission and goals of the plan.
3. If benchmarking partners (i.e., other companies in your peer grouping who agree to be part of your effort) are to be used, specific criteria for their involvement should be noted. In addition, a list of any benchmarking partners should be provided. Characteristics of benchmarking partners important to note include: policies and procedures, organizational structure, financials, locations, quality, productivity, competitive environment, products/services. There is no BYOD industry. Thus, finding partners for benchmarking will be achieved with some degree of difficulty. Still, partners might be found within the purview of asset management or even knowledge management interest groups or associations.
4. Define a data collection plan and determine how the data will be used, managed, and ultimately distributed.
5. Finally, your plan should discuss how implementation of any improvements resulting from the benchmarking effort will be accomplished.

Collect

The collection phase of a benchmarking effort is very similar to the requirements elicitation phase of software engineering. The goal is to collect data and turn it into knowledge.

During the collection phase the focus is on developing data collection instruments. The most widely used is the questionnaire with follow-up telephone interviews and site visits. Other methods include interviewing, observation, participation, documentation, and research. Appendix H provides a quick primer on "elicitation" techniques from a software engineering perspective.

Analyze

Once the data has been collected it should be analyzed. Hopefully, you've managed to secure the cooperation of one or more benchmarking partners so that your analysis will be comparative rather than introspective.

The goal of data analysis is to identify any gaps in performance. Once you find these you will need to do the following:

1. Identify the operational best practices and enables. In other words, what are your partners doing right that you're not? Then you need to find out exactly "how" they're doing it.
2. Formulate a strategy to close these gaps by identifying opportunities for improvement.
3. Develop an implementation plan for these improvements.

The analysis phase uses the outputs of the data collection phase—for example, the questionnaires, interviews, and observations. It is during this phase that process mapping and the development of requisite process performance measurements is performed.

Process performance measurements should have the following characteristics:

1. Be tied to customer expectations
2. Be aligned with strategic objectives
3. Be clearly reflective of the process and not influenced by other factors
4. Be monitored over time

Adapt

Once the plan has been formulated and receives approval from management it will be implemented in this phase. Traditional project management techniques should be used to control, monitor, and report on the project. It is also during this phase that the continuous improvement plan is development. In this plan, new benchmarking opportunities should be identified and pursued.

The Benchmarking Maturity Matrix might be used for a periodic review of the benchmarking initiative. To understand an initiative's current state and find opportunities for improvement, the organization must examine its approach, focus, culture, and results. The Benchmarking Maturity Matrix demonstrates the maturity of 11 key elements derived from five core focus areas: management culture (e.g., expects long-term improvement), benchmarking focal point (e.g., team), processes (e.g., coaching), tools (e.g., BYOD), and results.

The 11 key elements within the matrix are as follows:

1. Knowledge management/sharing
2. Benchmarking
3. Focal point
4. Benchmarking process
5. Improvement enablers
6. Capture storage
7. Sharing dissemination
8. Incentives
9. Analysis
10. Documentation
11. Financial impact

The following are the five maturity levels, from lowest to highest:

1. Internal financial focus, with short-term focus that reacts to problems.
2. Sees need for external focus to learn.
3. Sets goals for knowledge sharing.
4. Learning is a corporate value.
5. Knowledge sharing is a corporate value.

Based on these two grids, a series of questions are asked and a score calculated:

Key 1: Which of the following descriptions best defines your organization's orientation toward learning?

Key 2: Which of the following descriptions best defines your organization's orientation toward improving?
Key 3: How are benchmarking activities and/or inquiries handled within your organization?
Key 4: Which of the following best describes the benchmarking process in your organization?
Key 5: Which of the following best describes the improvement enablers in place in your organization?
Key 6: Which of the following best describes your organization's approach for capturing and storing best practices information?
Key 7: Which of the following best describes your organization's approach for sharing and disseminating best practices information?
Key 8: Which of the following best describes your organization's approach for encouraging the sharing of best practices information?
Key 9: Which of the following best describes the level of analysis done by your organization to identify actionable best practices?
Key 10: How are business impacts that result from benchmarking projects documented within your organization?
Key 11: How would you describe the financial impact resulting from benchmarking projects?

Generally, there are six steps in a benchmarking initiative:

1. Select the process and build support. It's more than likely that there will be many processes to benchmark. It is advisable that you break down a large project into discrete manageable subprojects. These subprojects should be prioritized, with those critical to the goals of the organization taking priority.
2. Determine current performance. Quite a few companies decide to benchmark because they've heard the wonderful success stories of Motorola or General Electric. During my days with the New York Stock Exchange, the chairman was forever touting the latest current management fad and insisting that we all follow suit. The problem is that all organizations are different and, in the case of benchmarking, extremely issue-specific. Before embarking on a benchmarking effort the planners need to really investigate and understand the business environment and the impact of specific business processes on overall performance.

3. Determine where performance should be. Perhaps just as importantly, the organization should benchmark itself against one of its successful competitors. This is how you can determine where "you should be" in terms of your own organization's performance. Both competitive analysis and phantom analysis, discussed later on in this chapter, are useful tools for this purpose.
4. Determine the performance gap. You now know where you are (#2 on this list) as well as where you'd like to be (#3 on this list). The difference between the two is referred to as the **performance gap**. The gap must be identified, organized, and categorized. In other words, the causal factor should be attributed to people, process, technology, or cultural influences and then prioritized.
5. Design an action plan. Technologies are most comfortable with this step as an action plan is really the same thing as a project plan. It should list the chronological steps for solving a particular problem as identified in #4 above. Information in this plan should also include problem-solving tasks, who is assigned to each task, and time frame.
6. Continuously improve. In the process improvement business there are two catchphrases: "process improvement" and "continuous improvement." The former is reactive to a current set of problems and the later is proactive, meaning that the organization should continuously be searching for ways to improve.

USING BALANCED SCORECARD TO MEASURE BYOD EFFECTIVENESS

From an organizational perspective, the concepts of performance management are very much the base that supports the balanced scorecard framework. Indeed, the balanced scorecard approach becomes very understandable when one realizes that, instead of being a radical new approach to performance management and measurement, it merely brings together and organizes tried and true performance-enhancing "best practices" that companies have been practicing for decades.

Heralded by the Harvard Business Review as one of the most significant management ideas of the past 75 years, balanced scorecard, shown in Figure 3.1, has been implemented in companies to both measure as well as manage the IT effort—and by extension BYOD.

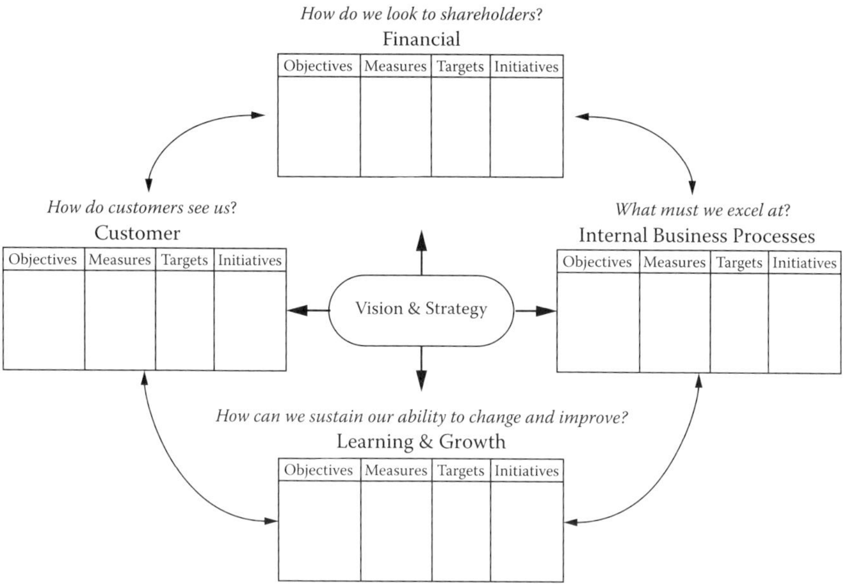

FIGURE 3.1
The balanced scorecard and its four perspectives.

Robert S. Kaplan and David P. Norton developed the balanced scorecard approach in the early 1990s to compensate for their perceived shortcomings of using only financial metrics to judge corporate performance. They recognized that in this New Economy, it was also necessary to value intangible assets, such as the satisfaction an end-user gains because she is permitted to use her own device. Because of this they urged companies to measure such esoteric factors as quality and customer satisfaction. By the middle 1990s, balanced scorecard became the hallmark of a well-run company. Kaplan and Norton often compare their approach for managing a company to that of pilots viewing assorted instrument panels in an airplane cockpit—both have a need to monitor multiple aspects of their working environment.

In the scorecard scenario, a company organizes its business goals into discrete, all-encompassing perspectives: Financial, Customer, Internal Process, and Learning/Growth. The company then determines cause-effect relationships—e.g., satisfied customers buy more goods, which increases revenue. Next, the company lists measures for each goal, pinpoints targets, and identifies projects and other initiatives to help reach those targets.

Departments create scorecards tied to the company's targets, and employees and projects have scorecards tied to their department's targets. This cascading nature provides a line of sight between each individual, what they're working on, the unit they support, and how that impacts the strategy of the whole enterprise.

The balanced scorecard approach is more than just a way to identify and monitor metrics. It's also a way to manage change and increase a company's effectiveness, productivity, and competitive advantage. Essentially, a company that uses the scorecard to identify and then realize strategic goals is a strategy-focused organization.

For IT managers, the balanced scorecard is an invaluable tool that permits IT to link to the business side of the organization using a "cause and effect" approach. Some have likened balanced scorecard to a new language, which enables IT and business line managers to think together about what IT can do to support business performance. A beneficial side effect of the use of the balanced scorecard is that, when all measures are reported, one can calculate the strength of relations between the various value drivers. For example, the relationship between BYOD usage and cost levels might infer that the usage of BYOD does not sufficiently contribute to results as expressed by the other (e.g., financial) performance measures.

Table 3.2 demonstrates a balanced scorecard approach to measuring the usage of BYOD.

Martinsons, Davison, and Tse (1999) suggest that the four balanced scorecard perspectives might require some modification to be effective as an IT scorecard. Their reasoning is that the IT department is typically an internal rather than external service supplier and projects are commonly carried out for the benefit of both the end-users and the organization as a whole—rather than individual customers within a large market.

Their suggested four perspectives include the following:

1. User orientation (end-user view)
   a. Mission: deliver value-adding products and services to end-users
   b. Objectives: establish and maintain a good image and reputation with end-users, exploit IT opportunities such as BYOD, establish good relationships with the user community, satisfy end-user requirements, and be perceived as the preferred supplier of IT products and services
2. Business value (management's view)
   a. Mission: contribute to the value of the business

TABLE 3.2

Sample Balanced Scorecard Including BYOD Metrics

Customer Perspective (End Users)	Internal Business Processes Perspective
Effective BYOD Service % of customers satisfied with the responsiveness, cooperation, and communication skills of IT support	**Effective Quality Control System** Number of problems with BYOD devices or services
	Effective Use of Procurement Practices Number of employees using internal services to help procure their devices and/or software
Learning and Growth Perspective	**Financial Perspective**
Information Availability for Strategic Decision Making The extent of reliable management information about BYOD usage	**Minimizing BYOD Costs** Cost to spend ratio
Quality Workforce % of employees using BYOD effectively	**Maximizing Contract Cost Avoidance** Cost avoidance through use of BYOD
Employee Satisfaction: Quality Work Environment % of employees satisfied with BYOD	

   b. Objectives: establish and maintain a good image and reputation with management, ensure that IT projects provide business value, control IT costs, sell appropriate IT products and services to third parties, and perform BYOD ROI
3. Internal processes (operations-based view)
   a. Mission: deliver IT products and services in an efficient and effective manner
   b. Objectives: anticipate and influence requests from end-users and management, be efficient in planning and developing IT applications, be efficient in operating and maintaining IT applications, be efficient in acquiring and testing new hardware and software, and provide cost-effective training and support that satisfies end-users
4. Future readiness (innovation and learning view)
   a. Mission: deliver continuous improvement and prepare for future challenges

b. Objectives: anticipate and prepare for IT problems that could arise, continuously upgrade IT skills through training and development, regularly upgrade IT applications portfolio, regularly upgrade hardware and software, and conduct cost-effective research into emerging technologies and their suitability for the business (e.g., BYOD, cloud services)

Martinsons et al. then drill down to provide IT-specific measures for each of these four perspectives. Most of the metrics have been derived from mainstream literature as shown in Table 3.3. You'll note that many of them are quite applicable to BYOD. You will also want to review Appendix E, which provides a standard set of IT metrics.

Martinsons et al. explain that the three key balanced scorecard principles of

1. Cause-and-effect relationships
2. Sufficient performance drivers
3. Linkage to financial measures

are built into their IT scorecard. They explain that cause-and-effect relationships can involve one or more of the four perspectives. For example, better staff skills (future readiness perspective) will reduce the frequency of bugs in an application (internal operations perspective).

Progressive scorecard practitioners track metrics in five key categories:

1. Financial performance. IT spending in the content of service levels, project progress, and so on. Sample metrics include cost of data communications per seat and relative spending per portfolio category.
2. Project performance. Sample metrics include percentage of new development investment resulting in new revenue streams and percentage of IT R&D investment leading to IT service improvements.
3. Operational performance. Instead of concentrating measurement efforts on day-to-day measures, best-in-class practitioners seek to provide an aggregate, customer-focused view of IT operations. Sample metrics include peak time availability and critical process uptime.
4. Talent management. This category of metrics seeks to manage IT human capital. Measures include staff satisfaction and retention as well as attractiveness of the IT department to external job seekers.

TABLE 3.3

IT Scorecard Metrics

Perspective	Metric
User orientation	Customer satisfaction
Business Value	
Cost control	% over/under IT budget
	Allocation to different budget items
	IT budget as a % of revenue
	IT expenses per employee
	Costs saved due to BYOD
Business value of an IT project	Traditional measures (e.g., ROI, payback)
	Business evaluation based on information economics: value linking, value acceleration, value restructuring, technological innovation
	Strategic match with business contribution to: product/service quality, customer responsiveness, management information, process flexibility
Risks	Unsuccessful strategy risk, IT strategy risk, definitional uncertainty (e.g., low degree of project specification), technological risk (e.g., bleeding edge hardware or software), development risk (e.g., inability to put things together), operational risk (e.g., resistance to change), IT service delivery risk (e.g., human/computer interface difficulties), BYOD risk stemming from lost devices, hackers, etc.
Business value of the IT department/functional area	% resources devoted to strategic projects
	% time spent by IT manager in meetings with corporate executives
	Perceived relationship between IT management and top management
Internal Processes	
Planning	% resources devoted to planning and review of IT activities
Development	% resources devoted to applications development
	Time required to develop a standard-sized new application
	% of applications programming with re-used code
	Time spent to repair bugs and fine-tune new applications
Operations	Number of end-user queries handled
	Average time required to address an end-user problem

(continued)

TABLE 3.3 (CONTINUED)

IT Scorecard Metrics

Perspective	Metric
Future Readiness	
IT specialist capabilities	IT training and development budget as a % of overall IT budget
	Expertise with specific technologies
	Expertise with emerging technologies
	Age distribution of IT staff
Satisfaction of IT staff	Turnover/retention of IT employees
	Productivity of IT employees
Applications portfolio	Age distribution
	Platform distribution
	Technical performance of applications portfolio
	User satisfaction with applications portfolio
Research into emerging technologies	IT research budget as percentage of IT budget
	Perceived satisfaction of top management with the reporting on how specific emerging technologies may or may not be applicable to the company

Metrics include retention of high-potential staff and external citations of IT achievement.

5. User satisfaction. Sample metrics include focused executive feedbacks and user perspective.

The Working Council also found that best-of-breed practitioner included two additional metric categories:

1. Information security. These metrics monitor remediation efforts for known vulnerabilities and track proactive policy and certification efforts. Sample metrics include percentage of staff receiving security training, percentage of external partners in compliance with security standards, and percentage of BYOD-related breaches.
2. Enterprise initiatives. Best-of-breed practitioners also use the scorecard to highlight IT's contributions to initiatives of corporate strategic importance, including the introduction and support of novel technological practices such as BYOD. Sample metrics include

percentage of acquired company systems integrated in merger and acquisition category and number of business process steps enabled by technology in Process Reengineering category.

Van Grembergen, Saull, and De Haes (2003) did an intensive study of the methodology used by Canada-based Great-West Life to develop their IT balanced scorecard. Great-West Life is the result of a merger of three financial services companies, each with its own IT services department. Stakeholders were quite concerned that they would lose control of their IT groups after the merger, so the merged IT department decided to utilize balanced scorecard to formalize the controls and measures required to ensure IT success.

The merged IT department consisted of seven units: career centers, management services, account management, application delivery, technology services, corporate technology, and the eBusiness solutions center. At the time of the study, the IT department employed 812 full-time and part-time employees.

The organizational structure of the IT department is quite interesting. Application delivery was created as a stand-alone unit to focus on continuous improvement of delivery performance. Account management was created to ensure effective communications with the company's end-users. This department takes great pains to educate end-users on IT corporate agendas and translate business needs into IT processes. As its name implies, the career center is focused on the professional development of IT staff. The corporate technology group utilizes a centralized approach to the development of a common enterprise architecture and technology policies. Finally, the management services group focuses on running IT as a business and provides for effective financial reporting and adherence to the IT scorecard.

As you can see, the organizational structure of the IT department roughly parallels that of the four perspectives of the balanced scorecard:

Financial perspective—Management services
Customer perspective—Account management
Internal perspective—Application delivery, technology services, corporate technology, eBusiness solutions
Learning and growth perspective—Career centers

Senior management of the three companies questioned the benefits of large investments in IT and wanted IT to be better aligned with corporate strategy. The following were some of the concerns of the different stakeholder groups:

1. Senior management
    a. Does IT support the achievement of business objectives?
    b. What value does the expenditure on IT deliver?
    c. Are IT costs being managed effectively?
    d. Are IT risks being identified and managed?
    e. Are targeted inter-company IT synergies being achieved?
2. Business unit executives
    a. Are IT services delivered at a competitive cost?
    b. Does IT deliver on its service-level commitments?
    c. Do IT investments positively affect business productivity or the customer experience?
    d. Does IT contribute to the achievement of our business strategies?
3. Corporate compliance internal audit
    a. Are the organization's assets and operations protected?
    b. Are the key business and technology risks being managed?
    c. Are proper processes, practices, and controls in place?
4. IT organization
    a. Are we developing the professional competencies needed for successful service delivery?
    b. Are we creating a positive workplace environment?
    c. Do we effectively measure and reward individual and team performance?
    d. Do we capture organizational knowledge to continuously improve performance?
    e. Can we attract/retain the talent we need to support the business?

One of the most important initiatives the new CIO undertook was to migrate the new information services group to a strategic partner as opposed to an IT services provider. As articulated by Venkatraman (1999), and summarized in Table 3.4, there are some important differences.

Great-West Life's IT scorecard, as described by Van Grembergen, Saull, and De Haes (2003), encompasses the following four quadrants:

Customer orientation—To be the supplier of choice for all information services, either directly or indirectly through supplier relationships.

TABLE 3.4

Moving IT from Service Provider to Strategic Partner

Service Provider	Strategic Partner
IT is for efficiency	IT for business growth
Budgets are driven by external benchmarks	Budgets are driven by business strategy
IT is separable from the business	IT is inseparable from the business
IT is seen as an expense to control	IT is seen as an investment to manage
IT managers are technical experts	IT managers are business problem solvers

Corporate contribution—To enable and contribute to the achievement of business objectives through effective delivery of value added information services.

Operational excellence—To deliver timely and effective services at targeted service levels and costs.

Future orientation—To develop the internal capabilities to continuously improve performance through innovation, learning, and personal organization growth.

The relationship between IT and business can be more explicitly expressed through a cascade of balanced scorecards, as shown in Figure 3.2.

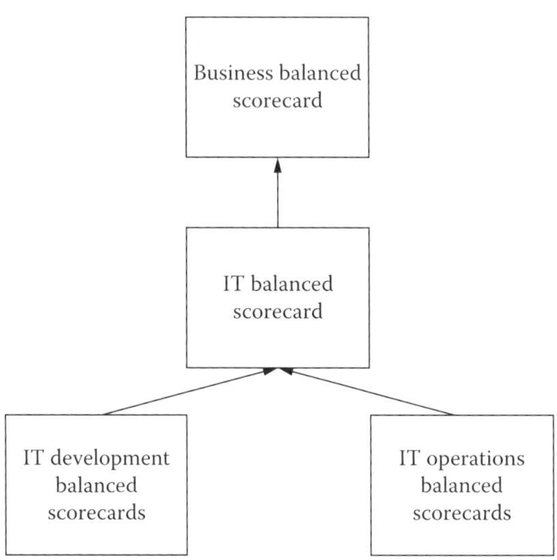

FIGURE 3.2
Cascade of balanced scorecards.

TABLE 3.5

Corporate Contribution Scorecard Evaluates IT from the Perspective of Senior Management

Objective	Measures	Benchmarks
Business/IT alignment	1. Operational plan/budget approval	1. Not applicable
Value delivery	2. Measured in business unit performance	2. Not applicable
Cost management	3. Attainment of expense and recovery targets	3. Industry expenditure comparisons
	4. Attainment of unit cost targets	4. Compass operational "top performance" levels
Risk management	5. Results of internal audits	5. Defined sound business practices
	6. Execution of security initiative	6. Not applicable
	7. Delivery of disaster recovery assessment	7. Not applicable
Inter-company synergy achievement	8. Single system solutions	8. Merger and acquisition guidelines
	9. Target state architecture approval	9. Not applicable
	10. Attainment of targeted integrated cost reductions	10. Not applicable
	11. IT organization integration	11. Not applicable

Cascading was used effectively at Great-West Life, similarly to the example in Figure 3.2, with the addition of "governance services" scorecards. You will notice the use of the term *scorecards*—plural. Each set of scorecards is actually composed of one or more unit scorecards. For example, the IT Operations scorecard also includes a scorecard for IT service desk. Great-West Life's four-quadrant IT scorecard consists of the following objectives, measures, and benchmarks, as shown in Tables 3.5 through 3.8.

The measures of each of these unit scorecards are aggregated in the IT balanced scorecard. This, in turn, is fed into and evaluated against the business balanced scorecard.

TABLE 3.6

Customer Orientation Scorecard Evaluated the Performance of IT from the Perspective of Internal Business Users

Objective	Measures	Benchmarks
Customer satisfaction	1. Business unit survey ratings a. Cost transparency and levels b. Service quality and responsiveness c. Value of IT advice and support d. Contribution to business objectives	1. Not applicable
Competitive costs	2. Attainment of unit cost targets	2. Compass operational "Top Level Performing" levels
	3. Blended labor rates	3. Market comparisons
Development services performance	4. Major project success scores	4. Not applicable
	5. Recorded goal attainment	
	6. Sponsor satisfaction ratings	
	7. Project governance rating	
Operational services performance	8. Attainment of targeted service levels	5. Competitor comparisons

REPRESENTATIVE IT BALANCED SCORECARD VALUE METRICS

There are a wide variety of metrics that an organization can utilize. Arveson (1998), writing for the Balanced Scorecard Institute, recommends the following metrics listed in Table 3.9.

Table 3.10 demonstrates the facility of modifying standard metrics to fit the BYOD paradigm.

Hopefully by now you understand the importance of developing cascading sets of interlinked balanced scorecards. From a departmental perspective, you will need to review, understand, and adhere to the organizational balanced scorecard from a macro perspective. However, you will need to review the departmental and system-level scorecards from a micro level.

TABLE 3.7

Operational Excellence Scorecard Views IT from the Perspective of IT Managers and Audit and Regulatory Bodies

Objective	Measures	Benchmarks
Development process performance	1. Function point measures of: a. productivity b. quality c. delivery rate	1. To be determined
Operational process performance	2. Benchmark based measures of: a. productivity b. responsiveness c. change management effectiveness d. incident occurrence levels	2. Selected compass benchmark studies
Process maturity	3. Assessed level of maturity and compliance in priority processes within: a. planning and organization b. acquisition and implementation c. delivery and support d. monitoring	3. To be defined
Enterprise architecture management	4. Major project architecture approval 5. Product acquisition compliance to technology standards 6. "State of the infrastructure" assessment	4. Sound business practices

KEEPING TRACK OF WHAT'S GOING ON

Operational awareness is the continuous attention to those activities that enable an organization to determine how well it is meeting pre-determined performance objectives. It is a necessary component of scorecard-type endeavors.

Factors influencing the level of operational awareness include: the nature of the work, the type of organization, and past performance. Accordingly, oversight organizations should maintain a relationship with the overseen organization and its management staff that affords ongoing awareness of that organization's strengths and weaknesses, if any. This monitoring or surveillance is a fundamental part of operational awareness.

TABLE 3.8

Future Orientation Perspective Shows IT Performance from the Perspective of the IT Department Itself: Process Owners, Practitioners, and Support Professionals

Objective	Measures	Benchmarks
Human resource management	1. Results against targets: a. staff complement by skill type b. staff turnover c. staff "billable" ratio d. professional development days per staff member	Market comparisons and industry standards
Employee satisfaction	2. Employee satisfaction survey scores in: a. compensation b. work climate c. feedback d. personal growth e. vision and purpose	Market comparisons and industry standards
Knowledge management	3. Delivery of internal process improvements to library 4. Implementation of "lessons learned" sharing process	1. Not applicable 2. Not applicable

Surveillance includes both formal and informal activities. Formal surveillance activities, based on specific criteria, are typically established in writing and provided to the organization. Surveillance, general in nature and usually conducted and reported orally, is an effective approach when circumstances require flexibility to accommodate changing emphasis, shifting priorities, or establishing rapport. There should be scheduled activities that provide for sufficient levels of operational awareness, a sampling of which follows:

1. Hold periodic meetings between management staff with agenda items designed to fully communicate subjects such as current initiatives, status of problem areas and actions taken to date, scheduled and planned training, policy and procedure revision status of organizational or contract change implementation, as appropriate.
2. Review status reports and trend analyses of performance measures, Perform limited on-site review (if applicable) of selected areas of significant risk as appropriate, and

TABLE 3.9

Recommended Metrics

System/Service/Function	Possible Metric(s)
R&D	Innovation capture
	# of quality improvements
	Customer satisfaction
Process improvement	Cycle time, activity costs
	# supplier relationships
	total cost of ownership
Resource planning, account management	Decision speed
	Lowering level of decision authority
Groupware	Cycle time reduction
	Paperwork reduction
Decision support	Decision reliability
	Timeliness
	Strategic awareness
	Lowering level of decision authority
Management information systems	Accuracy of data
	Timeliness
eCommerce	Market share
	Price premium for products/services
Information-based products and services	Operating margins
	New business revenues
	Cash flow
	Knowledge retention

3. Maintain awareness and involvement at a level such that a "for cause" issue is not a surprise.

When a "for cause" condition exists, certain surveillance activities may be assigned to other disciplines or functional areas. In these instances, supporting documentation resulting from the findings should be provided to the organization. Reports generated as a result of internal audits should be considered valuable diagnostic tools.

Selected significant risk areas typically refer to those actions or activities that require compliance with laws, regulations, and contract terms and conditions. There should be various control systems employed as necessary to ensure compliance and to test the currency and adequacy of the business system.

TABLE 3.10

Metrics for BYOD

Category	Focus	Purpose	Measure of Success
Budget Performance	Revisions to cost estimates of supporting BYOD.	Assess and manage project cost.	100% of revisions are reviewed and approved.
	Dollars spent vs. dollars budgeted.	Measure cost efficiency.	Project completed within approved cost parameters.
	Return on investment (ROI).	Track and assess performance of project investment portfolio.	ROI (positive cash flow) begins according to plan.
	Acquisition cost control.	Assess and manage acquisition dollars.	All applicable acquisition guidelines followed.
Product Quality	Defects in devices identified through quality activities.	Track progress in, and effectiveness of, defect removal.	90% of expected defects identified.
	Number of service calls.	Track customer problems.	75% reduction after three months of operation.
	BYOD user satisfaction index.	Identify trends.	95% positive rating.
	BYOD user satisfaction trend.	Improve user satisfaction.	5% improvement each quarter.
	Number of problems reported by users.	Assess quality of project deliverables.	100% of reported problems addressed within 72 hours.
Compliance	Compliance with Enterprise Architecture model requirements—e.g., integrate devices into architectural framework (data access).	Track progress toward department-wide architecture model.	Zero deviations without proper approvals.
	Compliance with Interoperability requirements.	Track progress toward system interoperability.	Product works effectively within system portfolio.

(continued)

TABLE 3.10 (CONTINUED)

Metrics for BYOD

Category	Focus	Purpose	Measure of Success
	Compliance with standards.	Alignment, interoperability, consistency.	No significant negative findings during architect assessments.
Cost Avoidance	System is easily upgraded—e.g., Apps, operating system, cloud services.	Take advantage of e.g., COTS upgrades.	Subsequent releases do not require major "glue code" project to upgrade.
	Avoid software costs due to usage of apps.	Reduce IT costs.	100% of redundant systems have been identified and eliminated.
	System is maintainable.	Reduce maintenance costs.	New version (of COTS) does not require "glue code."
Employee Satisfaction	System availability (up time).	Measure system availability.	100% of requirement is met.
	System functionality (meets user's needs).	Measure how well user needs are being met.	Positive trend in user satisfaction survey(s).
	Absence of defects (that impact customer).	Number of defects removed during project life cycle.	90% of defects expected were removed.
	Ease of learning and use.	Measure time to becoming productive.	Positive trend in training survey(s).
	Time it takes to answer calls for help.	Manage/reduce response times.	95% of severity one calls answered within 3 hours.
	Rating of training course.	Assess effectiveness and quality of training.	90% of responses of "good" or better.

VALIDATION AND VERIFICATION

Validation is the process of determining the degree of accuracy and completeness of the measurement techniques and the resulting data. Assessment practices and results should be periodically validated. The success of the self-assessment will depend largely on the mutually agreed and understood performance objectives, measures, and expectations; the scope, depth, and effectiveness of the self-assessment; and the integrity of the self-assessment.

Verification is the process of substantiating a set of data results by such means as checking stated facts, citations, measurements, or attendant circumstances.

Verification of data resulting, for example, from the self-assessment and other operational awareness activities will, in part, formulate the basis of the approval of the business system. The data should be analyzed to determine its accuracy and that comparisons or benchmarks are valid.

Verification of narrative or statistical data should be tailored by data type. For example, reports and documentation could substantiate the self-assessment results of measures designed to demonstrate efficiency. Likewise, interviews with selected internal and external customers and the organization's employees may also verify reported survey results. Trend analysis of the self-assessment results should reflect the factual information provided by the interviews with staff.

The following suggestions can assist in the validation and verification of the self-assessment process and results:

1. Mutually understand what and how the organization will measure performance.
2. Be familiar with the data sources and methods that will be used in the calculations.
3. Confirm that the collection methodology is accurate, complete, and timely.
4. Confirm that the data is properly controlled.
5. Become familiar with the trend analysis techniques to be used and gain assurances that the organization's personnel are qualified in this area.

If you don't measure, you'll never truly know how successful your BYOD program is.

REFERENCES

Arveson, P. (1998). The Value of Corporate IT Initiatives. http://www.balanced-scorecard.org/bscit/value_add.html.

Balanced Scorecard Collaborative. (2004). htpp://www.bscol.com.

Martinsons, M., Davison, R., and Tse, D. (1999, February). The balanced scorecard: A foundation for the strategic management of information systems. *Decision Support Systems, 25*(1), pp. 71–88.

Van Grembergen, W., Saull, R., and De Haes, S. (2003). Linking the IT balanced scorecard to the business objectives at a major Canadian financial group. *Journal of Information Technology Cases and Application, 5*(1).

Venkatraman, N. (1999). Valuing the IS contribution to the business. *Computer Sciences Corporation Report.* http://lef.csc.com/publications/245

4

Assessment and Mitigation of Risks in a BYOD Environment

BYOD solutions include not just the device and the applications (apps) on that device. Mobile devices (e.g., laptops, phones, tablets) are also used to connect to organizational systems. This chapter, which is based on information provided by the National Institute of Standards and Technology (NIST), illustrates how a hypothetical organization deals with computer security issues in its enterprise operating environment. In the real world, many solutions exist for computer security problems. No single solution can solve similar security problems in all environments. Likewise, the solutions presented in this example may not be appropriate for all environments. Essentially, there are two methodologies that are used to ensure that mobile devices are securely accessing the network: Agent-based solutions and Network-based Mobile Device Management (MDM). In the Network-based MDM paradigm, no agents are actually stored on the client device. Instead, network devices are intelligent enough to make security decisions based on user identity, device type, location, and time. Both should be supported. This chapter does not delve into these specific issues. That will be discussed in Chapter 5, which provide guidelines for managing and securing mobile devices in the enterprise.

This example can be used to help understand how security issues are examined, how some potential solutions are analyzed, how their cost and benefits are weighed, and ultimately how management accepts responsibility for risks.

This case study about a fictitious company we will call "A Typical Organization" is provided for illustrative purposes only, and should not be construed as guidance or specific recommendations to solving specific security issues. Because a comprehensive example attempting to illustrate all security topics would be inordinately long, this example necessarily simplifies the issues presented and omits many details. For instance, to highlight the similarities and differences among controls in the different processing environments, it addresses some of the major types of processing platforms linked together in a distributed system: personal computers, local-area networks, wide-area networks, and mainframes; it does not show how to secure these platforms.

This chapter also highlights the importance of management's acceptance of a particular level of risk—this will, of course, vary from organization to organization. It is management's prerogative to decide what level of risk is appropriate, given operating and budget environments and other applicable factors.

INITIATING THE RISK ASSESSMENT

A Typical Organization has information systems that comprise and are intertwined with several different kinds of assets valuable enough to merit protection. System components owned and operated by A Typical Organization are assets, as are personnel information, contracting and procurement documents, draft regulations, internal correspondence, and a variety of other day-to-day business documents, memos, databases, and reports. A Typical Organization's assets include intangible elements as well, such as reputation of the organization and the confidence of its employees that information will be handled properly.

A recent change in the directorship of A Typical Organization has brought in a new management team. Among the new Chief Information Officer's first actions was appointing a Computer Security Program Manager who immediately initiated a comprehensive risk analysis to assess the soundness of A Typical Organization's computer security program in protecting the organization's assets and its compliance with organizational and regulatory directives. This analysis drew upon prior risk assessments, threat studies, and applicable internal control reports. The Computer Security Program Manager also established a timetable for periodic reassessments.

Since the wide-area network and mainframe used by A Typical Organization are owned and operated by other organizations, they were not treated in the risk assessment as A Typical Organization's assets. And although A Typical Organization's personnel, buildings, and facilities are essential assets, the Computer Security Program Manager considered them to be outside the scope of the risk analysis.

After examining A Typical Organization's computer system, the risk assessment team identified specific threats to A Typical Organization's assets, reviewed A Typical Organization's safeguards against those threats, identified the vulnerabilities of those policies, and recommended specific actions for mitigating the remaining risks to A Typical Organization's computer security. The following sections provide highlights from the risk assessment. The assessment addressed many other issues at the programmatic and system levels.

A TYPICAL ORGANIZATION'S COMPUTER SYSTEM

A Typical Organization relies on the distributed computer systems and networks shown in Figure 4.1. They consist of a collection of components, some of which are systems in their own right. Some belong to A Typical Organization, but others are owned and operated by other organizations.

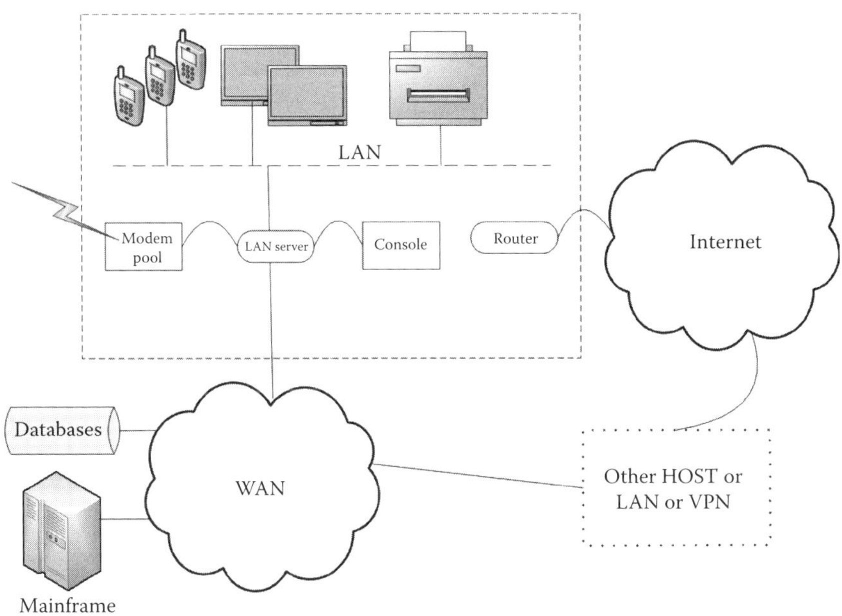

FIGURE 4.1
Typical system architecture.

This section describes these components, their role in the overall distributed system architecture, and how they are used by A Typical Organization.

SYSTEM ARCHITECTURE

A Typical Organization's staff (a mix of clerical, technical, and managerial staff) are provided with personal computers (PCs) located in their offices. Some employees use their own devices out in the field or at home, which typically consists of tablets, laptops, and smartphones.

The devices are connected to a local area network (LAN) so that users can exchange and share information. The central component of the LAN is a LAN server, a more powerful computer that acts as an intermediary between devices on the network and provides a large volume of disk storage for shared information, including shared application programs. The server provides logical access controls on potentially sharable information via elementary access control lists. These access controls can be used to limit user access to various files and programs stored on the server. Some programs stored on the server can be retrieved via the LAN and executed on a PC or other device; others can only be executed on the server. To initiate a session on the network or execute programs on the server, users must log into the server and provide a user identifier and password known to the server. Then they may use files to which they have access.

Since A Typical Organization lets employees access information via BYOD devices, the LAN also provides a connection to the Internet via a router. The router is a network interface device that translates between the protocols and addresses associated with the LAN and the Internet. The router also performs network packet filtering, a form of network access control.

SYSTEM OPERATIONAL AUTHORITY/OWNERSHIP

The system components contained within the large dashed rectangle shown in Figure 4.1 are managed and operated by an organization within A Typical Organization known as the Computer Operations Group (COG).

Devices connect to the organization for word processing, data manipulation, and other common applications, including spreadsheet and project management tools. Many of these tasks are concerned with data that are sensitive with respect to confidentiality or integrity. Some of these documents and data also need to be available in a timely manner.

THREATS TO A TYPICAL ORGANIZATION'S ASSETS

Different assets of A Typical Organization are subject to different kinds of threats. Some threats are considered less likely than others, and the potential impact of different threats may vary greatly. The likelihood of threats is generally difficult to estimate accurately. Both A Typical Organization and the risk assessment's authors have attempted to the extent possible to base these estimates on historical data, but have also tried to anticipate new trends stimulated by emerging technologies.

A Typical Organization's building facilities and physical plant are several decades old and are frequently under repair or renovation. As a result, power, air-conditioning, and LAN, VPN, or WAN connectivity for the server are typically interrupted several times a year for periods of up to one workday. For example, on several occasions, construction workers have inadvertently severed power or network cables. Fires, floods, storms, and other natural disasters can also interrupt computer operations, as can equipment malfunctions.

Another threat of small likelihood, but significant potential impact, is that of a malicious or disgruntled employee or outsider seeking to disrupt time-critical processing (e.g., payroll) by deleting necessary inputs or system accounts, misconfiguring access controls, planting computer viruses, or stealing or sabotaging computers or related equipment. Such interruptions, depending upon when they occur, can prevent time and attendance data from getting processed and transferred to the mainframe before the payroll processing deadline.

Other kinds of threats may be stimulated by the growing market for information about an organization's employees or internal activities. Individuals who have legitimate work-related reasons for access to the master employee database may attempt to disclose such information to other employees or contractors or to sell it to private investigators, employment recruiters, the press, or other organizations. A Typical Organization considers such threats to be moderately likely and of low to high potential impact, depending on the type of information involved.

Many of the human threats of concern to A Typical Organization originate from insiders. Nevertheless, A Typical Organization also recognizes the need to protect its assets from outsiders. Such attacks may serve many different purposes and pose a broad spectrum of risks, including unauthorized disclosure or modification of information, unauthorized use of services and assets, or unauthorized denial of services.

As shown in Figure 4.1, A Typical Organization's systems are connected to the three external networks: (1) the Internet, (2) the Interorganization WAN, and (3) the public-switched (telephone) network. Although these networks are a source of security risks, connectivity with them is essential to A Typical Organization's mission and to the productivity of its employees; connectivity cannot be terminated simply because of security risks.

In each of the past few years before establishing its current set of network safeguards, A Typical Organization had detected several attempts by outsiders to penetrate its systems. Most, but not all of these, have come from the Internet, and those that succeeded did so by learning or guessing user account passwords. In two cases, the attacker deleted or corrupted significant amounts of data, most of which were later restored from backup files. In most cases, A Typical Organization could detect no ill effects of the attack, but concluded that the attacker may have browsed through some files. A Typical Organization also conceded that its systems did not have audit logging capabilities sufficient to track an attacker's activities. Hence, for most of these attacks, A Typical Organization could not accurately gauge the extent of penetration.

In one case, an attacker made use of a bug in an e-mail utility and succeeded in acquiring System Administrator privileges on the server—a significant breach. A Typical Organization found no evidence that the attacker attempted to exploit these privileges before being discovered two days later. When the attack was detected, COG immediately contacted A Typical Organization's Incident Handling Team, and was told that a bug fix had been distributed by the server vendor several months earlier. To its embarrassment, COG discovered that it had already received the fix, which it then promptly installed. It now believes that no subsequent attacks of the same nature have succeeded.

Although A Typical Organization has no evidence that it has been significantly harmed to date by attacks via external networks, it believes that these attacks have great potential to inflict damage. A Typical Organization's management considers itself lucky that such attacks have not harmed A Typical Organization's reputation and the confidence of the

TABLE 4.1

Threat Assessment

Potential Threat	Probability	Impact
Accidental loss/release of disclosure-sensitive information	Medium	Low/Medium
Accidental destruction of information	High	Medium
Loss of information due to virus contamination	Medium	Medium
Misuse of system resources	Low	Low
Theft	High	Medium
Unauthorized access to telecom resources	Medium	Medium
Natural disaster	Low	High

citizens it serves. It also believes the likelihood of such attacks via external networks will increase in the future.

A Typical Organization's systems also are exposed to several other threats that, for reasons of space, cannot be fully enumerated here. Examples of threats and A Typical Organization's assessment of their probabilities and impacts include those listed in Table 4.1.

CURRENT SECURITY MEASURES

A Typical Organization has numerous policies and procedures for protecting its assets against the above threats. These are articulated in A Typical Organization's Computer Security Manual. Readers will want to review the Security Glossary, found in Appendix A.

A Typical Organization's Computer Operations Group (COG) is responsible for controlling, administering, and maintaining the computer resources owned and operated by A Typical Organization. These functions are depicted in Figure 4.1 enclosed in the large, dashed rectangle. Only individuals holding the job title System Administrator are authorized to establish log-in IDs and passwords on multiuser A Typical Organization systems (e.g., the LAN server). Only A Typical Organization's employees and contract personnel may use the system, and only after receiving written authorization from the department supervisor (or, in the case of contractors, the contracting officer) to whom these individuals report.

COG issues copies of all relevant security policies and procedures to new users. Before activating a system account for new users, COG requires that they (1) attend a security awareness and training course or complete an interactive computer-aided-instruction training session, and (2) sign an acknowledgment form indicating that they understand their security responsibilities.

Authorized users are assigned a secret log-in ID and password, which they must not share with anyone else. They are expected to comply with all of A Typical Organization's password selection and security procedures (e.g., periodically changing passwords). Users who fail to do so are subject to a range of penalties.

Users creating data that are sensitive with respect to disclosure or modification are expected to make effective use of the automated access control mechanisms available on A Typical Organization computers to reduce the risk of exposure to unauthorized individuals. (Appropriate training and education are in place to help users do this.) In general, access to disclosure-sensitive information is to be granted only to individuals whose jobs require it.

A Typical Organization requires various organizations within it to develop contingency plans, test them annually, and establish appropriate administrative and operational procedures for supporting them. The plans must identify the facilities, equipment, supplies, procedures, and personnel needed to ensure reasonable continuity of operations under a broad range of adverse circumstances.

COG CONTINGENCY PLANNING

COG is responsible for developing and maintaining a contingency plan that sets forth the procedures and facilities to be used when physical plant failures, natural disasters, or major equipment malfunctions occur sufficient to disrupt the normal use of A Typical Organization's PCs, LAN, server, router, printers, and other associated equipment.

The plan prioritizes applications that rely on these resources, indicating those that should be suspended if available automated functions or capacities are temporarily degraded. COG personnel have identified backup facilities sufficient to support A Typical Organization's system-based operations for a few days during an emergency.

No communication devices or network interfaces may be connected to A Typical Organization's systems without written approval of the COG Manager.

To protect against accidental corruption or loss of data, COG personnel back up the LAN server's disks onto magnetic tape every night and transport the tapes weekly to a sister organization for storage. A Typical Organization's policies also stipulate that all BYOD users are responsible for backing up weekly any significant data stored on their devices. For the past several years, COG has issued a yearly memorandum reminding users of this responsibility.

To prevent more limited computer equipment malfunctions from interrupting routine business operations, COG maintains an inventory of spare devices. COG is also responsible for reviewing audit logs generated by the server, identifying audit records indicative of security violations, and reporting such indications to the Incident-Handling Team. The COG Manager assigns these duties to specific members of the staff and ensures that they are implemented as intended.

The COG Manager is responsible for assessing adverse circumstances and for providing recommendations to A Typical Organization's Director. Based on these and other sources of input, the Director will determine whether the circumstances are dire enough to merit activating various sets of procedures called for in the contingency plan.

DIVISIONAL CONTINGENCY PLANNING

A Typical Organization's divisions also must develop and maintain their own contingency plans. The plans must identify critical business functions, the system resources and applications on which they depend, and the maximum acceptable periods of interruption that these functions can tolerate without significant reduction in A Typical Organization's ability to fulfill its mission. The head of each division is responsible for ensuring that the division's contingency plan and associated support activities are adequate.

For each major application used by multiple divisions, a chief of a single division must be designated as the application owner. The designated official (supported by his or her staff) is responsible for addressing that application in the contingency plan and for coordinating with other divisions that use the application.

If a division relies exclusively on computer resources maintained by COG (e.g., the LAN), it need not duplicate COG's contingency plan, but is responsible for reviewing the adequacy of that plan. If COG's plan does not adequately address the division's needs, the division must communicate its concerns to the COG Director. In either situation, the division must make known the criticality of its applications to the COG. If the division relies on computer resources or services that are not provided by COG, the division is responsible for (1) developing its own contingency plan or (2) ensuring that the contingency plans of other organizations (e.g., the WAN service provider) provide adequate protection against service disruptions.

The LAN server operating system's access controls provide extensive features for controlling access to files. These include group-oriented controls that allow teams of users to be assigned to named groups by the System Administrator. Group members are then allowed access to sensitive files not accessible to nonmembers. Each user can be assigned to several groups according to need to know. (The reliable functioning of these controls is assumed, perhaps incorrectly, by A Typical Organization.)

All users undergo security awareness training when first provided accounts on the server. Among other things, the training stresses the necessity of protecting passwords. It also instructs users to log off the server before going home at night or before leaving the PC unattended for periods exceeding an hour.

PROTECTION AGAINST NETWORK-RELATED THREATS

A Typical Organization's current set of external network safeguards has only been in place for a few months. The basic approach is to tightly restrict the kinds of external network interactions that can occur by funneling all traffic to and from external networks through interfaces that filter out unauthorized kinds of interactions.

Figure 4.1 shows that the network router is the only direct interface between the LAN and the Internet. The router is a dedicated special-purpose computer that translates between the protocols and addresses associated with the LAN and the Internet. Internet protocols, unlike those used on the WAN, specify that packets of information coming from or going to the Internet must carry an indicator of the kind of service that is being requested or used to process the information. This makes it possible for the router to distinguish e-mail packets from other kinds of packets—for example, those associated with a remote login request. The router has been configured by COG to carefully authorize all remote log-in sessions.

A Typical Organization relies on systems and components that it cannot control directly because they are owned by other organizations. A Typical Organization has developed a policy to avoid undue risk in such situations. The policy states that system components controlled and operated by organizations other than A Typical Organization may not be used to process, store, or transmit A Typical Organization information without obtaining explicit permission from the application owner and the COG Manager. Permission to use such system components may not be granted without written commitment from the controlling organization that A Typical Organization's information will be safeguarded commensurate with its value, as designated by A Typical Organization. This policy is somewhat mitigated by the fact that A Typical Organization has developed an issue-specific policy on the use of the Internet, which allows for its use for e-mail with outside organizations and access to other resources (but not for transmission of A Typical Organization's proprietary data).

VULNERABILITIES REPORTED BY THE RISK ASSESSMENT TEAM

The risk assessment team found that many of the risks to which A Typical Organization is exposed stem from (1) the failure of individuals to comply with established policies and procedures or (2) the use of automated mechanisms whose assurance is questionable because of the ways they have been developed, tested, implemented, used, or maintained. The team also identified specific vulnerabilities in A Typical Organization's policies and procedures for protecting against payroll fraud and errors, interruption of operations, disclosure and brokering of confidential information, and unauthorized access to data by outsiders.

When a person enters a password to the server, the password is sent to the server by broadcasting it over the LAN "in the clear." This allows the password to be intercepted easily by any other device connected to the LAN. In fact, so-called password sniffer programs that capture passwords in this way are widely available. Similarly, a malicious program planted on a PC could also intercept passwords before transmitting them to the server. An unauthorized individual who obtained the captured passwords could then run applications. Users might also store passwords in a log-on script file.

According to the risk assessment, the server's access controls, with prior caveats, probably provide acceptable protection against unauthorized modification of data stored on the server. The assessment concluded that a WAN-based attack involving collusion between an employee of A Typical Organization and an employee of the WAN service provider, although unlikely, should not be dismissed entirely, especially since A Typical Organization has only cursory information about the service provider's personnel security practices and no contractual authority over how it operates the WAN.

The access control on the mainframe is strong and provides good protection against intruders breaking into a second application after they have broken into a first. However, previous audits have shown that the difficulties of system administration may present some opportunities for intruders to defeat access controls.

The risk assessment concluded that A Typical Organization's safeguards against accidental corruption and loss of time and attendance data were adequate, but that safeguards for some other kinds of data were not. The assessment included an informal audit of a dozen randomly chosen devices (PCs and other devices) and users in the organization. It concluded that many users store significant data on their devices, but do not back them up. Based on anecdotes, the assessment's authors stated that there appear to have been many past incidents of loss of information stored on devices and predicted that such losses would continue.

A Typical Organization takes a conservative approach toward protecting information about its employees. Since information brokerage is more likely to be a threat to large collections of data, A Typical Organization risk assessment focused primarily, but not exclusively, on protecting the mainframe.

The risk assessment concluded that significant, avoidable information brokering vulnerabilities were present—particularly due to A Typical Organization's lack of compliance with its own policies and procedures. Documents were typically not stored securely after hours, and few PCs were routinely locked. Worse yet, few were routinely powered down, and many were left logged into the LAN server overnight. These practices make it easy for an A Typical Organization employee wandering the halls after hours to browse or copy information on another employee's desk, PC hard disk, or LAN server directories.

The risk assessment pointed out that information sent to or retrieved from the server is subject to eavesdropping by other PCs and devices on the LAN. The LAN hardware transmits information by broadcasting it to all connection points on the LAN cable. Moreover, information sent to or retrieved from the server is transmitted in the clear—that is, without encryption. Given the widespread availability of LAN "sniffer" programs, LAN eavesdropping is trivial for a prospective information broker and, hence, is likely to occur.

Last, the assessment noted that A Typical Organization's databases stored on the mainframe, where they might be a target for information brokering by employees of the organization that owns the mainframe. It might also be a target for information brokering, fraudulent modification, or other illicit acts by any outsider who penetrates the mainframe via another host on the WAN.

The risk assessment concurred with the general approach taken by A Typical Organization, but identified several vulnerabilities. It reiterated previous concerns about the lack of assurance associated with the server's access controls and pointed out that these play a critical role in A Typical Organization's approach. The assessment noted that the e-mail allows a user to include a copy of any otherwise accessible file in an outgoing mail message. If an attacker accessed the server and succeeded in logging in as A Typical Organization employee, the attacker could use the mail utility to export copies of all the files accessible to that employee. In fact, copies could be mailed to any host on the Internet.

The assessment also noted that the WAN service provider may rely on microwave stations or satellites as relay points, thereby exposing A Typical Organization's information to eavesdropping. Similarly, any information, including passwords and mail messages, transmitted during a dial-in session is subject to eavesdropping.

RECOMMENDATIONS FOR MITIGATING THE IDENTIFIED VULNERABILITIES

The discussions in the following subsections were chosen to illustrate a broad sampling of topics. Risk management and security program management themes are integral throughout, with particular emphasis given to the selection of risk-driven safeguards.

To remove the vulnerabilities related to unauthorized access to data, the risk assessment team recommended the use of stronger authentication mechanisms based on smart tokens to generate one-time passwords that cannot be used by an interloper for subsequent sessions. Such mechanisms would make it very difficult for outsiders (e.g., from the Internet) who penetrate systems on the WAN to use them to attack the mainframe. The assessment team also recommended improving the server's administrative procedures and the speed with which security-related bug fixes distributed by the vendor are installed on the server.

While the immaturity of the LAN server's access controls was judged a significant source of risk, COG was only able to identify one other PC LAN product that would be significantly better in this respect. Unfortunately, this product was considerably less friendly to users and application developers, and incompatible with other applications used by A Typical Organization. The negative impact of changing PC LAN products was judged too high for the potential incremental gain in security benefits. Consequently, A Typical Organization decided to accept the risks accompanying use of the current product, but directed COG to improve its monitoring of the server's access control configuration and its responsiveness to vendor security reports and bug fixes.

A Typical Organization concurred that risks of fraud due to unauthorized modification of data at or in transit to the mainframe should not be accepted unless no practical solutions could be identified. After discussions with the mainframe's owning organization, A Typical Organization concluded that the owning organization was unlikely to adopt the advanced authentication techniques advocated in the risk assessment.

The assessment recommended that COG institute a program of periodic internal training and awareness sessions for COG personnel having contingency plan responsibilities. The assessment urged that COG undertake a rehearsal during the next three months in which selected parts of the plan would be exercised. The rehearsal should include attempting to initiate some aspect of processing activities at one of the designated alternative sites. A Typical Organization's management agreed that additional contingency plan training was needed for COG personnel and committed itself to its first plan rehearsal within three months.

After a short investigation, A Typical Organization divisions owning applications that depend on the WAN concluded that WAN outages, although inconvenient, would not have a major impact on A Typical Organization. This is because the few time-sensitive applications that required WAN-based communication with the mainframe were originally designed to work with magnetic tape instead of the WAN, and could still operate in that mode; hence courier-delivered magnetic tapes could be used as an alternative input medium in case of a WAN outage. The divisions responsible for contingency planning for these applications agreed to incorporate into their contingency plans both descriptions of these procedures and other improvements.

A Typical Organization's management agreed to improve adherence to its virus-prevention procedures. It agreed (from the point of view of the entire organization) that information stored on external devices is frequently lost. It estimated, however, that the labor hours lost as a result would amount to less than a person year—which A Typical Organization management does not consider to be unacceptable. After reviewing options for reducing this risk, A Typical Organization concluded that it would be cheaper to accept the associated loss than to commit significant resources in an attempt to avoid it.

A Typical Organization concurred with the risk assessment's conclusions about its exposure to information-brokering risks, and adopted most of the associated recommendations. The assessment recommended that A Typical Organization improve its security awareness training (e.g., via mandatory refresher courses) and that it institute some form of compliance audits. The training should be sure to stress the penalties for noncompliance.

The assessment recommended that an activity log be installed on the server (and regularly reviewed). Moreover, it would avoid unnecessary reliance on the server's access-control features, which are of uncertain assurance. The assessment noted, however, that this strategy conflicts with the desire to store most information on the server's disks so that it is backed up routinely by COG personnel. (This could be offset by assigning responsibility for someone other than the PC owner to make backup copies.) Since the security habits of A Typical Organization's PC users have generally been poor, the assessment also recommended use of hard-disk encryption utilities to protect disclosure-sensitive information on unattended PCs from browsing by unauthorized individuals. Also, ways to encrypt information on the server's disks would be studied.

The assessment recommended that A Typical Organization require stronger authentication for remote access, which would prevent a user from including files in outgoing mail messages; replace its current modem pool with encrypting modems, and provide each dial-in user with such a modem; and work with the mainframe organization to install a similar encryption capability for server-to-mainframe communications over the network.

SUMMARY

As illustrated, effective computer security requires clear direction from upper management. Upper management must assign security responsibilities to organizational elements and individuals and must formulate or elaborate the security policies that become the foundation for the organization's security program. These policies must be based on an understanding of the organization's mission priorities and the assets and business operations necessary to fulfill them. They must also be based on a pragmatic assessment of the threats against these assets and operations. A critical element is assessment of threat likelihoods. These are most accurate when derived from historical data, but must also anticipate trends stimulated by emerging technologies.

A good security program relies on an integrated, cost-effective collection of physical, procedural, and automated controls. Cost-effectiveness requires targeting these controls at the threats that pose the highest risks while accepting other residual risks. The difficulty of applying controls properly and in a consistent manner over time has been the downfall of many security programs. This chapter has provided numerous examples in which major security vulnerabilities arose from a lack of assurance or compliance. Hence, periodic compliance audits, examinations of the effectiveness of controls, and reassessments of threats are essential to the success of any organization's security program.

REFERENCE

NIST. Preface. *Special Publication 800-12: An introduction to computer security—The NIST handbook*. Retrieved from http://csrc.nist.gov/publications/nistpubs/800-12/800-12-html/chapter20-printable.html.

5

Guidelines for Managing and Securing Mobile Devices in the Enterprise

The purpose of this chapter is to help organizations centrally manage and secure mobile devices, such as smartphones and tablets. This chapter, which is aligned with NIST guidance, provides recommendations for selecting, implementing, and using centralized management technologies, and it explains the security concerns inherent in mobile device use and provides recommendations for securing mobile devices throughout their life cycles.

The scope of this chapter includes both organization-provided and personally owned (bring your own device) mobile devices.

MOBILE DEVICE OVERVIEW

Mobile device features are constantly changing, so it is difficult to define the term *mobile device*. However, as features change, so do threats and security controls, so it is important to establish a baseline of mobile device features. The following hardware and software characteristics collectively define the baseline for the purposes of this discussion:

1. A small form factor
2. At least one wireless network interface for Internet access (data communications). This interface uses Wi-Fi, cellular networking, or other technologies that connect the mobile device to network infrastructures with Internet connectivity.
3. Local built-in (non-removable) data storage

4. An operating system that is not a full-fledged desktop or laptop operating system
5. Applications available through multiple methods (provided with the operating system, accessed through web browser, acquired, and installed from third parties)
6. Built-in features for synchronizing local data with a remote location (desktop or laptop computer, organization servers, telecommunications provider servers, other third party servers, etc.)

The list below details other common, but optional, characteristics of mobile devices. These features do not define the scope of devices included in the publication, but rather indicate features that are particularly important in terms of security risk. This list is not intended to be exhaustive, and is merely illustrative of common features of interest as of this writing.

1. Network services
2. One or more wireless personal area network interfaces, such as Bluetooth or near-field communications
3. One or more wireless network interfaces for voice communications, such as cellular
4. Global Positioning System (GPS), which enables location services
5. One or more digital cameras
6. Microphone
7. Storage
8. Support for removable media
9. Support for using the device itself as removable storage for another computing device

HIGH-LEVEL THREATS AND VULNERABILITIES

Mobile devices typically need to support multiple security objectives. These can be accomplished through a combination of security features built into the mobile devices and additional security controls applied to the mobile devices and other components of the enterprise IT infrastructure. The most common security objectives for mobile devices are as follows:

- Confidentiality—ensure that transmitted and stored data cannot be read by unauthorized parties.
- Integrity—detect any intentional or unintentional changes to transmitted and stored data.
- Availability—ensure that users can access resources using mobile devices whenever needed.

To achieve these objectives, mobile devices should be secured against a variety of threats. Mobile devices often need additional protection because their nature generally places them at higher exposure to threats than other client devices (e.g., desktop and laptop devices only used within the organization's facilities and on the organization's networks). Before designing and deploying mobile device solutions, organizations should develop system threat models for the mobile devices and the resources that are accessed through the mobile devices. Threat modeling involves identifying resources of interest and the feasible threats, vulnerabilities, and security controls related to these resources, then quantifying the likelihood of successful attacks and their impacts, and finally analyzing this information to determine where security controls need to be improved or added. Threat modeling helps organizations to identify security requirements and to design the mobile device solution to incorporate the controls needed to meet the security requirements. Major security concerns for these technologies that would be included in most mobile device threat models are listed below.

Mobile devices are typically used in a variety of locations outside the organization's control, such as employees' homes, coffee shops, hotels, and conferences. Even mobile devices only used within an organization's facilities are often transported from place to place within the facilities. The devices' mobile nature makes them much more likely to be lost or stolen than other devices, so their data is at increased risk of compromise. When planning mobile device security policies and controls, organizations should assume that mobile devices will be acquired by malicious parties who will attempt to recover sensitive data either directly from the devices themselves or indirectly by using the devices to access the organization's remote resources.

The mitigation strategy for this is layered. One layer involves protecting sensitive data—either encrypting the mobile device's storage so that sensitive data cannot be recovered from it by unauthorized parties, or not storing sensitive data on mobile devices. Even if a mobile device is always in the possession of its owner, there are other physical security risks, such as an attacker looking over a teleworker's shoulder at a coffee shop and viewing sensitive data on the mobile device's screen (e.g., a password being entered). A second mitigation layer involves requiring authentication before gaining access to the mobile device or the organization's resources accessible through the device. A mobile device usually has a single authenticator—not a separate account for each user of the device—as it is assumed that the device only has one user. So there is no username, just a password, which is often a PIN. More robust forms of authentication, such as domain authentication, can be used instead of or in addition to the built-in device authentication capabilities.

USE OF UNTRUSTED MOBILE DEVICES AND NETWORKS

Many mobile devices, particularly those that are personally owned (bring your own device, BYOD), are not necessarily trustworthy. Current mobile devices lack the root of trust features that are increasingly built into laptops and other types of hosts. There is also frequent jailbreaking and rooting of mobile devices, which means that the built-in restrictions on security, operating system use, and so on, have been bypassed. Organizations should assume that all phones are untrusted unless the organization has properly secured them before user access and monitors them continuously while in use with enterprise applications or data.

There are several additional possible mitigation strategies related to use of untrusted mobile devices. One option is to restrict or prohibit use of BYOD devices, thus favoring organization-issued devices. Another effective technique is to fully secure each organization-issued phone before allowing it to be used; this gets the phone in as trusted a state as possible when initially deployed, and deviations from this secure state can be monitored and addressed. There are also technical solutions for achieving degrees of trust, such as running the organization's software in a secure, isolated sandbox on the phone, or using device integrity scanning applications.

Because mobile devices primarily use non-organizational networks for Internet access, organizations normally have no control over the security of the external networks the devices use. Communications systems may include broadband networks, such as cable, and wireless mechanisms such as Wi-Fi and cellular networks. These communications systems are susceptible to eavesdropping, which places sensitive information transmitted at risk of compromise. Man-in-the-middle attacks may also be performed to intercept and modify communications. Unless it is absolutely certain that the mobile device will not be used on any networks not controlled by the organization or any other untrusted networks, organizations should plan their mobile device security on the assumption that the networks between the mobile device and the organization cannot be trusted.

Risk from use of unsecured networks can be reduced by using strong encryption technologies to protect the confidentiality and integrity of communications, as well as using mutual authentication mechanisms to verify the identities of both endpoints before transmitting data.

USE OF APPLICATIONS CREATED BY UNKNOWN PARTIES

Mobile devices are designed to make it easy to find, acquire, install, and use third-party applications. This poses obvious security risks, especially for mobile device platforms that do not place security restrictions or other limitations on third-party application publishing. Organizations should plan their mobile device security on the assumption that unknown third-party mobile device applications downloadable by users should not be trusted.

Risk from these applications can be reduced in several ways, such as prohibiting installation of all third-party applications, implementing whitelisting to prohibit installation of all unapproved applications, or implementing a secure sandbox that isolates the organization's data and applications from all other data and applications on the mobile device. Another general recommendation is to perform a risk assessment on each third-party application before permitting its use on the organization's mobile devices.

It is important to note that even if these mitigation strategies are implemented for third-party applications, users can still access untrusted web-based applications through browsers built into their mobile devices. The risks inherent in this can be reduced by prohibiting or restricting browser access, or by using a separate browser within a secure sandbox for all browser-based access related to the organization, leaving the mobile device's built-in browser for other uses.

INTERACTION WITH OTHER SYSTEMS

Mobile devices may interact with other systems in terms of data synchronization and storage. Local system interaction generally involves connecting a mobile device to a desktop or laptop via a cable for charging and/or syncing. Remote system interaction most often involves automatic backups of data to a cloud-based storage solution. When all of these components are under the organization's control, risk is generally acceptable, but often one or more of these components are external. Examples include attaching a personally owned mobile device to an organization-issued laptop, attaching an organization-issued mobile device to a personally owned laptop, and attaching an organization-issued mobile device to a remote backup service. In all of these scenarios, the organization's data is at risk of being stored in an unsecured location outside the organization's control; transmission of malware from device to device is also a possibility.

The mitigation strategies depend on the type of attachment. Preventing an organization-issued mobile device from syncing with a personally owned computer necessitates security controls on the mobile device that restrict what devices it can synchronize with. Preventing a personally owned mobile device from syncing with an organization-issued computer necessitates security controls on the organization-issued computer, restricting the connection of mobile devices. Finally, preventing the use of remote backup services can possibly be achieved by blocking use of those services (e.g., not allowing the domain services to be contacted) or by configuring the mobile devices not to use such services.

USE OF UNTRUSTED CONTENT

Mobile devices may use untrusted content that other types of devices generally do not encounter. An example is Quick Response (QR) codes. They are specifically designed to be viewed and processed by mobile device cameras. Each QR code is translated to a URL, so malicious QR codes could direct mobile devices to malicious websites. This could allow for targeted attacking, such as placing malicious QR codes at a location where targeted users gather.

A primary mitigation strategy is to educate users on the risks inherent in untrusted content and to discourage users from accessing untrusted content with any mobile devices they use for work. It is also possible to restrict peripheral use on mobile devices, such as disabling camera use in order to prevent QR codes from being processed.

USE OF LOCATION SERVICES

Mobile devices with GPS capabilities typically run what are known as location services. These services map a GPS-acquired location to the corresponding businesses or other entities close to that location. Location services are heavily used by social media, navigation, web browsers, and other mobile-centric applications. In terms of organization security, mobile devices with location services enabled are at increased risk of targeted attacks because it is easier for potential attackers to determine where the user and the mobile device are, and to correlate that information with other sources about who the user associates with and the kinds of activities they perform in particular locations.

This situation can be mitigated by disabling location services or by prohibiting use of location services for particular applications such as social networking or photo applications. Users may also be trained to turn off location services when in sensitive areas. However, a similar problem can occur even if GPS capabilities or location services are disabled. It is increasingly common for websites and applications to determine a person's location based on their Internet connection, such as a Wi-Fi hotspot or IP address range. The primary mitigation for this is to opt out of location services whenever possible.

TECHNOLOGIES FOR MOBILE DEVICE MANAGEMENT

Centralized mobile device management technologies are a growing solution for controlling the use of both organization-issued and personally owned mobile devices by enterprise users. In addition to managing the configuration and security of mobile devices, these technologies offer other features, such as providing secure access to enterprise computing resources. This section provides an overview of the current state of these technologies, focusing on the technologies' components, architectures, and capabilities.

Components and Architectures

There are two basic approaches to centralized mobile device management: use a messaging server's management capabilities (often from the same vendor that makes a particular brand of phone), or use a product from a third party, which is designed to manage one or more brands of phone. It may be possible with the latter approach to have a single product that can manage multiple brands of phones desired for use within an enterprise. However, a product provided by a phone manufacturer may have more robust support for the phones than third party products. It is outside the scope of this publication to recommend one approach over the other; both approaches can provide the necessary centralized management functionality.

Architecturally, both approaches to centralized mobile device management are quite similar. The typical solution has straightforward client/server architecture. The enterprise contains one or more servers that provide the centralized management capabilities, and one or more client applications are installed on each mobile device and configured to run in the background at all times. If the device is organization issued, the client application typically manages the configuration and security of the entire device. If the device is BYOD, the client application typically manages only the configuration and security of itself and its data, not the entire device. The client application and data are essentially sandboxed from the rest of the device's applications and data, both helping to protect the enterprise from a compromised device and helping to preserve the privacy of the device's owner.

The centralized mobile device management may make use of other enterprise services, such as domain authentication services and virtual private networking (VPN) services.

If there is not a centralized management solution, or certain mobile devices cannot use it, then mobile devices have to be managed individually and manually. In addition to the additional resources expended, there are two major security problems with this:

1. The security controls provided by a mobile device often lack the rigor of those provided by a centralized mobile device management client application. For example, a mobile device often supports only a short passcode for authentication and may not support strong storage encryption. This will necessitate acquiring, installing, configuring, and maintaining a variety of third-party security controls that provide the missing functionality.
2. It may not be possible to manage the security of the device when it is not physically present within the enterprise. It is possible to install utilities that manage devices remotely, but it will require significantly more effort to use such utilities to manually apply updates and perform other maintenance and management tasks with out-of-office mobile devices.

CAPABILITIES

This section describes security services commonly provided for mobile devices. These services apply to the entire mobile device (if it is wholly managed) or to the mobile device's secure sandbox, unless explicitly noted otherwise. These services are equally relevant for centrally managed or individually managed mobile devices.

Most organizations will not need all of the security services listed in this section. Organizations deploying mobile devices should consider the merits of each security service, determine which services are needed for their environment, and then design and acquire one or more solutions that collectively provide the necessary services.

General Policy

The centralized technology can enforce enterprise security policies on the mobile device, including (but not limited to) other policy items listed. General policy restrictions of particular interest for mobile device security include the following:

1. Restrict user and application access to hardware, such as the digital camera, GPS, Bluetooth interface, USB interface, and removable storage.
2. Restrict user and application access to the built-in web browser, e-mail client, application installation services, and so on.

3. Manage wireless network interfaces (Wi-Fi, Bluetooth, etc.).
4. Automatically monitor, detect, and report when policy violations occur.

Data Communication and Storage

1. Strongly encrypt data communications between the mobile device and the organization. This is most often in the form of a VPN, although it can be established through other uses of encryption.
2. Strongly encrypt stored data on both built-in storage and removable media storage. Removable media can also be "bound" to particular devices such that encrypted information can only be decrypted when the removable media is attached to the device, thereby mitigating the risk of offline attacks on the media.
3. Remotely wipe the device (to scrub its stored data) if it is suspected that the device has been lost, stolen, or otherwise fallen into untrusted hands and is at risk of having its data recovered by an untrusted party. A device often can also be configured to wipe itself after a certain number of incorrect authentication attempts.

User and Device Authentication

1. Require a password/passcode and/or other authentication (e.g., domain authentication) before accessing the organization's resources. This includes basic parameters for password strength and a limit on the number of retries permitted without negative consequences (e.g., locking out the account, wiping the device).
2. If device account lockout is enabled or the device password/passcode is forgotten, an administrator can reset this remotely to restore access to the device.
3. Have the device automatically lock itself after it is idle for a period (e.g., 5 minutes).

Applications

1. Restrict which applications may be installed through whitelisting (preferable) or blacklisting.
2. Install, update, and remove applications.
3. Restrict the use of synchronization services (e.g., local device synchronization, remote synchronization services, and websites).

4. Digitally sign applications to ensure that only applications from trusted entities are installed on the device and that code has not been modified.
5. Distribute the organization's applications from a dedicated mobile application store.
6. Limit or prevent access to the enterprise based on the mobile device's operating system version (including whether the device has been rooted/jailbroken) or its mobile device management software client version (if applicable). Note that this information may be spoofable.

SECURITY FOR THE ENTERPRISE MOBILE DEVICE SOLUTION LIFE CYCLE

This section explains how the concepts already presented should be incorporated throughout the entire life cycle of enterprise mobile device solutions, involving everything from policy to operations. The section references a five-phase life cycle model to help organizations determine at what point in their mobile device solution deployments a recommendation may be relevant. Organizations may follow a project management methodology or life cycle model that does not directly map to the phases in the model presented here, but the types of tasks in the methodology and their sequencing are probably similar. The phases of the life cycle are as follows:

Phase 1: Initiation. This phase involves the tasks that an organization should perform before it starts to design a mobile device solution. These include identifying needs for mobile devices, providing an overall vision for how mobile device solutions would support the mission of the organization, creating a high-level strategy for implementing mobile device solutions, developing a mobile device security policy, and specifying business and functional requirements for the solution.

Phase 2: Development. In this phase, personnel specify the technical characteristics of the mobile device solution and related components. These include the authentication methods and the cryptographic mechanisms used to protect communications and stored data. The types of mobile device clients to be used should also be considered, since they can affect the desired policies. Care should be taken to ensure that the mobile device security policy can be employed and enforced by all clients. At the end of this phase, solution components are procured.

Phase 3: Implementation. In this phase, equipment is configured to meet operational and security requirements, including the mobile device security policy documented in the system security plan, installed and tested as a prototype, and then activated on a production network. Implementation includes integration with other security controls and technologies, such as security event logging and authentication servers.

Phase 4: Operations and Maintenance. This phase includes security-related tasks that an organization should perform on an ongoing basis once the mobile device solution is operational, including log review and attack detection.

Phase 5: Disposal. This phase encompasses tasks that occur when a mobile device solution or its components are being retired, including preserving information to meet legal requirements, sanitizing media, and disposing of equipment properly.

This section highlights security considerations of particular interest for mobile device solutions. These considerations are not intended to be comprehensive, nor is there any implication that security elements not listed here are unimportant or unnecessary.

Initiation

The initiation phase involves many preparatory actions, such as identifying current and future needs, and specifying requirements for performance, functionality, and security. A critical part of the initiation phase is the development of a mobile device security policy for an organization. The section lists elements that a mobile device security policy should contain and, where relevant, describes some of the factors that should be considered when making the decisions behind each element.

A mobile device security policy should define which types of mobile devices are permitted to access the organization's resources, the degree of access that various classes of mobile devices may have (e.g., organization-issued devices versus personally owned devices), and how provisioning should be handled. It should also cover how the organization's centralized mobile device management servers are administered and how policies in those servers are updated. The mobile device security policy should be documented in the system security plan. To the extent feasible and appropriate, the mobile device security policy should be consistent with and complement security policy for non-mobile systems.

An organization's mobile device security policy often limits the types of mobile devices that may be used for enterprise access; this is done for a variety of reasons, including security concerns and technology limitations. For example, an organization might permit only organization-owned mobile devices to be used. Some organizations have tiered levels of access, such as allowing organization-issued mobile devices to access many resources, BYOD mobile devices running the organization's mobile device management client software to access a limited set of resources, and all other BYOD mobile devices to access only a few web-based resources, such as e-mail. This allows an organization to limit the risk it incurs by permitting the most-controlled devices to have the most access and the least-controlled devices to have only minimal access.

Each organization should make its own risk-based decisions about what levels of access should be permitted from which types of mobile devices. Factors that organizations should consider when setting mobile device security policy for this include the following:

Sensitivity of work. Some work involves access to sensitive information or resources, while other work does not. Organizations may have more restrictive requirements for work involving sensitive information, such as permitting only organization-issued devices to be used. Organizations should also be concerned about the legal issues involved in remotely scrubbing sensitive information from BYOD mobile devices.

The level of confidence in security policy compliance. Meeting many of an organization's security requirements can typically be ensured only if the organization controls the configuration of the mobile devices. For devices not running the organization's mobile device management client software, some requirements can possibly be verified by automated security health checks conducted by the mobile device management server when mobile devices attempt to connect, but other requirements cannot be verified.

Cost. Costs associated with mobile devices will vary based on policy decisions. The primary direct cost is issuing mobile devices and client software. There are also indirect costs in maintaining mobile devices and in providing technical support for users.

Work location. Risks will generally be lower for devices used only in the enterprise environment than for devices used in a variety of locations.

Technical limitations. Certain types of mobile devices may be needed, such as for running a particular application. Also, an organization's mobile device management client software may only support certain types of mobile devices.

Compliance with mandates and other policies. Organizations may need to comply with mobile device–related requirements from mandates and other sources, such as a federal department issuing policy requirements to its member agencies. An example of a possible requirement is restrictions on using mobile devices in foreign countries that have strong known threats against federal agency systems; in such cases, it may be appropriate to issue "loaner" mobile devices or to prohibit mobile device use altogether.

Organizations may choose to specify additional security requirements that are tied to factors such as the sensitivity of work. Many organizations require more stringent security controls for work situations that are particularly high-risk, such as permitting the work only from organization-issued and secured mobile devices, and requiring the use of multi-factor authentication for access to the mobile device and to enterprise resources. Another possible security control is to migrate high-risk resources to servers that assume responsibility for protecting them; for example, a mobile device could connect to a server that holds sensitive data that the user needs to access, instead of the sensitive data being stored locally on the mobile device. In high-risk situations, organizations may also choose to reduce risk by prohibiting mobile devices from accessing particular types of information, such as sensitive personally identifiable information.

Every year, there are many changes in mobile device capabilities, the security controls available to organizations, the types of threats made to different types of devices, and so on. Therefore, organizations should periodically reassess their policies for mobile devices and consider changing which types of mobile devices are permitted and what levels of access they may be granted. Organizations should also be aware of the emergence of new types of mobile device solutions and of major changes to existing mobile device management technologies, and ensure that the organization's policies are updated accordingly as needed.

Organizations often have additional security considerations for mobile devices that, while helpful in mitigating threats, cannot necessarily be directly enforced by the organization. Organizations should educate users on the importance of these additional security measures and define users' responsibilities for implementing these measures in policy and mobile device agreements.

One possible security consideration involves wireless personal area networks (WPAN), which are small-scale wireless networks that require no infrastructure to operate. Examples of WPAN technologies are using a wireless keyboard or mouse with a computer, printing wirelessly, synchronizing a mobile device with a computer wirelessly, and using a wireless headset or earpiece with a smartphone. The two most commonly used types of WPAN technologies are Bluetooth and near-field communications. For devices within proximity of significant threats, mobile device users should disable these technologies when not needed to prevent misuse by unauthorized parties.

Development

Once the organization has established a mobile device security policy, identified mobile device needs, and completed other preparatory activities, the next steps are to determine which types of mobile device management technologies should be used and to design a solution to deploy. There are many considerations for designing a solution, most of which are generally applicable to any IT technology. This section focuses on the technical security considerations that are most important for designing mobile device management solutions. Major considerations include the following:

Architecture. Designing the architecture includes the selection of mobile device management server and client software, and the placement of the mobile device management server and other centralized elements.

Authentication. Authentication involves selecting device and/or user authentication methods, including determining procedures for issuing and resetting authenticators and for provisioning users and/or client devices with authenticators.

Cryptography. Decisions related to cryptography include selecting the algorithms for encryption and integrity protection of mobile device communications, and setting the key strength for algorithms that support multiple key lengths.

Configuration requirements. This involves setting minimum security standards for mobile devices, such as mandatory host hardening measures and patch levels, and specifying additional security controls that must be employed on the mobile device, such as a VPN client.

Application vetting and certification requirements. This sets security, performance, and other requirements that applications must meet and determines how proof of compliance with requirements must be demonstrated.

The security aspects of the mobile device solution design should be documented in the system security plan. The organization should also consider how incidents involving the mobile device solutions should be handled and document those plans as well.

Implementation

After the mobile device solution has been designed, the next step is to implement and test a prototype of the design, before putting the solution into production. Aspects of the solution that should be evaluated for each type of mobile device include the following:

Connectivity. Users can establish and maintain connections from the mobile device to the organization. Users can connect to all of the organization's resources that they are permitted to and cannot connect to any other organization resources.

Protection. Information stored on the mobile device and communications between the mobile device and the organization are protected in accordance with the established requirements.

Authentication. Authentication is required and cannot be readily compromised or circumvented. All device, user, and domain authentication policies are enforced.

Applications. The applications to be supported by the mobile device solution function properly. All restrictions on installing applications are enforced.

Management. Administrators can configure and manage all components of the solution effectively and securely. The ease of deployment and configuration is particularly important. Another concern is the ability of users to alter device/client software settings, which could weaken mobile device security.

Logging. The mobile device solution logs security events in accordance with the organization's policies.

Performance. All components of the solution provide adequate performance during normal and peak usage. It is important to also consider the performance of intermediate devices, such as routers and firewalls.

Security of the implementation. The mobile device implementation itself may contain vulnerabilities and weaknesses that attackers could exploit. Organizations with high security needs may choose to perform extensive vulnerability assessments against the mobile device solution components. At a minimum, all components should be updated with the latest patches and configured following sound security practices. Also, jailbroken and rooted phones should be automatically detected to prohibit their use, for cases in which detection is feasible.

Default settings. Implementers should carefully review the default values for each mobile device setting and alter the settings as necessary to support security requirements. Implementers should also ensure that the mobile device solution does not unexpectedly "fall back" to insecure default settings for interoperability or other reasons.

Organizations should fully secure each organization-issued mobile device before allowing a user to access it. Any already-deployed mobile device with an unknown security profile (e.g., unmanaged device) should be recovered, restored to a known good state, and fully secured before returning it to its user.

Operations and Maintenance

Operational processes that are particularly helpful for maintaining mobile device security, and thus should be performed regularly, include the following:

1. Checking for upgrades and patches to the mobile device software components, and acquiring, testing, and deploying the updates.
2. Ensuring that each mobile device infrastructure component (mobile device management servers, authentication servers, etc.) has its clock synced to a common time source so that its timestamps will match those generated by other systems.

3. Reconfiguring access control features as needed based on factors such as policy changes, technology changes, audit findings, and new security needs.
4. Detecting and documenting anomalies within the mobile device infrastructure. Such anomalies might indicate malicious activity or deviations from policy and procedures. Anomalies should be reported to other systems' administrators as appropriate.
5. Providing training and awareness activities for mobile device users on threats and recommended security practices.

Organizations should also periodically perform assessments to confirm that the organization's mobile device policies, processes, and procedures are being followed properly. Assessment activities may be passive, such as reviewing logs, or active, such as performing vulnerability scans and penetration testing.

Disposal

Before a mobile device component permanently leaves an organization (such as when a leased server's lease expires or when an obsolete mobile device is being recycled), the organization should remove any sensitive data from the host. The task of scrubbing all sensitive data from storage devices such as hard drives and memory cards is often surprisingly difficult because of all the places where such data resides and the increasing reliance on flash memory instead of magnetic disks. An organization should strongly consider erasing all organization-issued storage devices completely.

CASE STUDY

NASA's Center for Internal Mobile Applications (CIMA) has worked to ensure the security of data exchanged via any CIMA-provided mobile application. CIMA relies upon Mobile Application Management (MAM), as opposed to Mobile Device Management (MDM), to secure the mobile application. Furthermore, an in-house-developed Secure Mobile Access Point (SMAP) and secure Identity, Credential, and Access Management (ICAM) services are leveraged for authenticating and accessing all CIMA mobile applications. This multilayered security approach relies upon

Launchpad for authentication and an application-level personal identification number (PIN) for accessing CIMA-hosted mobile applications. It secures or removes all data at rest and provides a secure channel between the mobile application and the protected NASA enterprise services. Developers can leverage SMAP for their applications to provide the NASA data and services they need in a secure and timely manner.

The following are the features of SMAP:

1. Provides a secure mobile public-access point for accessing protected NASA services and data.
2. Allows mobile devices outside of NASA locations to access protected NASA services and data.
3. Offers full whitelist and blacklist filtering by user, device, application, application version, and Center.
4. Provides secure web proxy services for the CIMA mobile application web wrapper, allowing wrapped websites to be accessed by mobile devices outside of NASA locations.

The Secure Mobile Access Point implemented by CIMA is effective in securing the mobile application, but CIMA's efforts don't stop there. Currently, CIMA is working with the ICAM team to further enhance the security of the installed mobile applications by implementing an ICAM certificate–based authentication for mobile devices. This additional security measure is expected to be deployed at the end of the calendar year.

While other Federal agencies are struggling with the idea of Bring Your Own Device (BYOD) and how to manage those devices, CIMA's approach to securing your data is to manage the mobile application as opposed to the mobile device. This is referred to as Mobile Application Management (MAM). MAM is application-centric, making it easier to target the things that matter most to NASA—the mobile apps and the inherent data—while leaving the personal device and data alone.

Readers will also want to review the following:

Appendix B, Employee Mobile Device Agreement
Appendix C, Mobile Device Security Checklist
Appendix D, Security Configuration Recommendations for Apple iOS 5 Devices
Appendix G, Computer Use Policy
Appendix I, Wireless Device Agreement

6

Cloud Best Practices

BYOD implies mobile computing and those on the run often use the cloud to store and access both personal and organizational documents. Thus, it is worthwhile to consider the cloud dynamic, including selection, legal issues, and security. The federal government's CIO Council carefully considered these issues (2012). This chapter aligns with their findings and recommendations. Readers are also urged to review Cloud Procurement Questions, Appendix F, which provides a comprehensive worksheet for cloud vendor selection. Readers will also be interested in reviewing Appendix K, which provides a detailed security checklist that can be used when accessing cloud vendors and web service providers.

The adoption of cloud computing represents a dramatic shift in the way organizations buy IT—a shift from periodic capital expenditures to lower cost and predictable operating expenditures. With this shift comes a learning curve regarding the effective procurement of cloud-based services.

Cloud computing presents a paradigm shift that is larger than IT, and while there are technology changes with cloud services, the more substantive issues that need to be addressed lie in the business and contracting models applicable to cloud services. This new paradigm requires organizations to re-think not only the way they acquire IT services in the context of deployment, but also how the IT services they consume provide mission and support functions on a shared basis. Organizations should begin to design and/or select solutions that allow for purchasing based on consumption in the shared model that cloud-based architectures provide.

Cloud computing allows consumers to buy IT in a new, consumption-based model. Given the dynamic nature of end-user needs, the traditional method of acquiring IT has become less effective in ensuring the organization effectively covers all of its requirements. By moving from purchasing IT in a way that requires capital expenditures and overhead, and instead purchasing IT "on-demand" as an organization consumes services, unique requirements have arisen that organizations need to address when contracting with cloud service providers (CSPs).

SELECTING A CLOUD SERVICE

The primary driver behind purchasing any new IT service is to effectively meet a commodity, support, or requirement that the organization has. Part of the analysis of that need or problem is determining the appropriate solution. Choosing the cloud is only the first step in this analysis. It is also critical for organizations to decide which cloud service and deployment model best meets their needs.

The National Institute of Standards and Technology (NIST) has defined three cloud computing service models: Infrastructure as a Service, Platform as a Service, and Software as a Service.

These service models can be summarized as follows:

1. **Infrastructure**: the provision of processing, storage, networking, and other fundamental computing resources
2. **Platform**: the deployment of applications created using programming languages, libraries, services, and tools supported by a cloud provider
3. **Software**: the use of applications running on a cloud infrastructure environment

Each service model offers unique functionality depending on the class of user, with control of the environment decreasing as you move from Infrastructure to Platform to Software. Infrastructure is most suitable for users like network administrators as organizations can place unique platforms and software on the infrastructure being consumed. Platform is most suitable for users such as server or system administrators in development and deployment activities. Software is most appropriate for end-users since all functionalities are usually offered out of the box. Understanding the degree of functionality and what users will consume the services is critical for organizations in determining the appropriate cloud service to procure.

NIST has also defined four deployment models for cloud services: Private, Public, Community, and Hybrid. These service deployments can be summarized as follows:

1. Private: For use by a single organization
2. Public: For use by general public
3. Community: For use by a specific community of organizations with a shared purpose
4. Hybrid: A composition of two or more cloud infrastructures (public, private, community)

These deployment models determine the number of consumers (multi-tenancy), and the nature of other consumers' data that may be present in a cloud environment. A public cloud does not allow a consumer to know or control who the other consumers of a cloud service provider's environment are. However, a private cloud can allow for ultimate control in selecting who has access to a cloud environment. Community clouds and Hybrid clouds allow for a mixed degree of control and knowledge of other consumers. Additionally, the cost for cloud services typically increases as the control over other consumers and knowledge of these consumers increases. When consuming cloud services, it is important for organizations to understand what type of data they will be placing in the environment, and select the deployment type that corresponds to the appropriate level of control and data sensitivity.

To choose a cloud service that will properly meet a unique need, it is vital to first determine the proper level of service and deployment. Organizations should endeavor to understand not only what functionality they will receive when using a cloud service but also how the deployment model a cloud service utilizes will affect the environment in which data is placed.

CSP AND END-USER AGREEMENTS

CSPs enforce common acceptable use standards across all users to effectively maintain how a consumer uses a CSP environment. Thus, use of a CSP environment usually end-users to sign Terms of Service Agreements (TOS). Additionally, organizations can also require CSPs to sign Non-Disclosure Agreements (NDAs) to enforce acceptable CSP personnel behavior when dealing with data. TOS and NDAs need to be fully contemplated and agreed upon by both CSPs and organizations to ensure that all parties fully understand the breadth and scope of their duties when using cloud services. These agreements are new to many IT contracts because of the nature of the interaction of end-users with CSP environments.

Terms of Service Agreements

Organizations need to know if a CSP requires an end-user to agree to TOS in order to use the CSP's services prior to signing a contract. TOS restrict the ways consumers can use CSP environments. They include provisions that detail how end-users may use the services, responsibilities of the CSP, and how the CSP will deal with customer data. Provisions within a TOS may contradict organizational policies. Given that, organizations are advised to work with CSPs to understand what they require in order for end-users to access a CSP environment and at the same time ensure that any TOS document incorporated into the contract is acceptable to the organization. If the TOS are not directly within the contract but referenced within the contract, the TOS should be negotiated and agreed upon prior to contract award.

Additionally, TOS sometimes include provisions relating to CSP responsibilities, controlling law, indemnification, and other issues that are more appropriate for the terms and conditions of the contract. If these provisions are included within service agreements, they should be clearly defined. Furthermore, any agreements must address time requirements that a CSP will need to follow to comply with rules and regulations.

Non-Disclosure Agreements

Some organizations require CSP personnel to sign NDAs when dealing with data. These are usually requested by organizations in order to ensure that CSP personnel protect non-public information that is procurement-sensitive, or affects pre-decisional policy, physical security, and so on. Organizations will need to consider the requirements and enforceability of NDAs with CSP personnel. The acceptable behavior prescribed by NDAs requires oversight, including examining the NDAs' requirements in the rules of behavior and monitoring of end-users activities in the cloud environment. CSP and end-user agreements such as TOS and NDAs are important to both organizations and CSPs in order to clearly define the acceptable behavior by end-users and CSP personnel when using cloud services. These agreements should be fully contemplated by both CSPs and organizations prior to cloud services being procured. All such agreements should be incorporated, either by full text or by reference, into the CSP contract in order to avoid the usually costly and time-consuming process of negotiating these agreements after the enactment of a cloud computing contract.

Service Level Agreements

Service Level Agreements (SLAs) are agreements under the umbrella of the overall cloud computing contract between a CSP and an organization. SLAs define acceptable service levels to be provided by the CSP to its customers in measurable terms. The ability of a CSP to perform at acceptable levels is consistent among SLAs, but the definition, measurement, and enforcement of this performance varies widely among CSPs. Organizations should ensure that CSP performance is clearly specified in all SLAs, and that all such agreements are fully incorporated, either by full text or by reference, into the CSP contract.

Terms and Definitions

SLAs are necessary between a CSP and customer to contractually agree upon the acceptable service levels expected from a CSP. SLAs across CSPs have many common terms, but definitions and performance metrics can vary widely among vendors. For instance, CSPs can differ in their definition of uptime (one measure of reliability) by stating uptime is not met only when services are unavailable for periods exceeding one hour. To further complicate this, many CSPs define availability (another measure of reliability sometimes used within the definition of uptime) in a way that may exclude CSP planned service outages. Organizations need to fully understand any ambiguities in the definitions of cloud computing terms in order to know what levels of service they can expect from a CSP.

Measuring SLA Performance

When organizations place data in a CSP environment, they are inherently giving up control over certain aspects of the services that they consume. As a best practice, SLAs should clearly define how performance is guaranteed (such as response time resolution/mitigation time, availability, etc.) and require CSPs to monitor their service levels, provide timely notification of a failure to meet the SLAs, and provide evidence that problems have been resolved or mitigated. SLA performance clauses should be consistent with the performance clauses within the contract. Organizations should enforce this by requiring in the reporting clauses of the SLA and the contract that CSPs submit reports or provide a dashboard where organizations can continuously verify that service levels are being met. Without this provision, an organization may not be able to measure CSP performance.

SLA Enforcement Mechanisms

Most standard SLAs provided by CSPs do not include provisions for penalties if an SLA is not met. The consequence to a customer if an SLA is not met can be catastrophic (unavailability during peak demand, for example). However, without a penalty for CSPs in the SLA, CSPs may not have sufficient incentives to meet the agreed-upon service levels. In order to incentivize CSPs to meet the contract terms, there should be a credible consequence (e.g., a monetary or service credit) so that a failure to meet the agreed to terms creates an undesired business outcome for the CSP in addition to the customer.

With many of the high-profile cases of cloud service provider failures relating to provisions covered by SLAs, as a best practice, organizations need SLAs that provide value and can be enforced when a service level is not met. SLAs with clearly defined terms and definitions, performance metrics measured and guaranteed by CSPs, and enforcement mechanisms for meeting service levels, will provide value to organizations and incentives for CSPs to meet the agreed-upon terms.

CSP, ORGANIZATION, AND INTEGRATOR ROLES AND RESPONSIBILITIES

Many organizations procure cloud services through integrators. In these cases, integrators can provide a level of expertise within CSP environments that organizations may not have, thus making an organization's transition to cloud services easier. Integrators may also provide a full range of services from technical support to help desk support that CSPs might not provide. When deciding to use an integrator, the organization may procure services directly from a CSP and separately with an integrator, or it may procure cloud services through an integrator, as the prime contractor and the CSP as subcontractor. Whichever method the organization decides to use, the addition of an integrator to a cloud computing implementation creates contractual relationships with at least three unique parties, and the roles and responsibilities for all parties need to be clearly defined.

Contracting with Integrators

Integrators can be contracted independently of CSPs or can act as an intermediary with CSPs. This flexibility allows organizations to choose the most effective method for contracting with integrators to help implement their cloud computing solutions. As a best practice, organizations need to consider the technical abilities and overall service offerings of integrators and how these elements impact the overall pricing of an integrator's proposed services. Additionally, if an organization contracts with an integrator acting as an intermediary, the organization must consider how this affects the organization's continued use of a CSP environment when the contract with an integrator ends.

Clearly Defined Roles and Responsibilities

Whether an organization contracts with an integrator independently or uses one as an intermediary, roles and responsibilities need to be clearly defined. Scenarios that need to be clearly defined within a cloud computing solution that incorporate an integrator include how an organization interacts with a CSP to manage the CSP environment, what access an integrator has to data within a CSP environment, and what actions an integrator may take on behalf of an organization. Failure to address the roles and responsibilities of each party can hinder the end-user's ability to fully realize the benefits of cloud computing. For instance, if initiating a new instance of a virtual machine requires an organization to interact with an integrator, then this interaction breaks the on-demand essential characteristic of cloud computing.

The introduction of integrators to cloud computing solutions can be a critical element of success for many organizations. However, the introduction of an additional party to a cloud computing contract requires organizations to fully consider the most effective method of contracting with an integrator and clearly define the roles and responsibilities among CSPs, organizations, and integrators.

STANDARDS

Standards are available in support of many of the functions and requirements for cloud computing. While many of these standards were developed in support of pre-cloud computing technologies, such as those designed for web services and the Internet, they also support the functions and requirements of cloud computing. Other standards are now being developed in specific support of cloud computing functions and requirements, such as virtualization.

SECURITY

Placing data on an information system involves risk, so it is critical for organizations to ensure that the IT environment in which they are storing and accessing data is secure.

Because of the variability in risk postures among different CSP environments and differing missions and needs, the determination of the appropriate levels of security vary across organizations and across CSP environments. Organizations must evaluate the type of data they will be placing into a CSP environment and categorize their security needs accordingly.

Based on the level of security that an organization determines a CSP environment must meet, the organization then must determine which security controls a CSP will implement within the cloud environment.

Within this framework, organizations need to explicitly state not only the security impact level of the system (i.e., the CSP environment must meet high, moderate, or low impact level), but organizations must also specify the security controls associated with the impact level the CSP must meet.

Continuous Monitoring

After organizations complete a security authorization of a system based on clear and defined security authorization requirements detailing the security controls a CSP must implement on their system, organizations must continue to ensure a CSP environment maintains an acceptable level of risk. In order to do this, organizations should work with CSPs to implement a continuous monitoring program. Continuous monitoring programs are designed to ensure that the level of security through a CSP's initial security authorization is maintained while organizational data resides within a CSP's environment.

Incident Response

Incident response refers to activities addressing breaches of systems, leaks/spillage of data, and unauthorized access to data. Organizations need to work with CSPs to ensure CSPs employ satisfactory incident response plans and have clear procedures regarding how the CSP responds to incidents as specified in the organization's computer security incident handling guidelines.

Organizations must ensure that contracts with CSPs include CSP liability for data security. An organization's ability to effectively monitor for incidents and threats requires working with CSPs to ensure compliance with all data security standards, laws, initiatives, and policies.

Generally, CSPs take ownership of their environment but not the data placed in their environment. As a best practice, cloud contracts should not permit a CSP to deny responsibility if there is a data breach within its environment. Organizations should make explicit in cloud computing contracts that CSPs indemnify organizations if a breach should occur and the CSP should be required to provide adequate capital and/or insurance to support their indemnity. In instances where expected standards are not met, then the CSP must be required to assume the liability if an incident occurs directly related to the lack of compliance. In all instances, it is vital for organizations to practice vigilant oversight.

When incidents do occur, CSPs should be held accountable for incident responsiveness to security breaches and for maintaining the level of security required by the organization. Organizations should work with CSPs to define an acceptable time period for the CSP to mitigate and re-secure the system.

At a minimum, organizations should ensure when implementing an incident response policy that:

1. They contractually ensure CSPs comply with organizational security guidelines.

2. CSPs must be accountable for incident responsiveness, including providing specific time frames for restoration of secure services in the event of an incident.

Key Escrow

Key escrow (also known as a fair cryptosystem or key management) is an arrangement in which the keys needed to decrypt encrypted data are held in escrow so that, under certain circumstances, an authorized third party may gain access to those keys. Procedural and regulatory regimes in environments where the organizations own the systems storing and transporting encrypted data are fairly well settled. These regimes, however, become increasingly complex when inserted into a cloud environment.

Organizations should carefully evaluate CSP solutions to understand completely how a CSP fully does key management to include how the key's encrypted data are escrowed and what terms and conditions of escrow apply to accessing encrypted data.

Forensics

When organizations use a CSP environment, the organization should ensure that a CSP only makes changes to the environment on pre-agreed upon terms and conditions; or as required by organization to defend against an actual or potential incident. Organizations should require CSPs to allow forensic investigations for regulatory, criminal, and non-criminal purposes, and these investigations should be able to be conducted without affecting data integrity and without interference from the CSP. In addition, CSPs should only be allowed to make changes to the cloud environment under specific standard operating procedures agreed to by the CSP and organization in the contract.

Audit Logs

Organizations must work with CSPs to ensure audit logs of a CSP environment are preserved with the same standards as is required by organizations. Organizations must outline which CSP personnel have access to audit logs prior to placing data in the CSP environment. All CSP personnel who have access to the audit logs must have the proper clearances as required by the organization. Essentially,

1. All audit/transaction files should be made available to authorized personnel in read-only mode;
2. Audit transaction records should never be modified or deleted;
3. Access to online audit logs should be strictly controlled. Only authorized users may be allowed to access audit transaction files; and
4. Audit/transaction records should be backed up and stored safely off site.

Privacy Impact Assessments (PIA)

The PIA process helps ensure that organizations evaluate and consider how they will mitigate privacy risks, and comply with applicable privacy laws and regulations governing an individual's privacy, to ensure confidentiality, integrity, and availability of an individual's personal information at every stage of development and operation. Typically, organizations conduct a PIA during the security authorization process for IT systems before operating a new system and update.

Some of the normal PIA considerations to include are the following:

1. What information will be collected and put into the CSP environment
2. Why the information is being collected
3. Intended use of the information
4. With whom the information might be shared
5. Whether individuals will be notified that their information will be maintained in a CSP environment and what opportunities individuals have to decline to provide information that will be maintained in a CSP environment
6. What ability individuals have to consent to particular uses of the information, and how individuals can grant consent
7. How the organization and CSP will secure information in the cloud

In addition, a cloud computing PIA should focus specific attention on the following:

1. The physical location of the data maintained by the CSP
2. The retention policies that apply to the data maintained in a CSP environment

3. The mechanism by which an organization maintains control over data (e.g., by contractual provisions, non-disclosure agreements) that is maintained by CSPs
4. The means by which the CSP will terminate storage and delete data at the end of the contract or project life cycle

Data Location

Many CSP environments involve the storage of data across multiple facilities, often across the globe. Where data resides changes an organization's applicable legal rights, expectations, and privileges based on the laws of the country where the data is located. Organizations need to first consider the type of data they plan to place in a cloud environment, and then the laws and policies of the country where the cloud providers' servers are located in order to fully understand who may have access to this data.

Almost every country has different standards and laws for handling personal information that CSPs must meet if they maintain facilities within their borders. Some countries allow persons with rights of access to personal information that may not directly align with the legal framework in the United States. Other countries may permit law enforcement to request more data from cloud providers than within the United States. It may not be clear how the privacy laws and protections apply in these situations. In any situation where a CSP environment goes outside of U.S. territories, there is a potential for conflict of law; and organizations must take sufficient time to proactively consult with legal counsel about the possible ramifications.

Breach Response

When placing data that contains PII in a CSP environment, organizations need to be aware of issues related to data loss incidents or breaches that are specific to the CSP environment. Organizations need to ensure that they can expand their breach policies and plans as required to ensure compliance with existing requirements for response. These policies must specify which parties are responsible for the cost and containment or mitigation of harm and for notifying affected individuals where required, as well as provide for instruction and requirements on terminating storage and deleting data upon expiration of the agreement, or agreement term and extension options.

It is important to ensure that an organization's breach policies and plans adequately address the new relationship between the organization and CSP, including the assignment of specific roles and tasks between the organization and the CSP, even before determination of ultimate responsibility in the case of a data breach. It is important to establish clear contractual duties and liability of the CSP for timely breach reporting, mitigation (i.e., administrative, technical, or physical measures to contain or remedy the breach), and costs, if any, of providing notice, credit monitoring, or other appropriate relief to affected individuals as appropriate under the circumstances. It is also important to address when the termination of services and assertion of the organization's rights of ownership, custody, transfer (return), or deletion of any data stored in a CSP environment will be invoked by the organization as a remedy for a breach. Finally, it is important to ensure that there are appropriate audit rights to permit compliance reviews.

REFERENCE

CIO Council. (2012, February 24). *Creating effective cloud computing contracts for the federal government: Best practices for acquiring IT as a service.* https://cio.gov/wp-content/uploads/downloads/2012/09/cloudbestpractices.pdf

7

Configuration Management in a BYOD Environment*

Configuration management (CM) provides the means to manage technology-related processes in a structured, orderly, and productive manner. As an engineering discipline, CM provides a level of support, control, and service to the organization. CM is a support function in that it supports the program, the corporation, and, in a number of situations, the customer.

CM is a control function in that it controls specifications, documents, drawings, requirements, tools, software, and other deliverables. It can also be extended to include BYOD devices and the software that runs on those devices.

The process of CM has not really changed much during the past 20 to 30 years. However, the environment that CM operates within has changed significantly and is likely to continue to change. Over the past few decades, we have migrated from centralized mainframes using just a few programming languages such as COBOL and FORTRAN to decentralized, networked environments with thousands of devices using hundreds of software packages/apps and dozens of programming languages. It is also worthwhile to note that BYOD is not just a composite of hardware devices and off-the-shelf applications. It can be expected that many organizations will create their own apps for use on these devices. Thus, CM within the context of BYOD does require the management of both hardware as well as software.

Regardless of this amazing diversity, the process of CM is basically immutable—that is, the process does not change, only what is being managed changes. What this means is that CM is as applicable to a mainframe

* This chapter is based on Keyes, J. (2004). *Software configuration management.* Boca Raton, FL: Auerbach Publications.

shop as it is to a shop supporting employees who bring their own devices. The key is in the process.

CM AND PROCESS IMPROVEMENT

Improvement depends upon changing current processes along with the accompanying environment. CM, then, provides the underlying structure for change and process improvement. We refer to this as process-based configuration management.

For example, the first step to improve the product is to know how the product is currently produced. The second step for improvement is to foster an atmosphere in which change can be readily accommodated. If change does not appear possible, then improvement is also unlikely. CM measurements of current practices and their associated metrics can help identify where processes are working and where they need to be improved. Such change efforts should lead to increased productivity, integrity, conformance, and customer satisfaction.

Configuration management (CM) can be defined as the process of managing the full spectrum of an organization's products, facilities, and processes by managing all requirements, including changes, and assuring that the results conform to those requirements. By this definition, CM can also be called process configuration management because it includes the process of managing an organization's processes and procedures.

Many organizations can be characterized as Level 1 organizations as defined in the Software Engineering Institute's Software Capability Maturity Model. These Level 1 organizations rely heavily on "heroes" to accomplish the work. The organization's processes are not documented, and few people know how the work is accomplished, how things are organized, and even where things might be located. The process is characterized as ad hoc, and occasionally even chaotic.

An effective CM program organizes all of this. Any changes, updates, and need additions are tracked and documented. Adhering to these policies and procedures will reduce the likelihood or problems with employees using unapproved hardware, software, and processes.

MEASUREMENT AND METRICS

The status accounting aspect of CM provides management visibility into the state of technology usage. A measure can be defined as a standard of measurement, the extent, dimensions, capacity, and so on, of anything, especially as determined by a standard, an act or process of measuring, a result of measurement. Examples of measure from a BYOD perspective would be number of BYOD devices in use and number of devices supported by in-house IT staff.

A metric can also be a composite of measures that yields systematic insight into the state of processes or products and drives appropriate actions. Measures (measurements) and metrics can be used to identify areas of the process that require attention, such as number of BYOD users experiencing problems versus non-BYOD users experiencing problems.

A metrics program should include the following fundamentals:

1. A motive that is compelling, not simply conformism
2. Benchmarks
3. Goals that define the purpose of the metrics program
4. Strategy for achieving the goals
5. Collection of data
6. Analysis of the data to find patterns: patterns imply consistency and consistency implies process
7. Action on the analysis—change in the process to achieve better results
8. Implementation ethics, including trust, value, communication, and understanding

One desired outcome of compiling and using these metrics to improve processes is the improvement of the value-to-cost ratio. If a change in a process yields an increase in production during a specific time frame, or yields the same production in a decreased time frame, the value-to-cost ratio is improved.

BENEFITS OF BYOD CM

There are many benefits to be gained by an organization that practices CM. Benefits from the BYOD perspective include the following:

1. Organizes tasks and activities that maintain the integrity of BYOD framework (i.e., devices, software, network)
2. Helps manage assets
3. Provides ability to track modifications
4. Ensures correct device/software configurations of software
5. Ensures that any changes are being made into the correct "baseline" or version
6. Limits legal liability by recording all—including memos, decisions, meeting minutes, etc., providing a "paper trail"
7. Allows responsibility to be traced to the source
8. Provides for consistent conformance to organizational requirements and mandates
9. Enhances compliance with standards being applied
10. Provides an environment in which meaningful measures can be gathered and used
11. Provides data for reports that can be easily generated
12. Allows quick and easy auditing
13. Provides the ability to reproduce circumstances/conditions under which the product was produced by retaining information relative to the production process
14. Provides communication channels between groups
15. Fosters an ability to improve without being punitive in nature

Essentially, CM provides visibility into the status of the evolving BYOD framework. Employees as well as managers benefit from CM information.

CM COMPONENTS

CM encompasses the everyday tasks within an organization. Changes are identified, controlled, and managed throughout the life of the device, or tenure of the employee.

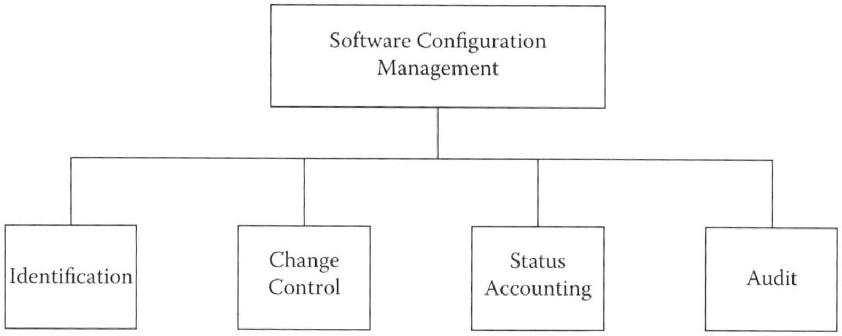

FIGURE 7.1
Functional elements of CM.

CM for BYOD should consist of the following activities:

1. Accessing and retrieving software (apps) and devices
2. Retrofitting changes across the development life cycle
3. Migrating changes across the development life cycle
4. Managing the compile and build process
5. Managing the distribution of changes
6. Obtaining approvals and sign-offs
7. Managing change requests
8. Coordinating communication between groups
9. Obtaining project status
10. Tracking bugs and fixes

CM is divided into the following functional areas, as shown in Figure 7.1.

CONFIGURATION IDENTIFICATION

Configuration identification involves identifying structure, uniquely identifying individual components, and making them accessible in some form. The goal of configuration identification is to have the ability to identify the components of a system throughout its life cycle and provide traceability between those components. Within the context of BYOD, identification answers the following questions: What is the configuration of my system? What devices are being used? What software is

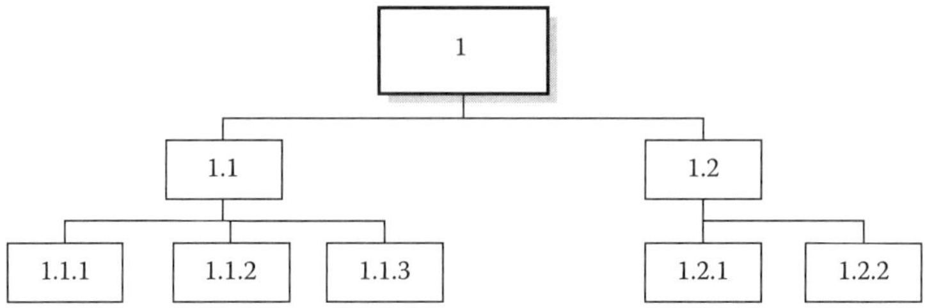

FIGURE 7.2
Configuration identification hierarchy.

being used? What network is being used? What enterprise files need to be accessed?

Configuration identification activities include the following:

1. Selecting items to be placed under CM control
2. Developing the hierarchy
3. Creating an identification scheme that reflects the hierarchy
4. Identifying which version of a component can or cannot be included
5. Uniquely identifying the various revisions of any products
6. Defining relationships and interfaces between the various software, hardware, and network products being used
7. Releasing configuration documentation
8. Establishing configuration baselines

Figure 7.2 presents a typical breakdown into its distinct parts and presents a numbering scheme that uniquely identifies each component of a baseline release. The number to the left of the dot is the last baseline or major release. The number to the right of the dot is the version since the last baseline or minor release. A hierarchical scheme is used.

Although key BYOD components to be managed are the devices and software, related documentation and data should be identified and placed under CM control. It is important to store and track all environment information and support tools used throughout so that the environment can be reproduced.

Effective configuration identification is a prerequisite for the other configuration management activities (configuration control, status accounting, and audit), which all use the products of configuration identification. If configuration items and their associated configuration documentation are not properly identified, it is impossible to control the changes to the items' configuration, to establish accurate records and reports, or to validate the configuration through audit.

CONFIGURATION CHANGE CONTROL

Configuration change control involves controlling the release and changes to any BYOD component throughout its life cycle. It is perhaps the most visible element of configuration management. It is the process to manage preparation, justification, evaluation, coordination, disposition, and implementation of proposed additions, changes, and deviations to affected configuration items and baselined configuration documentation.

The goal of configuration change control is to establish mechanisms that will help ensure the production of a quality environment for the employee and to ensure that the employee's device contains all necessary elements, and that all elements in a version will work correctly together. A generic change process is identified in Figure 7.3.

Configuration change control answers the following BYOD questions: what is controlled; how are the changes to the products controlled; who controls the changes; and when are the changes accepted, received, and verified?

Configuration change control activities include the following:

1. Defining the change process
2. Establishing change control policies and procedures
3. Maintaining baselines
4. Processing changes
5. Developing change report forms
6. Controlling release of the product

Changes made to the configuration management baselines or baselined configuration items should be done according to a documented change control process. The change control process should specify the following:

1. Who can initiate the change requests
2. What the criteria are for placing the components under formal change control
3. The "change impact" analysis expected for each requested change

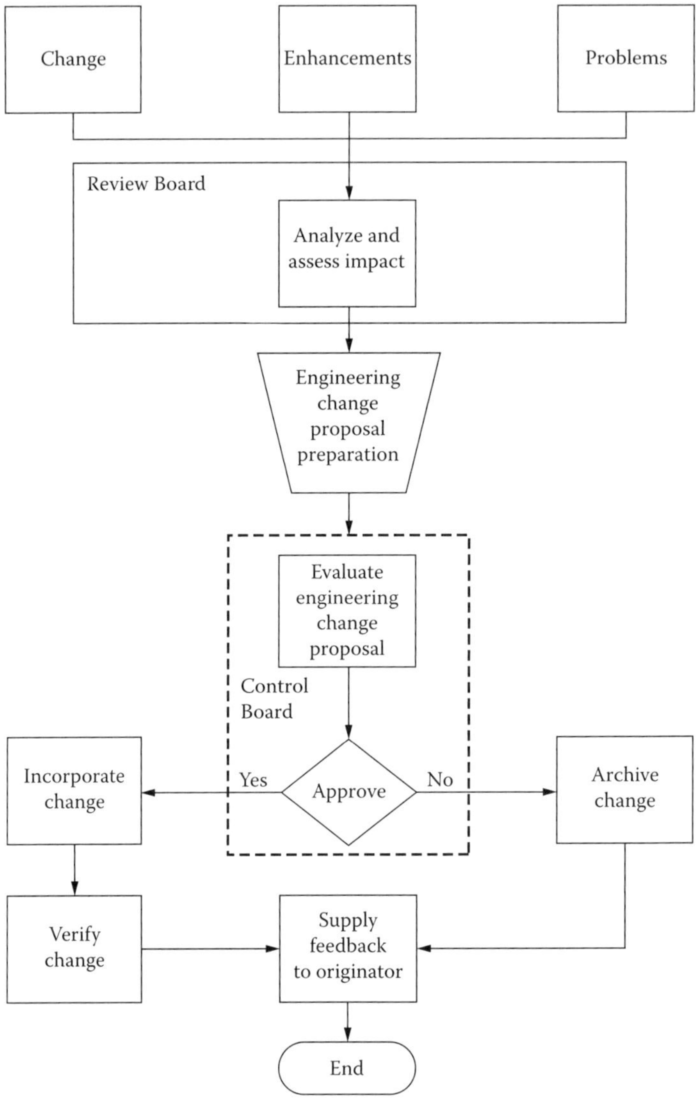

FIGURE 7.3
Generic change process.

4. How revision history should be kept
5. The process that the Configuration Control Board (CCB) follows to approve changes
6. How change requests will be linked to the Trouble Reporting System
7. How change requests are tracked and resolved

To control changes made to configuration items or the system, many organizations establish a Configuration Control Board (CCB). This board reviews each proposed change; approves or disapproves it; and if approved, coordinates the change with the affected groups.

Another key concept of change control is the use of baselines. A baseline is a specification or product that has been formally reviewed and agreed upon, that thereafter serves as the basis for further modification, and that can be changed only through formal change procedures. When an item is baselined, it becomes frozen and can only be changed by creating a new version.

From a BYOD perspective, a baseline would consist of the version of the software (apps, custom, or public) being used by the employee. In other words, an example of a baseline might be a particular version of Salesforce.com's iPhone app.

CONFIGURATION STATUS ACCOUNTING

Configuration status accounting involves the recording and reporting of the change process. The goal of status accounting is to maintain a continuous record of the status and history of all baselined items and proposed changes to them. It includes reports of the traceability of all changes to the baseline.

Configuration status accounting answers the following questions: what changes have been made to the system, what was affected by the change, and who was affected.

Configuration status accounting activities include the following:

1. Determining type of logs and reports required
2. Tracking the status of CM items
3. Tracking the status of changes
4. Generating status reports
5. Recording and reporting the activities of CM

Key information about the configuration items can be communicated to management and employees through status accounting. Employees can see what is included in which baseline. Managers can track completion of problem reports and various other maintenance activities. Minimal reports to be completed include transaction log, change log, and item "delta" report (i.e., summary of changes). Other typically common reports include resource usage, "stock status" (status of all configuration items), changes in process, and deviations agreed upon.

CONFIGURATION AUDITING

Configuration auditing verifies that the BYOD environment is built according to the requirements, standards, or contractual agreement. The goal of configuration audit is to verify that all products have been produced, correctly identified, and described, and that all change requests have been resolved according to established CM processes and procedures. Configuration audit answers the following questions: does the system satisfy the requirements and are all changes incorporated in this version?

Configuration audit activities include the following:

1. Defining audit schedule and procedures
2. Identifying who will perform the audits
3. Performing audits on the established baselines
4. Generating audit reports

IMPLEMENTING CM IN THE ORGANIZATION

One of the first steps in successfully implementing CM is to obtain management sponsorship. This means public endorsement for CM, and making sure the resources needed for success are allocated to the project. Management also needs to establish CM as a priority and help facilitate implementation.

An organization can maintain management sponsorship by identifying and resolving risks, reporting progress, managing CM implementation details, and communicating with all members of the organization.

The next step is to assess current CM processes. Every organization is practicing some type of CM. This may not be a formal process or even thought of as CM. After assessing your current processes, the next step is to analyze your requirements. What is it that your organization wants to accomplish? The requirement may be an ISO 9000 certification, some other standard or certification, or simply to improve.

Document the requirements for your organization, how you will implement them, and how you will measure success. Depending on the requirements of your organization, the various roles and formality of the CM team may differ. At a minimum there should be a point-of-contact for CM. Other recommended roles and functions include the following:

1. A control and review board should be in place to analyze and approve changes.
2. Managers and leaders also play a role in CM in establishing or following a CM plan, ensuring requirements are properly allocated, ensuring adequate tools are available to support activities, and conducting regular reviews.
3. A librarian is also necessary to track baselines and versions of files included in each release. A CM tool can assist in those activities.
4. Quality assurance (QA) can be used to verify that documented CM processes and procedures are followed.

MANAGE THE RISKS OF CM

With each new project or process there is some amount of associated risk, particularly in the case of BYOD. The same is true when implementing CM. Whether an organization is implementing a whole new system or just updating a few processes, there will be risks that must be addressed. Note that having risk is not bad—on the contrary, risk is a necessary part of CM.

Without risk, there is no opportunity for improvement. Risk-free CM processes are typically of little use. The very nature of CM requires risk-taking. Managing and controlling the risks associated with CM is essential to the success of CM processes in terms of cost, schedule, and quality.

It is always less expensive to be aware of and deal with risks than to respond to unexpected problems. A risk that has been analyzed and resolved ahead of time is much easier to deal with than one that surfaces unexpectedly.

In general a risk management program is comprised of six different activities, with communication being central to all of them. This program can be used when implementing CM to effectively manage the associated risks. Risk management should be viewed as an important part of the CM process. A brief summary of each activity follows:

1. Identify. Before risks can be managed, they must be identified. Identification surfaces risks before they become problems and adversely affect a project.
2. Analyze. Analysis is the conversion of risk data into risk decision-making information.
3. Plan. Planning turns risk information into decisions and actions (both present and future). Planning involves developing actions to address individual risk, prioritizing risk actions, and creating an integrated risk management plan.
4. Track. Tracking consists of monitoring the status of risks and actions taken to ameliorate risks.
5. Control. Risk control corrects for deviations from planned risk actions.
6. Communicate. Risk communication lies at the center of the model to emphasize both its pervasiveness and its criticality. Without effective communication, no risk management approach can be viable.

As part of an organization's risk management program, a plan should be developed that integrates the above outlined activities. An CM risk management plan may focus on addressing risks in three areas: business, people, and technology.

The business risks include the following:

1. Cost. The expense to incorporate CM encompasses far more than just the licensing fee for a tool. Management must be willing to make the necessary expenditures for people and resources.
2. Culture shock. Each organization has its own culture, to which the success of the business can be attributed. The procedures and products implemented for CM must match that culture. The person in charge of CM needs a broad understanding of software engineering principles and the cultural aspects of the organization.
3. Commitment. To establish a successful CM process, there must first be a strong commitment from management. The benefits of CM are not always immediately recognized. Deploying CM can be a long,

costly, and sometimes painful exercise. Counter this risk by building up steam in the project. Get momentum going quickly and keep feeding it.

The risks associated with people include the following:

1. Preferred tools. They may have a tool they want to use that is different from that of the organization, which is fairly typical in a BYOD environment. To mitigate these risks, try to get employees to be part of the decision-making process. Let them have input into the procedures and tools that will be used.
2. Resistance. The greatest barrier to overcome when CM is introduced into an organization is to change how people view CM. People generally react negatively toward it. In many organizations, CM has a low status, and CM personnel are not trained or qualified to perform their duties. People may perceive CM as intrusive and have little understanding of the long-term effects of not following CM procedures. Communication, training, and employee input to CM processes will help ensure CM principles are adopted by an organization.

The last area is technology. The technology risks include the following:

1. Loss of control. At times, it may seem that the CM procedures and tools are at the controls. There may also be reliance on tools where previously the needed data and information were obtained manually. Again, communication will help mitigate this risk. Management will have greater control over and information about their projects after successfully implementing CM.
2. Access. Controlling who can have access and make changes to various baselines, data repositories, software files, or documents is also a risk that must be managed. By thorough analysis and design, the procedures implemented may restrict access to approved individuals and give up-to-date information on many aspects of the project that is current and accurate.
3. Scalability. A project has the potential to outgrow the implemented tool. Counter this risk by selecting a tool that will adapt to the changing size of your organization over time.

The secret to CM risk management is to identify and resolve potential risks before they surface unexpectedly or become serious problems. Develop a program for identifying and managing risks. Incorporate a CM risk management plan that addresses risks to business, people, and technology. Central to everything is communication. Communicate as much as possible to as many people and organizations as possible.

CONFIGURATION MANAGEMENT AND DATA MANAGEMENT

In this age of rapidly developing information technology, data management and particularly the management of digital data constitute an essential prerequisite to the performance of configuration management. Digital data is information prepared by electronic means and made available to users by electronic data access, interchange, transfer, or on electronic/magnetic media, including mobile devices. There is virtually no data today, short of handwritten notes, that does not fall into this category. Configuration management (CM) of data is therefore part of data management activity.

Figure 7.4 is an activity model for configuration management of data. All the activities shown apply to configuration documentation. Most of the activities apply to all data. The model illustrates that the process is driven by business rules established based on the concept of operations for the processing of digital data, and specific data requirements.

When the data process is initiated to create or revise an item of data, or to perform any of the actions necessary to bring it from one status level to the next, the various rule sets illustrated in Figure 7.3 are triggered to facilitate the workflow. The result is a data product with the following:

1. Appropriate document, document representation, and data file identification
2. Version control
3. Clear and unambiguous relationships to the product configuration with which it is associated, and to the changes that delineate each configuration of the product

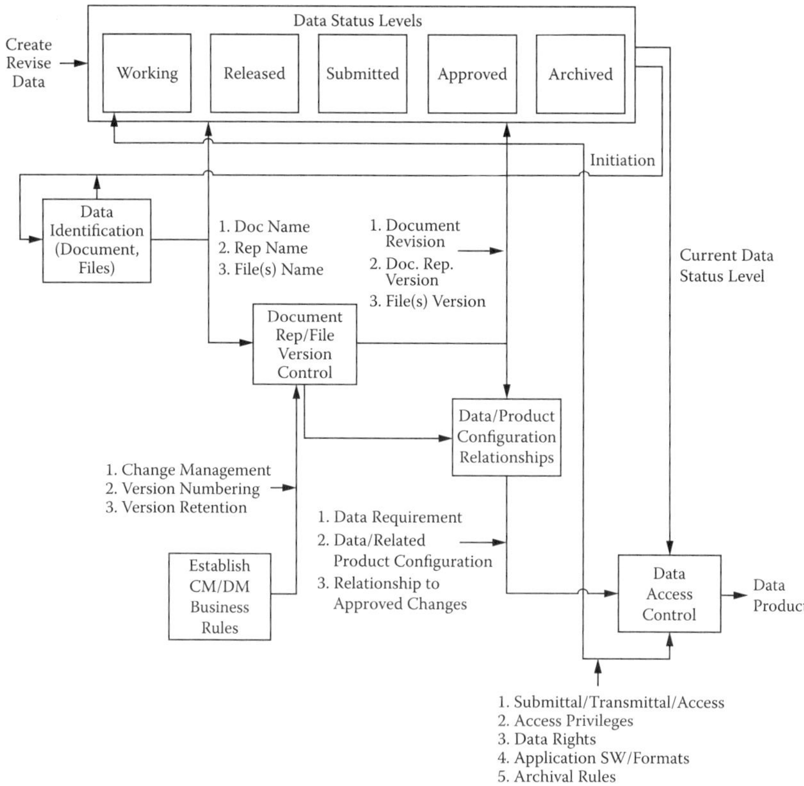

FIGURE 7.4
CM-related data management activity model.

In addition, the data is available for access in accordance with contractually agreed-to rules for submittal, transmission, or online access (as appropriate), in the prescribed format (document representation) that can be used by the application software available to the authorized user.

Configuration management principles ensure the integrity of digital representations of product information and other data, and enhance good data management practice. The concepts are described, as follows:

1. Document identification
2. Data status level management
3. Data and product configuration relationships
4. Data version control and management of review, comment, annotation, and disposition
5. Digital data transmittal
6. Data access control

Document Identification

Each document/file/app/etc. should be given a unique identifier so that it can be

1. Correctly associated with the applicable configuration (product identifier and revision) of the associated item
2. Referred to precisely
3. Retrieved when necessary

Document identifier formats include all or most of the following parameters:

1. Date
2. Assigned numeric or alphanumeric identifier unique to the document
3. Revision indicator
4. Type of document
5. Title or subject
6. Originator/organization

A document is digitally represented by one or more electronic data files. Each document representation is the complete set of all the individual digital data files (e.g., word processor, CAD/CAM, graphics, database, spreadsheet, software, app, website) constituting one document.

As shown in Figure 7.5, the same document can have several different, equally valid representations, such as different word processing or standard neutral formats (IGES, ASCII, SGML-tagged ASCII). Any individual file (such as a raster graphics file, an ASCII file, or a spreadsheet file) may be part of several document representations of the same document/same revision; same document/different revision; or different document. The business rules relating documents, documentation representations, and files are shown in Figure 7.5.

Each document iteration exists as one or more document representations, identified by the following:

1. Document identifier
2. Document representation identifier
3. Document representation revision identifier

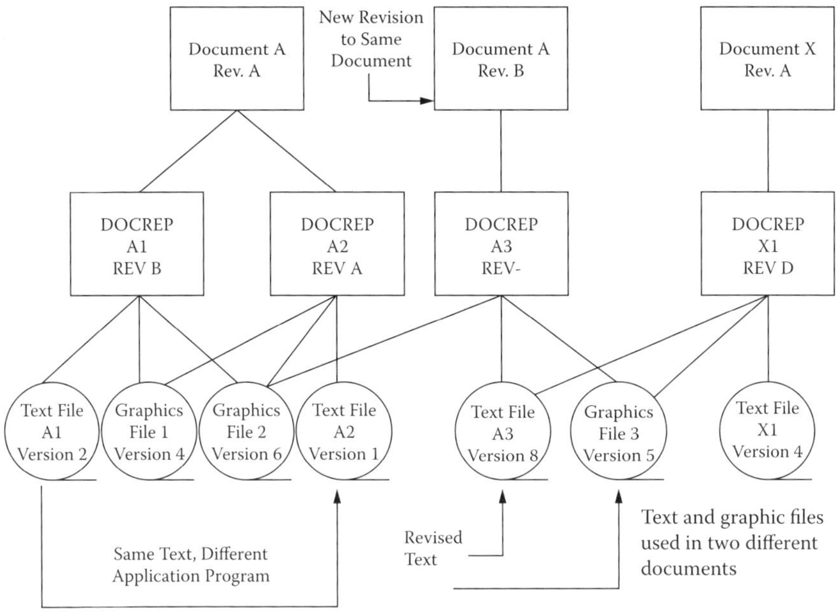

FIGURE 7.5
Illustration of document representation concepts.

Each document representation is comprised of zero or more files. To facilitate the proper relationships, apply the following digital data identification rules to maintain document, document representation, and file version relationships:

1. Assign a unique identifier to each file
2. Assign a unique identifier to each document representation
3. Assign a version identifier to each file
4. Maintain, in a database, the relationship between document identifier and its revision level, associated document representation(s), and file identifiers and versions
5. Retain multiple versions of files as necessary to re-create prior document revisions and provide a traceable history of each document
6. Identify the tool and version of the tool (e.g., Word 2010) used to generate the document when the document is not in neutral format

Data Status Level Management

Document status level is important as a foundation for the business rules defining access, change management, and archiving of digital data documents. It is the basis for establishing data workflow management and enhances data integrity. The standard data life-cycle model shows the data status levels (also referred to as states) that a specific document or document revision is processed through in its life cycle:

1. Working is the status used to identify data (document representations or document revisions) that is in preparation—a work in progress that is subject to unilateral change by the originator. Each design activity can define any number of subordinate states within the working category, to define the unique processes that different document types go through before release in their organization.
2. Released is the status of document representations, and revisions thereto, that have been reviewed and authorized for use (such as for manufacture, or for submittal to, or access by a customer or supplier). Released data is under originating organization (e.g., a contractor) change management rules, which prohibit a new revision of the document representation from replacing a released revision of a document representation until it has also been reviewed and authorized by the appropriate authority. The content of a document representation revision is fixed once it is in the released state. It is only changed by release of a superseding document representation revision. Once a document (or document revision) is in the approved state, changes are made only by release of a new document representation related to the next document revision.
3. Submitted data is a proposed or approved document revision in the form of a released document representation that has been made available for customer review. If a submitted document revision that has not been approved is commented to or disapproved, a new working revision of the related document representation can be started and eventually submitted to replace the original document representation without affecting the identifier proposed for the new document revision. If a submitted document revision that has been approved is commented to, or disapproved by the customer, a new working representation of the next document revision can be started and eventually replace the original document revision.
4. Approved is the status of documents and document revisions signifying that the data (document revision) has been approved by the Current Document Change Authority (CDCA) of the document. The

content of a document revision is fixed once it is in the approved state. It is only changed by approval of a superseding document revision.
5. Some CM tools include Archived as a data status for document representations and documents. This status is independent of the approval status (released, submitted, and approved) and merely means that the data has been removed from an active access storage mode.

No changes are allowed in the document representations that progress to the released state, or in document revisions that progress to the approved state. If there are changes to be made, they are accomplished by the generation and release or approval of a new revision. Documents must have at least one released document representation in order to be approved by the CDCA or submitted to a non-CDCA customer for review and adoption. Some data will exist only at the working level.

Business rules related to document or data status apply to each document type by defining requirements such as the following:

1. In which application software and data format is submittal or access required?
2. Who will be granted access privileges to the data in each of the applicable states?
3. What are the approval requirements (reviewers/approvers) and method of approval (e.g., electronic signature) to promote a document to the released state? The approved state?
4. What are the archiving rules for this document type (e.g., all released versions upon release of a superseding version, all released versions, 90 days after release of a superseding version)?

Data and Product Configuration Relationships

A product data management system must provide an effective system to maintain the key relationships between digital data, data requirements, and the related product configuration so that the correct revision of an item of data can be accessed or retrieved when needed.

Data files are related to documents via document representations. Each product document, with a specific source, document type, document identifier (title, name, and number), and document revision identifier, may have the following relationships:

1. Program/project or contractual agreement
2. Contract data item identifiers
3. Document revision/change authorization
4. Associated product (hardware or software) name
5. Associated product (end item), part, or software identifying number and revision/version identifier, where applicable
6. The effectivity in terms of end item serial numbers for the associated product, part, or software item
7. Status (working, released, submitted, approved, archived) of the data
8. Associated data (document name, document title, document revision number, and date)
9. Associated correspondence: document number, subject, date, references

The business rules for document retrieval should use these key relationships within a database to ensure the integrity of the data that users can extract. Thus, information concerning a given product or part is associated with the configuration and effectivity (serial number) of the end item that uses the part.

This capability is particularly significant during the operation and support phase, when data is needed to support maintenance activity and to determine the appropriate replacement parts for a specific end item.

Data Version Control

Disciplined version control of data files is the prerequisite to effective electronic management of digital data. Version occurs whenever a file is changed. The simplest form of version management is the file save feature incorporated in application software, which advances the file date and time identification each time a file is saved.

However, to retain the superseded version, it must be renamed. True version control business rules require automatic version identifier advance whenever a file is revised and not when the file is saved without change. Furthermore, they require all versions to be retained, subject to archiving guidelines and special rules pertinent to specific document types.

Because a single document representation can consist of many files, a very disciplined process is necessary to manage a document review process electronically. Version control rules facilitate the establishment of an audit trail of comments and annotations by reviewers, and the disposition of each comment. Each version of each document representation provided to, or received from, each reviewer is uniquely identified and associated with the source of the comment. Essentially, this means that a reviewer's version of a set of files (document representation) constituting a document being reviewed is renamed to enable the annotated comment copy to be distinguished from the official current version of the document.

Digital Data Transmittal

Part of the obligation of the sender of any document, regardless of transmission method, is to make sure that the document is in a format (document representation) that can be read by the receiver and converted to human-readable form. Guidelines include the following:

1. Identification of the files included in the transfer by file name, description, version, data status level, application/file type, and application version
2. Applicable references to associate the data with the basis (requirement) for its transmittal, approval, and payment, where applicable
3. If there are multiple files, such as separate text and graphics, how to assemble each included data item for reading, review, or annotation, as applicable
4. The naming convention for file versions and data status level distinguishes altered (e.g., annotated or red-line/strike-out) file versions from unaltered files
5. If and how changes from previous versions are indicated
6. How to acknowledge receipt of the data, provide comments, and/or indicate disposition of the data digitally
7. Time constraints, if any, relating to review and disposition

Data Access Control

Access to digital data involves retrieving the appropriate files necessary to compile the correct version of each digital data document, view it, and perform the prescribed processing. Seeking digital data access should be as user-friendly as possible. Users should be provided with data/documents they are entitled to in the correct revision/version. Before this can be accomplished, there are a number of pertinent parameters concerning access privileges, security, and protection of data rights that must be set up.

Access privileges limit access to applicable users. Access privileges vary according to the individual's credentials (security clearance, need-to-know, organizational affiliation, etc.), data status level, the document type, program milestones, and user need. Users of accessed data must respect all contractual and legal requirements for data rights, security, licenses, copyrights, and other distribution restrictions that apply to the data. The applicable distribution code, which represents the type of distribution statement, must be affixed to a document or viewable file to indicate the authorized circulation or dissemination of the information contained in the item.

Typically, working data should be made available only to the originating individual, group, or team (such as an integrated product development team), or to other designated reviewers of the data.

The following checklist of ground rules should be pre-established prior to initiating interactive access (i.e., predefined query and extraction of data):

1. How data is to be accessed
2. Request for access and logging of access for read-only or annotation
3. Naming of temporary working version of the file(s) for purpose of annotation/mark-up
4. Means of indicating whether a comment/annotation is essential/suggested
5. Re-identification of marked-up versions, as required
6. Method of indicating acceptance, approval, or rejection, as applicable
7. Time constraints, if any, on data acceptance
8. Tracking of disposition of required actions
9. Re-identification of changed files

8

Content Management, Mobile and Otherwise

Information is essential to running a successful business. Nowadays, information is acquired from many sources, including from employees out in the field using mobile devices, some of which are BYOD. All of this information needs to be managed using some form of content management.

There are four major elements to Enterprise Information Management, or EIM: correspondence management, workflow management, document management, and records management.

In a modern organization, these information assets might take the form of documents, multimedia objects, corporate public relations and advertising, technical documents, images, sounds, video, databases, e-mails, and knowledge bases stored either in-house or in the cloud.

EIM systems should be considered strategic investments, as they will affect the conduct of business throughout every part of the organization. Most implementers of EIM systems recommend that there be a single, clear vision of the desired end result of implementing the EIM. This vision must be understood and supported by those at the very highest levels of leadership.

There are several varieties of EIM systems that can be implemented, as shown in Figure 8.1:

1. Content management system (CMS): Usually focus on Intranet-based or Internet-based corporate content including data and knowledge bases.
2. Document management system (DMS): Focuses on the storage and retrieval of work documents (e.g., forms), in their original format.

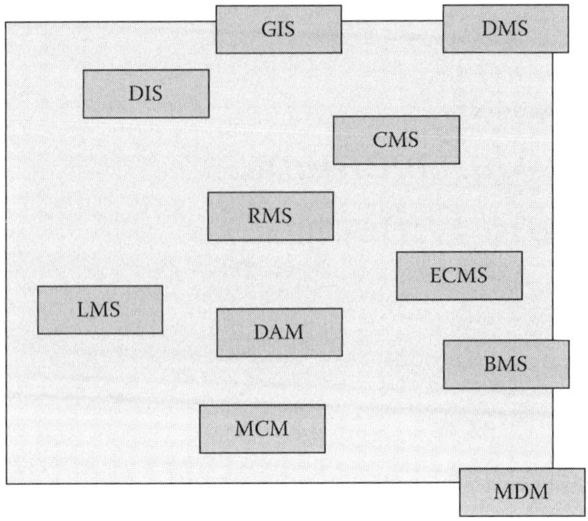

FIGURE 8.1
Enterprise Information System components.

3. Records management system (RMS): The management of both physical and electronic documents.
4. Digital asset management (DAM): Similar to RMS but focused on multimedia resources, such as images, audio, and video.
5. Brand management system (BMS): Management of advertising and promotional materials.
6. Library management system (LMS): The administration of a (corporate) library's technical functions and services.
7. Digital imaging system (DIS): Automates the creation of electronic versions of paper documents (e.g., PDF files) that are input to records management systems.
8. Learning management system (LMS): The administration of training and other learning resources. Learning content management systems (LCMS) combine content management systems with learning management systems.
9. Geographic information system (GIS): Computer-based systems for the capture, storage, retrieval, and analysis and display of spatial (i.e., location-referenced) data.
10. Mobile content management system (MCM): Allows secure document distribution and mobile access to corporate documents.
11. Mobile device management system (MDM): Allows the management of large-scale deployments of mobile devices.

Enterprise content management systems (ECMS) combine all of the above within an organizational setting. We will delve into the most important of these in greater detail. What you will find is that managing BYOD effectively requires MCM and MDM systems that work synergistically with enterprise content management systems.

CONTENT MANAGEMENT SYSTEM (CMS)

This digital content life cycle consists of six primary states: create, update, publish, translate, archive, and retire. For example, an instance of digital content is created by one or more authors. Over time that content may be edited. One or more individuals may provide some editorial oversight thereby approving the content for publication. Once published that content may be superseded by another form of content and thus retired or removed from use.

Content management is an inherently collaborative process. The process often consists of the following basic roles and responsibilities:

1. Content Author—responsible for creating and editing content. The author could reside in house or be out on the road contributing content via mobile device.
2. Editor—responsible for tuning the content message and the style of delivery.
3. Publisher—responsible for releasing the content for consumption.
4. Administrator—responsible for managing the release of the content ultimately placing it into a repository so that it can be found and consumed.

A critical aspect of content management is the ability to manage versions of content as it evolves (i.e., version control). Authors and editors often need to restore older versions of edited products due to a process failure or an undesirable series of edits.

A content management system is a set of automated processes that may support the following features:

1. Identification of all key users and their roles.
2. The ability to assign roles and responsibilities to different instances of content categories or types.

3. Definition of workflow tasks often coupled with messaging so that content managers are alerted to changes in content.
4. The ability to track and manage multiple versions of a single instance of content.
5. The ability to be aware of the location of the content.
6. The ability to publish the content to a repository in order to support the consumption of the content.

Content management systems take the following forms:

1. A web content management system is software for website management—which is often what is implicitly meant by this term.
2. A document management system.
3. A single source content management system—where content is stored in chunks, within a relational database.
4. Content management systems usually focus on Intranet-based or Internet-based corporate content including data and knowledge bases.
5. Mobile device management and mobile content management systems focus on the management of mobile devices and data.

DOCUMENT MANAGEMENT SYSTEMS/ ELECTRONIC DOCUMENT MANAGEMENT SYSTEMS (DMS/EDMS)

Document management systems (DMS) focus on the storage and retrieval of work documents (e.g., forms), in their original format. The key processes within the DMS are as follows:

1. Feed—Paper scanning or document importing.
2. Store—Every organization has its own particular storage needs, based on data volume, accessibility requirements, archival duration, etc. Choices include magnetic (such as typical desktop hard drives, RAID), optical (CD, DVD, WORM), magneto-optical storage technology or a combination of these devices. Nowadays, the cloud is an option as well.
3. Indexing—Tagging each document with some code for accessibility.

4. Control—One of the main advantages of an EDMS is that all documents of all types reside in the same computing environment. Yet in the context of a company's daily operations, it is quite probable that you would want for certain groups of employees to be granted access privileges to certain types of documents, while others may not.
5. Workflow—The EDMS is capable of mapping a company's organizational rules in the form of access controls to the document databases. EDMS tool suites often provide the means to model their operational procedures in the form of workflow management utilities.
6. Security— The EDMS exhibits a high degree of security at the client as well as enterprise level.
7. Search—An efficient EDMS will allow users to search documents via pre-set indices, keywords, full-text search, even via thesaurus and synonym support. A majority of the time, filters can be applied, search criteria may be nested, and Boolean and comparison operators may be used. We discuss this in more depth below.
8. Access—Once you've identified the documents you wish to review, the EDMS must be capable of retrieving them fast and transparently, regardless of where they are located. Documents may be distributed in multiple databases, in multiple locations. An efficient access strategy will give the end-user the impression that the documents are all stored in one location, on one computer.
9. Share—Collaborative capabilities prevent end-users from making duplicates, of the retrieved documents they've just retrieved.

The document management solution allows the user to deposit documents through multiple interfaces. Most users will access the document management system through a typical desktop configuration via a web interface or an existing proprietary application. However, within the context of our discussion, some users will certainly access the document management system through a mobile device. Access can also be obtained through imaging devices or through the organization's e-mail system, which archives e-mails as historical artifacts.

Search capabilities are typically built into the functionality of the document management system. Searches can be driven by a keyword search or through other designated parameters.

The web content management interface depicts how documents within the document management system are published onto a website. Access through this web content management interface would be independent of the access directly to a document management system, but defined accessibility and authentication would have to be established.

Originally, a document management system was a computer program (or set of programs) used to track and store images of paper documents. More recently, the term has been used to distinguish between imaging and records management systems that specialize in paper capture and records respectively. Document management systems commonly provide check-in, checkout, storage, and retrieval of electronic documents often in the form of word processor files and the like.

Typical systems have the user scan in the original paper document, and store the image of the document in the document management system, although increasingly many documents are starting life as digital documents. The image is often given a name containing the date and the user is often asked to type in additional "tags" in order to make finding the image easier. For instance, a user scanning in an invoice might want to tag it with "hardware, CompUSA invoice, 1/1/2013."

RECORDS MANAGEMENT SYSTEMS (RMS)

Records management systems (RMS) manage both physical and electronic documents.

As of 2005, records management has increased interest among corporations due to new compliance regulations and statutes. While government, legal, and health care entities have a strong, historical records management discipline, general record-keeping of corporate records has been poorly standardized and implemented. In addition, scandals such as the Enron/Andersen scandal, and more recently records-related mishaps at Morgan Stanley, have renewed interest in corporate records compliance, litigation preparedness, and issues. Statutes such as the U.S. Sarbanes–Oxley Act have created new concerns among corporate "compliance officers" that result in more standardization of records management practices within an organization.

The practice of records management involves all of the following activities:

1. Creating, approving, and enforcing records policies, including a classification system and a records retention policy

2. Developing a records storage plan, which includes the short- and long-term housing of physical records and digital information
3. Identifying existing and newly created records, classifying them, and then storing them according to standard operating procedures
4. Monitoring the access and circulation of records within and even outside of an organization
5. Executing a retention policy to archive and destroy records according to operational needs, operating procedures, statutes, and regulations

Trustworthy records are essential for an organization to meet its legal and internal business needs. Reliability, authenticity, integrity, and usability are the characteristics used to describe trustworthy records from a records management perspective.

Creating and maintaining trustworthy records requires resources. Organizations need to conduct a risk analysis to balance the level of trustworthiness of records against costs and risks.

The characteristics of trustworthy records include the following.

Reliability

A reliable website is one whose content can be trusted as a full and accurate representation of the transactions, activities, or facts to which it attests and therefore can be depended upon in the course of subsequent transactions or activities.

Authenticity

An authentic website is one that is proven to be what it purports to be and to have been created by the organization with which it is identified.

Website-related records should be created by individuals who have direct knowledge of the facts or by instruments routinely used within the business to conduct the transaction.

To demonstrate the authenticity of a website, organizations should implement and document policies and procedures that control the creation, transmission, receipt, and maintenance of website records to ensure that records creators are authorized and identified and that records are protected against unauthorized addition, deletion, and alteration (e.g., via hacking).

Integrity

The integrity of a web content record refers to it being complete and unaltered.

Web management policies and procedures for updating and modifying websites should be created. The ISO (International Standards Organization) specifies that records systems should maintain audit trails or other elements sufficient to demonstrate that records were effectively protected from unauthorized alteration or destruction. The web management policies should prescribe how changes to the website are to be documented.

Another aspect of integrity is the structural integrity of a website's content-related records. The structure of a website (i.e., its physical and logical format and the relationships between the pages and content elements composing the site) should remain physically or logically intact. Failure to maintain the website's structural integrity may impair its reliability and authenticity.

Usability

A usable website is one that can be located, retrieved, presented, and interpreted. In retrieval and use, you should be able to directly connect the website to the business activity or transaction that produced it. You should be able to identify both the site and its content within the context of broader business activities and functions. The links between content, contextual, and structural website-related records that document organizational website activities should be maintained. These contextual linkages should provide an understanding of the transactions that created and used them.

What Are the Records Management Risks Associated with Websites?

From a records management perspective, risk relates to (1) challenge to the trustworthiness of the records (e.g., legal challenge) that can be expected over the life of the record and (2) unauthorized loss or destruction of records. Consequences are measured by the degree of loss that the agency or citizens would suffer if the trustworthiness of the website-related records could not be verified or if there were unauthorized loss or destruction.

DIGITAL ASSET MANAGEMENT (DAM)

Digital asset management (DAM) is similar to RMS but focused on multimedia resources, such as images, audio, and video. This form of asset management is particularly relevant to mobile devices given their ability to quickly and efficiently create audio and video.

Digital asset management is still a new market with rapid technical evolution, hence many different types of systems will be labeled as DAM systems although they are designed to address slightly different problems or were created for a specific industry. A variety of commercial systems for DAM are available and numerous groups are trying to establish standards for DAM.

DAM systems generally support functions for ingesting, managing, searching, retrieving, and archiving of assets. DAM systems may also include version control and asset format conversion capabilities (i.e., dynamically downsizing a large, high-resolution image for display on a website). DAM systems are related to and can be considered a superset of content management systems.

DAM is a combination of workflow, software, and hardware that organizes and retrieves a company's digital assets.

There are three categories of digital asset management systems:

1. Brand asset management systems, with a focus on facilitation of content re-use within large organizations.
2. Library asset management systems, with a focus on storage and retrieval of large amounts of infrequently changing media assets, for example in video or photo archiving.
3. Production asset management systems, with a focus on storage, organization, and revision control of frequently changing digital assets, for example in digital media production.

From a technical perspective, DAM applications are divided into two basic categories: media catalogs and asset.

The primary characteristic of media catalogs is the utilization of proxies, such as thumbnails, in an indexed database that can be quickly searched by keyword. The actual source files are left untouched and under control of the operating system. The benefits of media catalogs include low cost, ease of installation and administration, and scalability across multiple divisions of an enterprise.

Since media catalogs do not actually manage the content itself, anyone with system access can typically view, change, move, or delete any content element. This usually precludes such features as check-in/check-out of content, rights management, and automatic versioning (e.g., the latest version of a print). Media catalogs can also become sluggish with very large catalogs, especially if distributed across multiple servers or geographic locations.

In asset repositories the content itself is physically stored inside a secure database. This results in a host of benefits, including security levels, replication, referential integrity, and centralized data management. Also included is the comfort of full hierarchical storage management and disaster recovery.

MOBILE DEVICE MANAGEMENT AND MOBILE CONTENT MANAGEMENT (MDM/MCM)

The advent of mobile devices within organizations has seen the need for the rise of a new administrative challenge. Mobile device management (MDM) administrators are responsible for provisioning devices and services, arranging for connectivity, and ensuring that IT security policies and other regulations are not violated.

MDM has a variety of capabilities:

1. Over-the-air (OTA) updates of applications
2. OTA updates of configuration settings
3. OTA updates of data
4. Ability to control which mobile devices are granted control access to which resources
5. Wipe a device remotely should it be lost

Aside from device management, the organization needs to address the information sharing and collaboration requirements of the remote or traveling worker. This is referred to as Mobile Content Management (MCM). MCM solutions should address multi-device support, data and device security, file sharing and updating, including check-in and checkout facilities, and app control.

Most organizations do not standardize on a particular mobile device. This is particularly true in organizations that support BYOD. Any MDM worth considering should support Android, Blackberry, and Apple iOS devices and permit the secure sharing of files across mobile and non-mobile platforms. File sharing should not be limited to a specific size. Mobile users should be able to access and share larger files, including audio, video, and graphics.

Security should be enforced at both the file and workspace levels, with strict access controls as well as encryption. File owners and administrators should be able to set expiration dates for files, so that damage is minimized if the device is left open or lost. Since BYOD translates to both personal and corporate data on a single device, a good MDM system has the ability to create a secure corporate sandbox to segregate personal from corporate. Appendix J provides a list of MDM vendors.

Aside from security, workspaces should be able to provide context for data. Context translates to the ability to track discussions and other activities. This enables the widely distributed mobile workforce to work collaboratively, which improves knowledge sharing throughout the organization.

Apple and Google both maintain app stores with thousands of devices. While Apple zealously guards their apps, Google does not. To avoid the risk of malicious apps compromising corporate transactions and information, the MDM should have the ability to control what apps are being downloaded (whitelisting).

Finally, there needs to be an administrative dashboard that provides IT with the ability to log and audit employees, teams, and departments in terms of file access rights and sharing activities.

Airwatch (http://www.air-watch.com) is representative of solution providers in this category. Its mobile content management solution allows for secure document distribution and mobile access to corporate documents through a native mobile app. Their Secure Content Locker (their sandbox) enables employees to access corporate resources from mobile devices. MCM functionality is shown in Table 8.1.

As you can see MCM combines the best practices of the content management systems discussed earlier in this chapter. Should the organization have in-house content management systems, records management systems, and so on, it would be expected that MCM would be integrated so that redundancy is avoided.

TABLE 8.1

Typical MCM Functionality

Security	Authentication	Authenticate users via basic or directory services-based authentication
	Encryption	Transmit documents over industry standard 256-bit SSL encrypted connections
	Compliance	Require devices to be compliant with corporate policies or enrolled in the MDM system
	Access	Disable access and delete documents if the device is compromised or non-compliant
	Sharing	Control user's ability to edit, copy/paste, or open files in unauthorized applications
Cloud Content Management	Store	Store documents in a cloud-based content management console
	Upload	Upload documents individually or through a bulk import
	Support	Support multiple document types: iWork, PDF, JPG, audio, video, etc.
	Organize	Organize content using custom document categories, sub-categories, tags, and metadata
	Capture	Capture information on author, description, notes, keywords, etc.
	Track	Track document versions and update history
	View	View which users have downloaded a file and when it was last viewed or deleted
	Set	Set documents as active or inactive
Secure Document Distribution	Publish	Publish files and updates to a single device or group of devices
	Enable	Enable documents to be downloaded automatically or on demand
	Define	Define effective and expiration dates for each document
	Define	Define settings for document transfers over cellular or Wi-Fi networks
	Set	Set the priority level in which a file will download in the document queue
	Enable	Enable users to view documents offline or only while online
	Prevent	Prevent user from deleting mandatory content
Easy Mobile Access	View	View organized content through custom categories
	Browse	Browse via smart views: all, new, recent, favorites

(continued)

TABLE 8.1 (CONTINUED)

Typical MCM Functionality

	Sort	Sort documents alphabetically or by importance
	Search	Search content based on specific keywords
	Click	Click links within documents and table of contents
	Store	Store downloaded content for offline viewing
	Receive	Receive automatic updates and notifications
	Update	Update all documents with a single click
IT Administration	Secure	Secure over-the-air distribution and access to corporate documents
	Restrict	Restrict editing, sharing, and opening in unauthorized applications
	Track	Track document version and updates and user activity
	Ensure	Ensure corporate content is up to date on end-user devices

It can be expected that MCM systems will work hand in hand with mobile device management systems (MDM). MDM allows the organization to manage large-scale deployments of heterogeneous mobile devices. Again, Airwatch's MDM product is being used as a baseline for this discussion. Expected MDM functionality is found in Table 8.2.

Of course, policies will be different depending on whether the device is corporate-owned or employee-owned (BYOD). So, it is important to make sure that any MCM or MDM being purchased is entirely configurable.

TABLE 8.2

Typical MDM Functionality

Enroll	Device Ownership	Enroll employee, corporate or shared devices in the enterprise environment
	Device Staging	Allow IT administrator to stage devices on behalf of other users to simplify enrollment
	Device Registration	Enable IT to register existing devices in bulk or end-users to self-register their own device
	User Authentication	Authenticate users via basic or directory-based authentication
	EULA	Create custom End-User License Agreements and require acceptance during enrollment
	Restrictions	Set up enrollment restrictions to block users or devices based on platform, version, etc.
Secure	Passcode	Require a device passcode with configurable complexity, length, lock, and wipe rules
	Encryption	Enforce full device and storage card encryption using industry standards
	Restrictions	Lock down an end-user's ability to use specific device features, apps, and web browsing
	Compliance	Set up rules for non-compliant activities and compromised devices with automated responses
Configure	Profiles	Configure device settings and use credentials for accessing enterprise resources
	Certificates	Integrate with certificates for secure distribution and management of profiles
	Accounts	Provision access to corporate e-mail, calendar, contacts, Wi-Fi, and VPN networks
	Applications	Distribute and manage internal/public/purchased apps via an app catalog
	Content	Distribution corporate documents and secure mobile access using a sandbox
Monitor	Privacy	Configure what data is collected and who can view it for different device groups
	Dashboard	Track and view real-time device information via interactive dashboard and portlets
	Alerts	Create event alerts with automated routing policies to notify IT administrators and end-users
	Rules Engine	Set up rules that define non-compliant events/activities and automated responses

(continued)

TABLE 8.2 (CONTINUED)

Typical MDM Functionality

	Reporting	Export data directly from the dashboard or generate reports with automated distribution
	Data Mart	Import device data to enterprise business intelligence tools to gain insightful metrics
Manage	Queries	Determine the frequency intervals at which the console captures device information
	Updates	Update configuration profiles on-demand and re-provision devices automatically
	Commands	Send commands on-demand to devices to request info, lock, or wipe a device
	Retirement	Un-enroll devices from the environment, remove corporate data and wipe device
Support	Messaging	Send a customized message to end-users with troubleshooting information
	Remote Diagnostics	Perform remote diagnostics to identify device issues in real time
	Remote View	View an end-user's device screen and take screen captures
	Remote Control	Take remote control of an end-user's device for troubleshooting
	Self-Service	Enable end-users to clear their passcode, locate their devices, etc.

9

Integrating BYOD into Resource Management[*]

Resource management provides the operational facilities for managing and securing an enterprise-wide, distributed, multi-platform data architecture. Nowadays, multi-platform includes mobile devices—many of which are BYOD. Resource management provides a common view of the data including definitions, stewardship, distribution, and currency, and allows those charged with ensuring operational integrity and availability the tools necessary to do so.

Resource management is particularly important from a BYOD perspective as supporting BYOD means that corporate data will be stored and transmitted by a device that might not be particularly trustworthy. It is also worthwhile to keep in mind that from a legal point of view, once data is on a mobile, unsecured device it can be easily leaked to an external party. Finally, those e-mails and documents stored on a mobile device can be relevant for litigation.

What most discussions on the integration of smart devices don't delve into is the fact that data is being created on these devices. Often, this data makes its way into the organization's data banks. Therefore, it's worth spending a bit of time delving into the process of resource management as a whole, while considering the integration of data that comes from outside of the organization through these sorts of devices.

Performing and maintaining the functions of data management is an integral part of most large organizations. The rapid and expansive development of information management technologies have opened the door to a vast world of information that can be processed and analyzed with

[*] This chapter was adapted from Keyes, J. (2006). *Knowledge management, business intelligence, and content management: The IT practitioner's guide.* Boca Raton, FL: CRC Press.

increasing speed and complexity. Ensuring that information (and the interpretations derived from it) is accurate is the key challenge for successful data management. Sound data management involves a series of actions that must be clearly defined, clearly understood, and diligently followed.

DATA MANAGEMENT ROLES

Achieving and maintaining data calls for the following role assignments in the organization: Data/project Sponsors, Data Stewards, Data and Database Administrators, and System Administrators. It will be these roles that facilitate the requirements of these data management functions.

Table 9.1 displays the relationship matrix between data management functions and personnel's corresponding roles. It is quite possible for roles to require both content knowledge and technical skills. As we move across the matrix from Data Sponsorship to System Administration, the required

TABLE 9.1

Relationships of Data Management Functions and Roles People Play

	Roles				
Functions	**Sponsor**	**Data Steward**	**Data Admin.**	**DBA**	**System Admin./ISM**
Development Requirements	C	C	C/T	T	T
Identification Enforcement Standards		C	C/T	T	
Design Implementation		C	C/T	T	T
Quality Control Data Integrity		C	C/T	T	T
Backup & Recovery			C/T		T
Data Sharing		C	C/T	T	T
Change Management Change Analysis		C	C/T		
Connectivity			C/T		T
Input & Update		C	C/T		
Security			C	T	T
Metadata			C/T	T	
Training		C	C/T		

Note: C = primarily content knowledge required; T = primarily technical knowledge required; C/T = both content and technical knowledge required.

skills phase from content in nature (program management level, data content level) to more highly technical in nature (systems, database management, etc.).

A description of each of these roles follows.

Data Sponsor

The Data Sponsor is an advocate for a particular information activity such as a spatial data set or application. The person in the organization representing this role has a vested interest in the information activity and provides an appropriate level of support to ensure its success. The Data Sponsor normally has decision authority (at the management level) and approves resources available to the project.

Sponsor duties include the following:

1. The review of project plans and assess relevancy to corporate information needs. The Sponsor must inform management about the scope and effect of the project and its impact on the organization. The sponsor needs to have a complete understanding as to how and where the information will be used, including any external devices (BYOD and not).
2. To serve as an advocate for the project. This advocacy role is not finished with the successful implementation of a data set or application; it continues through evaluation and support of required future developments related to information needs changes due to technological advancements.
3. To collaborate in setting goals and priorities.
4. To ensure that staffing, funds, and other resources are available, in addition to making sure the appropriate data management roles are assigned and fulfilled.
5. To review the project's progress and use of resources.

Sponsor coordination responsibilities include the following:

1. Project Sponsors must coordinate with counterparts at the Leadership Team level on budget and staffing issues. Implicit in this task is ensuring that adequate resources are available for the project.
2. Coordination is required at the planning level to ensure that priorities are clarified and that the project can proceed with the allotted resources.

3. The Sponsor also coordinates with the roles of Data Steward, Data Administrator, and Database Administrator at project initiation and periodically during the project life cycle.
4. Sponsors coordinate with higher-level counterparts in the program area that the projects fall within.
5. The Sponsor should validate the need for the data to be used by employees that might be accessing the data using mobile devices.

Other sponsor requirements include the following:

1. Every project must have clearly defined sponsorship.
2. Sponsorship is an on-going responsibility that does not end with a project's implementation; this role extends through the project life cycle as well. Prior to beginning an information activity, a commitment to this responsibility must be comprehended and accepted.

Data Steward

Effective resource management requires data that is current, accurate, and readily available. To achieve this goal, responsibility for effective data management must be assigned to Data Stewards from top to bottom within the organization. Data automation and data sharing has increased the necessity for accurate and immediate data accessibility. It is the Data Steward's role that is essential to meeting these requirements.

Data Steward duties include the following:

1. The development of procedures and standards that ensure the data is both acceptable and accurate in the applicable program area. It is imperative that only data relevant to the organization's mission is collected, and that the data is of sufficient quality. This also includes functioning as a liaison with the users of the data. The Data Steward must be assertive in asking for input when defining and managing corporate data sets. The Data Steward will coordinate with user representatives to understand the nature of any data collected by employees using mobile devices.
2. The implementation of data standards. Stewards must define how the standards will be applied to the resource(s) or program(s).
3. The development of new standards when necessary. This includes maintaining state-of-the-art knowledge of existing data standards

for the program. These standards must be extended to any data ported to or from mobile devices.

4. The development of quality assurance and quality control plans. Examples of this include data gathering, updates, and sampling protocols for alphanumeric databases and database edit rules. Data collected and used within the confines of a mobile device should still be required to adhere to applicable standards.
5. To check data and databases to address the needs of others who use and share the data.
6. Initiate data sharing and exchange agreements, where necessary. It must be determined whether any data collected by an employee using a mobile device is to be shared.
7. To follow the life cycle management/project planning and configuration management procedures in an application's development.
8. To determine user training needs and the resources necessary for user training (specific to the data and applications).
9. To determine data/application update needs and points of implementation. Included in this task is establishing periodic update cycles (either specific dates or frequency of updates) when relevant.
10. To establish and maintain data/application documentation; e.g., user manuals, data dictionaries, and metadata. Applications accessed by mobile devices are of three types: (1) internal applications; (2) commonly used applications on the Internet; and (3) apps downloaded to the smartphone. Documentation for using these applications should be maintained centrally and accessible through all devices.
11. To serve as a point of contact for data or application.
12. To define access and security requirements for data/applications.
13. To comply with map accuracy standards where applicable.

Data Steward coordination responsibilities include the following:

1. To coordinate with counterparts within the program area.
2. To coordinate with the user community of the data/application.
3. To coordinate with the Data Administrator, Database Administrator, and Data Sponsor roles.

Data Administration

Data Administration is responsible for the management of data-related activities. Two levels of data administration activities exist: system and project.

System level functions deal with management issues. System level functions include planning, developing data standards (in conjunction with Data Stewards), developing policies including policies for usage of organizational data via mobile device, establishing data integrity procedures, resolving data conflict issues, and managing data resource related DBMS.

At the system level, Data Administration policies ensure careful management of data—both at creation and during use. This management practice is necessary to maintain data integrity, maximize data use, and to minimize cost associated with data management and collection.

At the physical management level, we intentionally classify the Database Administrator (DBA) as a sub-component of the Data Administrator role. The Database Administrator differs from the Data Administration role in that the DBA supports the development and use of a specific database system. The DBA role must fulfill the following tasks: defining user requirements, developing data models, training and consulting, establishing and monitoring data integrity, monitoring database usage, and controlling database changes.

Data Administrator duties include the following:

1. Implement a program of data administration that meets the organization's vision with respect to consistency, shareability, and quality of data. This must reflect the business management requirements of the organization. From a BYOD perspective the data administrator must ask questions such as: how will data collected by users using smart devices for quality assured; will this data need to be shared and, if so, how; and how can the organization ensure consistency of data that derives from multiple entry points.
2. Develop strategies, policies, procedures, standards, guidance, and assistance needed for effective data administration.
3. Help to facilitate maximum data sharing capability and to eliminate data definition redundancies by promoting a common description and representation of data. Cooperation with Data Stewards is necessary to accomplish this task.

4. Promote data collection strategies to ensure that data is collected at the source, and that key data collection surveys meet identified integration and business needs.
5. Establish and support strategies governing access, retention, and disposition of data.
6. Establish a communication program with customers and suppliers of information resources.
7. Maintain a repository of active sponsors and stewards for all information activities and components. Also, be sure to ensure that stewardship responsibilities are properly established and maintained for the shared components.
8. Establish and support corporate strategies for data administration.
9. Promote a shared data environment that is both flexible and responsive to the changing business needs of the organization.
10. Establish an integrating framework (Enterprise Data Model) and work with development projects to ensure compatibility with the framework. The Enterprise Data Model will consist of a collection of models ranging from high-level strategic planning views through the implementation of shared databases. The Enterprise Data Model will also need to include a model for the mobile device view.
11. Develop data and function modeling standards and procedures.
12. Develop and enforce standards for maintaining corporate data.
13. Participate in the review of all software releases to ensure compliance with data administration policy, procedures, and standards.
14. Facilitate the "change management" process for all corporate data, including data in the cloud or stored in mobile devices.
15. Ensure that data administration standards comply with government and industry standards. In addition to providing for information exchange and operational compatibility.
16. Ensure compliance with metadata policy and facilitate the maintenance of official metadata records.
17. Facilitate customer access to metadata.
18. Promote data security. This task most notably includes identifying security requirements and assisting the identification of data security procedures and policies. We discuss security in detail in another chapter, but from a data perspective it is critical to assess security risks to data given the multitude of devices being supported.

Data Administration coordination responsibilities include the following:

1. The Data Administrator coordinates with the Database Administrators (DBA), Data Stewards, program area leads, project managers, and application developers by providing education, technical support, reviewing feedback, and developing good working relationships about the enterprise.
2. The Data Administrator role serves as an internal consultant to help employees, managers, and developers locate and retrieve data that meets their information needs. This consultation helps provide leverage to the organization's data investment.
3. The Data Administrator role serves as a coordination point between the various Data Stewards. By providing this type of coordination, data integration and standard consistency is maintained throughout the organization.

Database Administration

The focus of this section is the Database Administration sub-component of Data Administration. It should be noted that the duties of Data Administrator and Database Administrator may overlap; these duties can be performed by one or more persons in the organization.

Both the DBA, who utilizes a technical perspective, and Data Steward, who utilizes a content perspective, work together to build a framework that promotes and provides several data management functions. In simplest terms, the DBA is responsible for the database framework and all transactions (inputs and updates) associated with the data set.

At the physical (project) level, the Database Administrator must focus on the detailed needs of the applications and individual users, including mobile users. The database development aspect of data management shoulders the bulk of the responsibility for developing data models and database implementation. Data development involves the analysis (planning), design, building, maintenance, documentation, and monitoring aspect.

Database Administration (DBA) duties include the following:

1. Formulates a conceptual model of the database in conjunction with the system level Data Administration requirements. As a result, the DBA must be identified/assigned at a project's earliest stages to provide a background and establishes the project's scope needed in the model.

2. Works closely with the System Administrator to ensure the physical environment is conducive to design and development, e.g., identifying appropriate physical space, networking, and access criteria, including access requirements for mobile devices.
3. Coordinates the development and implementation of procedures that ensure data consistency, integrity, and quality with the Data Steward.
4. Builds a data structure conducive to an enforcement of standards—as developed at the system level of Data Administration and by Data Stewards. Although the ultimate responsibility for identification of standards related to the data and processes resides with the Data Steward, it is the responsibility of the DBA to build a data structure conducive to the enforcement of these standards.
5. Ensures data structures are suitable for analysis and application development. Performs database tuning to assure efficient input, update, and retrieval of data.
6. Monitors the data set/application use and routinely reports back to the Data Steward regarding the use of a particular data set/application.
7. Ensures the data set is readily available for sharing both internally and externally.
8. Coordinates the identification, assessment of impacts, strategy, and implementation of change management procedures for a data set.
9. Implements appropriate data security measures by aiding in the control of access at several levels. Works closely with the system administrator to ensure this security exists at the appropriate levels (network, platform, data, and application).
10. Assesses current and new technology merit (e.g., the new technology/tool's performance, the change's cost ramifications at all levels). Thus, any new mobile device type should be cleared through Database Administration.

Database Administration coordination responsibilities include the following:

1. Coordinates with project sponsors and Data Stewards to design and develop a data structure that meets their needs.
2. Coordinates with system administrators and other information support to ensure adequate physical environment and system security.

3. Coordinates the identification, impact assessment, strategy, and implementation of the "change management" procedures for the data set.

System Administration and System Support

System Administrator duties include the following:

1. Assesses existing computer resources and identifies additional needs.
2. Develops guidelines and offers consultation for optimal computer configurations, including mobile devices.
3. Determines the online storage capacity, computer memory, and server, workstation, PC, and other device configuration for the processing and management of data.
4. Monitors computer resources and makes recommendations for changes to the system.
5. Ensures that the systems are kept running and maintained with the latest technology.
6. Loads data onto the system and ensures its security. Provides security for corporate data via access control. Ensures integrity of data flowing to and from the mobile device.
7. Provides access for maintenance of corporate data.
8. Performs scheduled backups of the data.
9. Archives historical data.

Coordination responsibilities include the following:

1. Coordinates with the Data Administrator and Database Administrator to understand the nature and size of the data sets that will be worked with.
2. Coordinates with the Data Administrator and Database Administrator to ensure backups and archives are performed when necessary.
3. Works with the Data Administrator, Database Administrator, and Data Stewards to ensure needed security and data access.
4. Coordinates with all individuals involved in the process to ensure that the systems are meeting project and organizational needs.

DATA MANAGEMENT RESPONSIBILITIES

Data management consists of the following functions, as shown in Table 9.2.

Data functionality is defined in the following sections.

Development and Management Requirements

Development and management requirements refer to management leadership's commitment toward the process of data development and data management. To be successful, management leadership must be totally involved and prepared to commit people, time, and financial resources to the projects and their associated tasks they are sponsoring—not to mention using intelligent foresight during a project's resource analysis. It is important to make your resource specialists and managers available when the important issues are defined, and when working through analysis and data requirements. Although this may be a repetitive process, taking place at the planning stages of identifying information needs and continuing throughout the life of the project, it is imperative to a project's proper development.

The actual event of defining "development and management requirements" is quite common; it occurs every time the details of a project are defined. For the purposes of this discussion, we are focusing specifically on

TABLE 9.2

Data Management Functionality

	Data Management Functions
A.	Development and Management Requirements
B.	Identification and Enforcement Standards, Design, and Implementation
C.	Data and Mapping Standards
D.	Quality Control, Data Integrity, and Backup and Recovery
E.	Data Sharing
F.	Change Management and Impact Analysis
G.	Connectivity
H.	Input and Update
I.	Security
J.	Metadata
K.	Training

defining the level of involvement of the spatial/associated-natural-resource data component of project planning.

Identification and Enforcement Standards, Design, and Implementation

Identification standards simply are guidelines to help maintain data collection/updates, definition, and validation protocol. Enforcement standards are guidelines to help ensure the identification standards are followed. Both functions are based on the outcomes of the development and management requirement phase described in Table 9.2, under heading A.

Successful implementation of data management depends on intelligent up-front data design, e.g., following up on standard's agreements, constructing a data model, and setting up the actual system. The actual implementation should always follow the physical design process.

Data and Mapping Standards

To ensure that your databases, data entry forms, acceptable codes, applications, and so on, are all shareable, consistent, and scientifically sound, data standards should be designed in advance. Given the large amount of data processing, it should be apparent that data collection standards are essential for data integrity.

Quality Control, Data Integrity, and Backup/Recovery

Before data can become corporate or shared, the appropriate mapping standards and data definition standards must be complied with via quality control.

Another important procedure that must be performed regularly, especially when a project or corporate data set reaches a significant milestone, is data backup. Data backup protects the project's progress from any unanticipated system failures or user errors by saving it to the proper media and archiving it. To ensure real-time data integrity, recovery contingencies must also be in place. Backup of data stored on mobile devices must also be considered.

Data Sharing

Sharing data is essential to most organizations; multiple users must have access to the same data to make this type of data processing effective. Before data sharing can occur, the data, metadata, projection, and format must all be integrated. Data sharing has direct links with data security because certain users will have different types of access depending on their need, update responsibilities, or device type. Connectivity is also implicit in data sharing, which is discussed in Table 9.2, under heading G.

Change Management and Impact Analysis

Impacts from data standard changes or technological changes (hardware/software upgrades) must be anticipated and planned for. Understanding the possible ramifications on certain end users, organizations, and applications must be accounted for during a project's planning.

Connectivity

Connectivity is how data is shared and distributed in a networked architecture. User requirements determine the scale of connectivity that is required; these requirements may or may not be apparent to the user community.

Input and Update

The actual collection, input, and update of data may take place in several different locations and several different steps. The technical side of data sharing has to do with the various data types: different types of data require different approaches to updating. Static data is usually low maintenance, whereas dynamic data is usually high maintenance (monitored by the specialist, Data Steward, and the Database Administrator). Update cycles are largely dependent on the dynamic/static nature of the data. Input and update protocols must be developed so that Data Stewards have standard methodologies to follow.

Security

A number of security levels exist in a multiple user interface: network, platform, and data. Security levels are based on user requirements both internal and external to applications (e.g., databases). To help implement security access levels, a review process should be established.

Network security pertains to the different levels of security throughout the computer-network and with firewall(s) management. Platform security relates directly to access privileges according to the platform(s) you are operating on (e.g., IBM, DG, Prime, PC's and associated operating systems, mobile devices). Here is where the issue of data access restrictions appear—normally set by the system administrator. Since data security is application specific, Data Stewards must determine the ownership requirements and Database Administrators must then implement the requirements (e.g., Read/Write, Read).

Metadata

Metadata management requires proper documentation throughout the life cycle of any data set. Technically, metadata is data about data.

Training

Appropriate training is imperative for those collecting data, those entering data, those designing database(s), and certainly for those persons involved in the data management process. A certification processes for some roles can be very valuable to ensure that consistent, sound, and accurate data is being collected and entered into the corporate database.

GUIDELINES

These guidelines are intended to provide a guide in the evaluation, selection, design, construction, and implementation of the organizational data warehouse.

Guideline 1

Information is valued as an asset, which must be capable of being shared.

1. Need to develop policy pertaining to information stewardship. Requires determination of responsibility for accuracy, access authorization, historical trails, manipulation approval, definitions, and integrity relationships.
2. Information and its value must be identified by its current keepers. It must be authenticated and documented. Stewardship must be identified or assigned. The metadata must be capable of being universally available so the data contained within can be leveraged by all authorized to use it.
3. A mechanism is required to maintain identified metadata information that can be listed and categorized and to show stewardship, level of privacy/security, and location of information. Need for unified metadata information management to make it accessible for all agencies.
4. Need to establish supporting policies for security, privacy, confidentiality, and information sharing. Requires Data Use Agreements for in-house as well as mobile access.
5. Data needs to be structured for easy access and management by adopting enterprise data standards.
6. Existing identified data should be used from existing sources and not recaptured by new development.
7. Standards should be adopted to provide more global sharing capabilities.
8. Management tools will be required to maintain and manage a metadata repository.
9. Change control procedures need to be defined and adopted to ensure metadata repository is current.
10. Methodology is needed to publish and disseminate information on data available for sharing.
11. Requires creation of an enterprise data model.
12. Need to establish policy and procedures for maintaining timely and accurate enterprise-wide geographic information.
13. Policies for service level agreements need to be defined to determine availability and level of service. This is particularly important when the cloud is being used.
14. Need to provide enterprise-wide systems that support the creation, storage, and retrieval of documents, images, and other information-rich objects that are used within processes or are exchanged with external organizations and constituents.

Guideline 2

The planning and management of the enterprise-wide technical architecture must be unified and have a planned evolution that is governed across the enterprise.

1. A unified approach will require a change in cultural attributes.
2. Normal evolution will require prioritization and reprioritization across all IT initiatives.
3. Dependencies must be maintained.
4. The architecture must be continually re-examined and refreshed—i.e., to include new platforms such as mobile devices.
5. Short-term results versus long-term impact must be constantly considered.
6. Establishing enterprise architecture takes time and involves a lot of change.
7. Make sure that the chosen architecture has a broad range of capabilities to handle vast needs and best-of-breed solutions in the marketplace (Internet and smartphones and kiosk).
8. Planning for retirement of obsolete and non-standard products.
9. Requires retraining of staff moving from obsolete technologies.
10. Need to develop in-house software engineers, data architects, DBA, and warehouse experts.

Guideline 3

Architecture support and review structures shall be used to ensure that the integrity of the architecture is maintained as systems and infrastructure are acquired, developed, and enhanced.

1. A structured project level review process and authority will be needed to ensure that information systems comply with the IT architecture and related standards.
2. Processes incorporating the guidelines of this (technical) architecture must be developed for all application procurement, development, design, and management activities.
3. This compliance process must allow for the introduction of new technology and standards. Smartphones, BYOD moved into the mainstream rather quickly. It can be expected that technology innovation will occur even more rapidly in the future.

4. Conceptual Architecture and Technical Domain Guidelines should be used as evaluation criteria for purchasing as well as developing software.
5. Negotiate at the enterprise level to handle increase in compliant systems.
6. Need for open mindedness when reviewing for compliance, possible need to broaden existing architecture, or considerations for possible exceptions.
7. Develop phase out plans.
8. Inventory of who is using which architectures. This is critical. The asset management database should include a list of employees and what devices they are using, including BYOD.

Guideline 4

Organizations should leverage a data warehouse and data marts to facilitate the sharing of existing information. This data warehouse will contain the one single version of "the truth."

1. Data warehousing must become a core competency of IT.
2. Data warehousing both requires and supplies configuration standards that need to be developed and maintained.
3. End-user tools must be provided to relieve the burden on programmers to provide this functionality.
4. End-users become more knowledgeable about the information available to them. End-users become more aware of and knowledgeable of the tools they need to access and analyze it.
5. The processes and procedures refreshing the data warehouse will require high levels of reliability and integrity.
6. Warehousing is not meant to replace transaction applications shortcomings. Guidelines on maintaining data and data retention need to be developed.
7. Not all requests for data are simple in nature and appropriate for end-user tools. Not all data will be available to all users.
8. End-users should be able to access the data without knowledge of where it resides or how it is stored and using any device, including mobile.
9. Data warehouse architecture design requires an integrated design effort to provide usefulness. Full potential of a data warehouse will not be realized unless there is full participation throughout the enterprise.

10. User community must be made aware of the (un-)timeliness of information.

Guideline 5

IT systems should be implemented in adherence with all security, confidentiality, and privacy policies and applicable legal and regulatory requirements.

1. Need to identify, publish, and keep the applicable policies current.
2. Need to secure data elements.
3. Categorize access control; this may vary depending on the data and device as well as the audience.
4. Need to monitor compliance to policies.
5. Must make the requirements for security, confidentiality, and privacy clear to everyone.
6. Education on issues of privacy and confidentiality must become a routine part of normal business processes.
7. Audit capabilities of data access.
8. Understanding that part of the stewardship role interprets security, confidentiality, and privacy.
9. All access requests for data that is not publicly available should be made to the steward of the data.
10. Requires a means to publish and implement changes to the status of data's access requirements.

Guideline 6

The enterprise architecture must reduce integration complexity to the greatest extent possible.

1. Decreases the number of vendors, products, and configurations in the environment.
2. Must maintain configuration discipline.
3. Will sacrifice performance and functionality in some instances.
4. Will rely on components supplied by vendors, which will make the enterprise more vulnerable. Refer to Chapter 6 on Cloud Best Practices.
5. Need to factor cost of vendor dependency when figuring the total cost of ownership.

6. Determination of "the greatest extent possible" includes consideration of how reducing complexity can negatively impact providing critical client services.

Guideline 7

Consider re-use of existing tools and infrastructure before investing in new solutions.

1. Software license agreements and system development contracts should be written to allow for re-use across the enterprise.
2. Areas that provide clear advantages and business cost savings are likely to require quick adaptation.

Guideline 8

Systems must be designed, acquired, developed, or enhanced such that data and processes can be shared and integrated across the enterprise and with partners.

1. IT staff will need to consider the impacts on an enterprise-wide scale when designing applications.
2. IT will need a method for identifying data and processes that need integration, when integration should take place, who should have access to the data, and cost justification for integration.
3. It will be necessary to coordinate, maintain, and arbitrate a common set of domain tables, data definitions, and processes across the organization.
4. Over integration can lead to difficult data management and inefficient processes.
5. Use of metadata repository, which spans internal sources, the cloud, and delivery to mobile as well as in-house devices.
6. Enterprise integration teams comprised for dedicated enterprise data architects and applications architects are required to assist in integration efforts.
7. Stewardship review of integration.
8. There is a need to evaluate the practicality of an integrated project before development.

Guideline 9

New information systems will be implemented after business processes have been analyzed, simplified, or otherwise redesigned as appropriate.

1. Need to have an agreed-upon business re-engineering process.
2. Need to identify the business need for data.
3. Need to determine the legal requirement for retention of data.
4. New technology will be applied in conjunction with business process review.
5. Business processes must be optimized to align with business drivers.
6. Additional time and resources will have to be invested in analysis early in the systems life cycle.
7. Organizational change will be required to implement re-engineered work processes.
8. May require regulatory or legislative change.

Guideline 10

Adopt a total cost of ownership model for applications and technologies that balances the costs of development, support, training, disaster recovery, and retirement against the costs of flexibility, scalability, ease of use, and reduction of integration complexity.

1. Will require looking closely at technical and user training costs especially when making platform or major software upgrades during the lifetime of the system.
2. Requires designers and developers to take a systemic view.
3. Need to selectively sub-optimize individual IT components.
4. Need to develop a cost of ownership model.
5. Need to ensure coordinated retirements of systems.
6. Need to consider budget issues for staffing and training.
7. Need to develop a cost structure for providing access to shared information.
8. Need to provide funding for data costs that are not billable or recoverable.
9. Need to establish permanent, reliable funding mechanisms for developing enterprise-wide geographic information such as aerial photography, satellite imagery, transportation, and hydrographic data layers.

Guideline 11

Infrastructure and data access will employ re-usable components across the enterprise, using an *n*-tier model.

1. Component management must become a core competency.
2. Requires development of a culture of re-use.
3. Design reviews become crucial.
4. Data marts can be modularized without making components too small or too simple to do useful "work."

Guideline 12

The logical design of application systems and databases should be highly partitioned. These partitions must have logical boundaries established, and the logical boundaries must not be violated.

1. Applications need to be divided into coded entities (e.g., presentation, process, and data access).
2. For databases, there will be a need to develop competency in partitioning horizontally and vertically; this will result in more but simpler tables and views.

    - Design reviews must ensure logical boundaries are kept intact.
    - Increases data management responsibilities for DBAs.

3. Requires increased analytical skills of project analyst to determine when partitioning takes place based on expected data and/or access requirements.

Guideline 13

Online transaction processing (OLTP) should be separated from data warehouse and other end-user computing and Internet access.

1. Data marts represent a type of configuration standard for physical partitioning.
2. Data warehousing and data marts must become core competencies of IT.

3. Business and IT must agree on the purpose and objective of the data warehouses.
4. Data redundancy will be necessary.
5. Data marts will not reflect the most current data.
6. It is not always necessary or even desirable to physically partition data such as when there is a low scalability requirement.

Guideline 14

IT solutions will use industry-proven, mainstream technologies.

1. Need to establish criteria for vendor selection and performance measurement.
2. Need to establish criteria to identify the weak vendors and poor technology solutions.
3. Requires migration away from existing weak products in the technology portfolio.
4. Will reduce some solution choices.
5. Need to respond as changes in technology occur.

Guideline 15

Priority will be given to products adhering to industry standards and open architecture.

1. Need to establish criteria to identify standards and the products using them.
2. IT organizations will need to determine how they will transition to this mode.
3. Will reduce some solution choices.

Guideline 16

An assessment of business recovery requirements is mandatory when acquiring, developing, enhancing, or outsourcing systems, including to the cloud. Based on that assessment, appropriate disaster recovery and business continuity planning, design, and testing will take place.

1. Systems will need to be categorized according to business recovery needs (e.g., business critical, noncritical, not required).
2. Alternate computing capabilities need to be in place.
3. Systems should be designed with fault tolerance and recovery in mind.
4. Plans for work site recovery will need to be in place.
5. Costs may be higher.
6. Data must be capable of online backups to provide 24×7 availability.

Guideline 17

The underlying technology infrastructure and applications must be scalable in size, capacity, and functionality to meet changing business and technical requirements.

1. Scalability must be reviewed for both "upward" and "downward" capability.
2. May increase initial costs of development and deployment.
3. Will reduce some solution choices.

GLOSSARY OF DATA MANAGEMENT TERMS

Application: A set or logical grouping of data and automated procedures that support one or more business processes and information needs.

Attribute: Any detail that serves to qualify, identify, classify, quantify, or express the state of an entity. Any description of "a thing of significance."

Business Function: What a business does or needs to do, irrespective of how it does it.

Business Model: A collection of models representing a definition of a business. Components include models of objectives, functions, information, and technology.

Connectivity: How data is shared and distributed in a networked architecture.

Coordination: Sound working relationships between Data Stewards, the Librarian/DBA function, System Administration, and the Data Administration function need to be developed and supported. These relationships ensure that developed standards are adequately represented, maintained, and that access and database use is promoted.

Corporate Data: Data that is needed across the organization and that must be shared or combined among offices. It is most valuable to the organization if corporate data is standardized, kept current, and managed in such a way that it addresses the needs of the project and the decision-making process.

Customer: A user or recipient of information management products and services.

Data: Symbols representing facts, ideas, or values that may be processed to produce information.

Data Administration: The policies, procedures, and organizational responsibilities for managing the definition, security, access, and maintenance of data.

Database: A collection of interrelated data stored in a structured manner.

Data Development Life Cycle: The data development life cycle begins at the data requirement's phase. The data development life cycle consists of analysis of need, design of structure, building the structure, documenting the approach, and monitoring results.

Data Element: (see Attribute)

Data Management: The art of managing data and the processes for collecting, maintaining, and using it effectively to meet the organization's need to have solid information available. Data management consists of the daily and long-term development and upkeep of data on automated systems.

To effectively accomplish sound data management practices, an enterprise modeling approach needs to be implemented within each organization. This cannot be fully successful until information needs at different levels of the organization are represented. If grass roots standards are developed, there is a significant risk that the overall objectives of the organization may be missed and that developed applications will have a "stovepipe" narrow focus. If standards come down from above, it is quite possible they will not meet the field users' needs. Data stewards are responsible for developing standards within the context of these broader organizational business requirements. Clear responsibility for the data must be assigned in order to achieve good data management. Stewards must be identified at the levels of the organization (appropriate to the corporate data). Responsibility should be clarified through the establishment of performance expectations that specifically refer to the stewardship responsibility.

Data Model: A structured representation of an organization's information. It includes entities, attributes, and entity relationships.

Data Sharing: Usefulness to more than one user.

Data Steward: Those personnel who ensure that the data complies with the respective program integrity standards. A Data Steward provides oversight and coordination.

Development and Management Requirements: Performing an analysis of the resources that will be required to support a project. Takes place every time the details of a project are defined.

Enforcement Standards: Methods to ensure all standards are being adhered to.

Function: What an organization does, will do, or should do; defines what is done, not how or by whom. The types of activities that are required for us to perform sound data management practices.

Identification Standards: Following protocol of how we collect/update, define, and validate data.

Information: Data that has been processed or interpreted. A majority of data evolves to information, which may in turn become data for a subsequent generation of information.

Information Needs Assessment: (see Needs Assessment)

Information Structures: An end product of data modeling. Logical (versus taxonomic) representation of data components and their relationships.

Integrated Application: An application designed to share data, screens, or behind-the-screens code with at least one other application.

Integrated Database: (a) A set of tables designed to be shared among applications. (b) Where the official data tables for a given application reside.

Integrated Information Environment (IIE): The set of approaches, tools, and products that makes up an environment in which information is managed to achieve a high level of integration among systems and data.

Interpretation Rules: Record of the rationale (logical and intuitive) and assumptions used to create interpreted data.

Life Cycle Management: A structured method for managing an application or automated system for its entire life cycle (initiation, design, development, implementation, operation, cancellation, or replacement).

Management: To treat with care, handle or direct with skill (*Webster's Dictionary*).

Management Direction: A statement of multiple-use and other goals and objectives, the management prescriptions, and the associated standards and guidelines for attaining them.

Management Support: Management at all levels should be informed that data management and its component parts are an ongoing, never-ending process. Creating enterprise data models and developing data standards is a long process (multi-year) and the resulting products must be monitored and maintained over time.

Metadata: Data about data. Proper documentation of process and data content should take place throughout the life cycle of any data set.

Monitoring: To watch, observe, or check, especially for a specific purpose, such as to keep track of, regulate, or control (*Webster's Dictionary*).

Needs Assessment: The identification of the information need. This is generally a multidisciplinary effort and may be a formal Information Needs Assessment (INA). The INA developed with an enterprise modeling perspective relating the information need to the overall business requirement, and is often tied directly to outstanding issues driving the need for analysis at a given scale(s). The end result is that a specific data set is required to meet some information analysis requirement(s).

Network: An interconnected network of computers as referred to in distributed processing.

Normalization: A step-by-step process that produces either entity or table definitions that have (a) no repeating groups; (b) the same kind of values assigned to attributes or columns; (c) a distinct name; (d) distinct and uniquely identifiable rows.

Operation: In other methodologies the term *operation* has the same meaning as business function or elementary business function when used in a business context.

Physical Database Design: The database design that will support an organization's information requirement. It is derived from the analysis model and is driven by the technology used by the organization.

Physical Model: Synonymous with Physical Database Design.

Principal User: The person or group of people for whom the database is designed to serve. These may be resource specialists, resource managers, decision makers, or policy makers.

Process: In other methodologies, the term *process* has the same meaning as business function, or elementary business function when used in a business context.

Project Management Life Cycle: From the perspective of the resource manager, projects are conceived, born, implemented, and monitored for compliance to standards that have roots in laws, executive orders, congressional mandates, and public input. Issues are then identified, a plan is developed, followed by an implementation and monitoring process. An information needs assessment is one of the outflows of the project management life cycle process.

Prototyping: A technique for demonstrating a concept rapidly, to gain acceptance and check feasibility.

Relational Database: (a) A database in which data is organized into one or more relations that may be manipulated using relational algebra. A relation is a named table (row-by-column) that identifies the set of occurrences of entities that have the same or common attribute(s). Relational algebra includes a set of relational operators, such as join and projection, to manipulate relations and the axioms of those operators. (b) A data storage, manipulation, and retrieval system that helps integrate information by emphasizing the flexible relationships among the data.

Relationship: What one thing has to do with another. Any significant way in which two things of the same or different type may be associated. Relationships are named, to indicate their nature.

Repository: A database that acts as a storage place for knowledge about the business and information systems of an enterprise. The repository includes, but is not limited to, models, standards, requirements, definitions, and detailed designs.

Repository Database Administration: The policy, procedures, and organizational responsibility for managing the database implementation of the repository, which includes installing software; managing access to the database; performing backups; and tuning for performance.

Role: (a) A privilege assigned to allow specific users to perform specific functions. (b) A statement of the part a contact plays in relation to an interest.

Role-Based Access Management (RBAM): Simplifies access management by granting access to menus, applications, report generators, and parts thereof to specified roles; people are then assigned to the roles.

Shared Data: Data shared between databases, not a single organization-wide database. Flexibility exists in the individual systems to keep information beyond that which is shared.

Sponsor: (a) An individual or organization officially assigned responsibility for the development and maintenance of one or more information system. (b) An individual or organization who is responsible for ensuring that a particular information activity (such as a request to add a standard value or a request to develop an analysis program based on stored data) is carried out. The sponsor is not necessarily the exclusive provider of the resources for carrying out the activity. (c) The person or organization who sees to it that a particular information activity such as a change request is carried out. This entails setting goals; making available time, funds, and other resources; participating in setting priorities; supporting employee participation; creating and maintaining support for integration; ensuring the sponsored changes are carried through to completion; and facilitating the acquisition of resources from other stakeholders. It should be noted that the sponsor is not the exclusive provider of resources. Other stakeholders may provide resources if they want to have an active role in the information activity. (d) The role of project sponsorship provides the overall direction and approval of the collection and acquisition of natural resource data. Project sponsors are responsible for evaluating the relevancy of the proposed project or activity within the corporate database. They also act as the liaison to higher leadership. (e) Sponsors and stewards would monitor development of interdisciplinary teams to proceed with project development. Sponsors plan and establish priorities for project development and re-affirm their support and involvement with the national efforts.

Staffing: Adequate staffing must be provided to the process that identifies the business requirements, data models, and standards. This goes beyond the naming of and assigning responsibility to Data Stewards. Individuals who are empowered to do the work are needed to manage the modeling tools and data dictionaries. Much of this work falls under the Data Administration function.

Ongoing management of a diverse, integrated data resource cannot be accomplished with a staff of one person. The monitoring and maintenance of data models and data standards requires a data administration staff of appropriate size to effectively manage the workload.

Stakeholder: (a) A stakeholder is responsible for providing input to decisions about information management objects (such as application modules or data tables) that impact the rest of the stakeholder's job. Anyone who has such an interest in the object is automatically a stakeholder, whether or not the person ever fulfills the responsibility of the role. Stakeholders include the users, customers, and managers of the data, processes, and systems. (b) Any person or position with an interest in an Information System (IS) who would be affected by any change to that object. (c) A key member of an organization unit who defines and has a personal stake in achieving the goal of the unit. (d) Anyone who will be affected by the outcome of decision.

Standards: Standards should be an outgrowth of data modeling activities and not have a life all their own. Creating standards for a database, although beneficial in many ways, does not reap the expected rewards if done without the benefit of knowing how they relate to the enterprise data model. Data sharing is maximized when standards are developed in the broader context.

Steward: (a) A steward is responsible for ensuring that the assigned object (such as a data model, an application module, a set of data, or a business process) has a structure that is logically consistent and accurately reflects business requirements, and that the data updates, availability, and performance are all adequately monitored for the requirements achievement. This includes ensuring that relevant policy is followed and that data integrity is maintained. (b) A position or organizational unit officially assigned responsibility for the development and maintenance of one or more information assets on behalf of the organization. (c) One whose job description makes her/him responsible for an Information System object to ensure that the structure accurately reflects business requirements, the structure is logically consistent, and data updates, availability, and access speeds are adequate to meet business requirements. Stewardship can also be broken down into specific categories of Information System objects in order to further describe the associated responsibilities. (d) A position or organizational unit officially assigned responsibility for the development and maintenance of one or more information assets.

Stewardship: The management of someone else's property.

System: (a) A total collection of interrelated programs; or equipment; or people and machines and processes; or all of the above—it is a very broad term. (b) A defined and interacting collection of real-world facts, procedures, and processes, along with the organized deployment of people, machines, and other resources that carry out those procedures and processes. In a good system, the real-world facts, procedures, and processes are used to achieve their defined business purposes within acceptable tolerances.

System Administration: The policies, procedures, coordination, and organizational responsibilities for managing computer systems.

System Integration: The blending of separate, inconsistent, and overlapping applications and their data into an information system.

Systems Analysis: An approach to problem solving where the total system is considered before focusing on individual parts of the system. The term is used very broadly, such as to describe the analysis of global ecosystems or political systems; but it may also apply to the analysis of a specific problem to be solved by a computer application.

Technology: The hardware and software used in conjunction with information management, regardless of the technology involved, whether computers, telecommunications, micrographics, or others.

Tools: Tools to aid in the management of data are a key ingredient in the success of a data management policy. Primary tools are data modeling and data repository (data dictionary) tools. The acquisition of these tools must be given a high priority.

Unique Identifier: Any combination of attributes and/or relationships that serves, in all cases, to uniquely identify an occurrence of an entity. Or one or more columns that will always supply a single row from a table.

10

BYOD Means Social Networking

The collective take on social networking collaboration tools is that they need to be institutionalized to meet the demands of the business. Given the popularity of these sorts of tools among consumers, it is no wonder that a variety of these sorts of tools have cropped up that are geared to specific business disciplines. In this chapter we'll discuss some of the social networking tools that enterprises can endorse for employees who BYOD or use corporate-supplied tools.

Seton Hill University's IT administrators are able to manage any network device, anywhere, leveraging the very same forces that created the BYOD wave in the first place. Using Enterasys's ISAAC (Intelligent Socially Aware Automated Communications) toolset, they have the ability to respond in real time to network challenges, through social media. Using a smartphone or tablet, they can control their enterprise network infrastructure on Twitter, Facebook, or Salesforce.com Chatter.

ISAAC gives network engineers visibility into every mobile device connected to the network, anytime, anywhere. Network engineers can manage the connections by a simple tweet or chat conversation, using everyday language to communicate with the network and individual devices.

So, enterprise networking is both doable and controllable through BYOD.

TOOLS THAT PROVIDE NETWORKING CAPABILITIES

Salesforce.com, the enterprise customer relationship management (CRM) giant, has begun to involve itself in providing social networking capabilities. Its new Chatter service is available on Salesforce's real-time collaboration cloud. Users establish profiles and generate status updates. These might be questions, bits of information and/or knowledge, or relevant hyperlinks. All of this is then aggregated and broadcast to co-workers in their personal network. Essentially, a running feed of comments and updates flow to those in that particular network. Employees can also follow colleagues from around the company, not just in their own personal network, enabling cross-organizational knowledge sharing. Toward that end, Chatter also provides a profile database that users can tap into to find needed skills for a particular project. Chatter is accessible via desktop or mobile.

Like Salesforce.com, more than a handful of well-known software companies have developed collaboration tools, all supporting mobile/BYOD in some way. Oracle's Beehive provides a spate of tools such as instant messaging, e-mail, calendaring, and team workspaces. Microsoft's SharePoint is quite heavily used within many departments. Microsoft's Lync Server product, which permits users to communicate from anywhere via voice, video, or document share, is also becoming a contender. One of the first companies to dabble in the collaborative market—indeed they created it—was Lotus. Now owned by IBM, Lotus Notes brings together a wide array of tools: instant messaging, team rooms, discussion forums, and even application widgets.

There are also a wide variety of free tools available, which can be adapted for our purposes. LinkedIn has been widely used to provide networking capabilities for business people. A relevant feature is LinkedIn groups. A group can be created for any purpose, with permission granted to join. Thus, project teams can make use of the already developed facilities LinkedIn provides. For example, the Tata Research Development and Design Centre (TRDDC) was established in 1981 as a division of Tata Consultancy Services Limited, India's largest IT consulting organization. TRDDC is today one of India's largest research and development centers in software engineering and process engineering. TRDDC has its own membership-by-request LinkedIn group. It is quite easy to create a members-only LinkedIn group for a particular project, and limited to specific members, as shown in Figure 10.1.

Of all of the collaborative tools available, particularly those that are free, wikis are the most prominently used. Zoho.com provides a wide range of tools, including chat, discussions, meetings, and projects, but it is their wiki tool I'd like to focus on here.

In Figure 10.2 I created a wiki to store all of the artifacts for a typical software development project—i.e., project plan, systems requirement

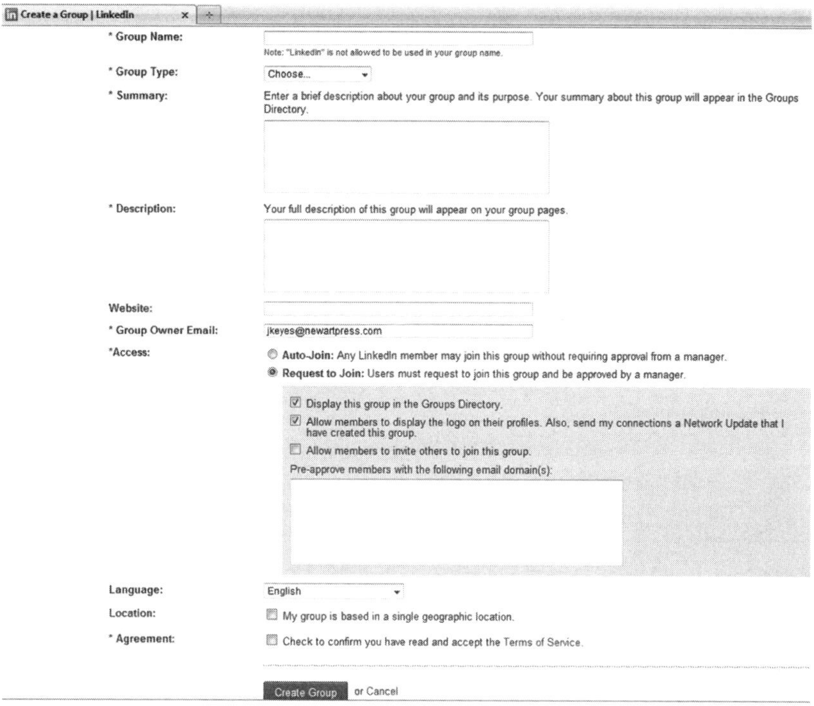

FIGURE 10.1
Creating a members-only LinkedIn group.

specification, analysis docs, and so on. In Figure 10.3 you can see the Project Plan artifact in wiki form. Note the ability to post comments.

Twitter, a social networking app made famous by celebrities who tweet hourly updates on what they are doing (e.g., eating lunch, shopping), has morphed into an enterprise social networking application called Yammer. With the ability to integrate with tools such as SharePoint, Yammer provides a suite of tools including enterprise microblogging, communities, company directory, direct messaging, groups, and knowledge base. SunGard employees actually started using Yammer on their own to share information about projects they were working on. Now it's been rolled out to all 20,000+ employees.

Much of what Yammer offers is free with their basic service. Their Gold subscription provides such corporate niceties as security controls, admin controls, broadcast messages, enhanced support, SharePoint integration, keyword monitoring, and virtual firewall solution.

Yammer can be used by the software development team to interactively discuss any aspect of a project, as shown in Figure 10.4.

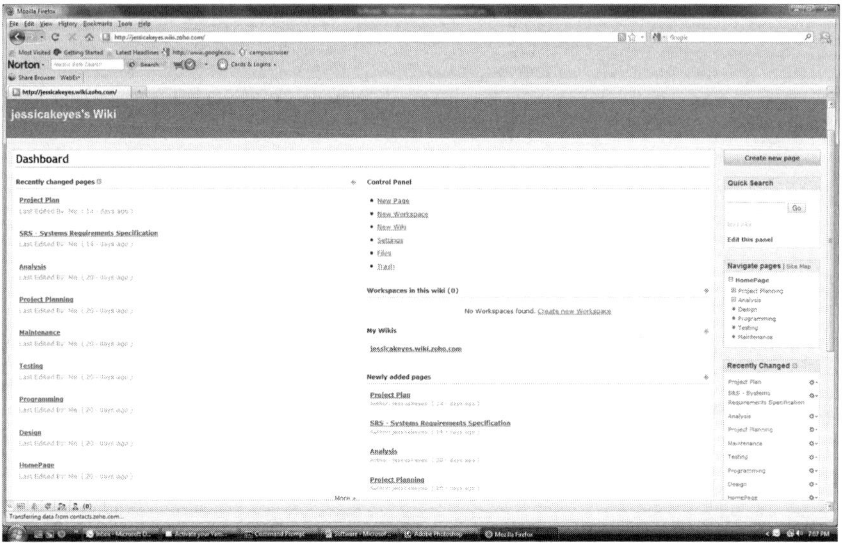

FIGURE 10.2
Project Artifact wiki.

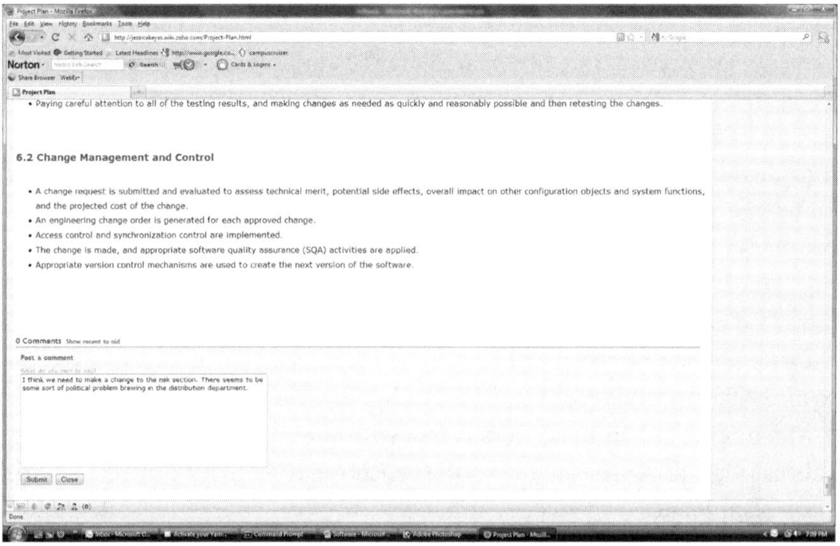

FIGURE 10.3
Project Plan wiki, demonstrating ability to include comments.

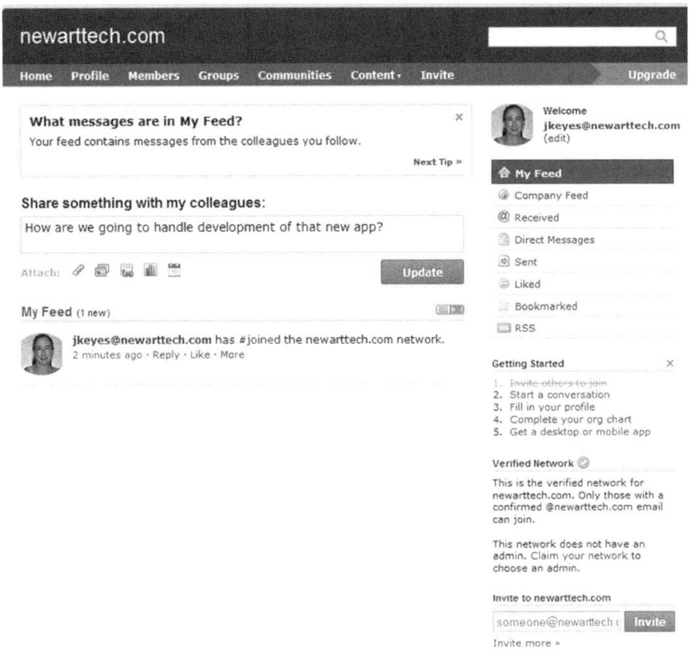

FIGURE 10.4
Dynamic discussion using Yammer.

Project groups have used wikis in some creative ways: writing up personal research and making comments on others' research; asking questions; posting links to resources that might be of interest to others in the group; adding details for upcoming events and meetings; letting each other know what they're up to; adding comments to other team members' information and pages; and recording minutes of meetings in real times. One might think that use of these sorts of ad hoc discussion tools would degenerate into chaos. In truth, this rarely happens—even in a social network of anonymous users. Anderson (2006) talks about the fact that the largest wiki of all, Wikipedia, is fairly resistant to vandalism and ideological battles. He stresses that the reason for this is "the emergent behavior of a Pro-Am (meaning professional and amateur) swarm of self-appointed curators." This group of curators has self-organized what Anderson terms the most comprehensive encyclopedia in history—creating order from chaos. Welcome to the world of "peer production."

WIKIS IN ACTION

Intellipedia (https://www.intelink.gov/wiki) is an online system for collaborative data sharing used by the United States Intelligence Community (IC). It consists of three different wikis with different levels of classification: Top Secret, Secret, and Sensitive but Unclassified. They are used by individuals with appropriate clearances from the 16 agencies of the IC and other national security–related organizations, including Combatant Commands and other federal departments. The wikis are not open to the public. Intellipedia includes information on the regions, people, and issues of interest to the communities using its host networks. Intellipedia uses MediaWiki, the same software used by the Wikipedia free-content encyclopedia project. Officials say that the project will change the culture of the U.S. intelligence community, widely blamed for failing to "connect the dots" before the September 11 attacks.

The Secret version predominantly serves Department of Defense and the Department of State personnel, many of whom do not use the Top Secret network on a day-to-day basis. Users on unclassified networks can access Intellipedia from remote terminals outside their workspaces via a VPN, in addition to their normal workstations. Open Source Intelligence (OSINT) users share information on the unclassified network.

Intellipedia was created to share information on some of the most difficult subjects facing U.S. intelligence and to bring cutting-edge technology into its ever-more-youthful workforce. It also allows information to be assembled and reviewed by a wide variety of sources and agencies, to address concerns that pre-war intelligence did not include robust dissenting opinions on Iraq's alleged weapons programs.

Some view Intellipedia as risky because it allows more information to be viewed and shared, but most agree that it is worth the risk. The project was greeted initially with a lot of resistance because it runs counter to past practice that sought to limit the pooling of information. Some encouragement has been necessary to spur contributions from the traditional intelligence community. However, the system appeals to the new generation of intelligence analysts because this is how they like to work and it's a new way of thinking.

The wiki provides so much flexibility that several offices throughout the community are using it to maintain and transfer knowledge on daily operations and events. Anyone with access to read it has permission to create and edit articles. Since Intellipedia is intended to be a platform for harmonizing the various points of view of the agencies and analysts of the Intelligence Community, Intellipedia does not enforce a neutral point of view policy. Instead, viewpoints are attributed to the agencies, offices, and individuals participating, with the hope that a consensus view will emerge.

During 2006–2007, Intellipedia editors awarded shovels to users to reward exemplary wiki “gardening” and to encourage others in the community to contribute. A template with a picture of the limited-edition shovel (actually a trowel) was created to place on user pages for Intellipedians to show their “gardening” status. The handle bears the imprint: “I dig Intellipedia! It’s wiki wiki, Baby.” The shovels have since been replaced with a mug bearing the tag line “Intellipedia: it’s what we know.” Different agencies have experimented with other ways of encouraging participation. For example, at the CIA, managers have held contests for best pages with prizes such as free dinners.

Chris Rasmussen, knowledge management officer at the Defense Department’s National Geospatial-Intelligence Agency (NGA), argues that “gimmicks” like the Intellipedia shovel, posters, and handbills encourage people to use Web 2.0 tools like Intellipedia and are effective low-tech solutions to promote their use. Also, Rasmussen argues that social software-based contributions should be written in an employee’s performance plan.

MEANING-BASED COMPUTING

Even before the advent of social networking, the sheer amount of data needed to be processed by a worker was overwhelming. Researchers and writers talked about information overload decades ago. Now data is coming in from many more directions, much of it unstructured and unordered (e.g., e-mail, IM, video, audio). Wall Street technologies have a solution for this sort of data overload. They use powerful computers to speed-read news reports, editorials, company websites, blogs posts, and even Twitter messages. Intelligent software then parses all of this and figures out what it means for the markets. If only we could have smart software like this for our IT-oriented blog, wiki, discussion group, and other messages!

Autonomy.com is a leader in the movement toward finding a way to add this sort of meaning to this disorganized chaos of data. Termed *meaning-based computing*, the goal here is to give computers the ability to understand the concepts and context of unstructured data, enabling users to extract value from the data where none could be found before. Meaning-based computing systems understand the relationships between seemingly disparate pieces of data and perform complex analyses on that data, usually in real time. Key capabilities of meaning-based computing systems are automatic hyperlinking and clustering, which enables users to be connected to documents, services, and products that are contextually linked to the original text. To be able to automatically collect, analyze, and organize data so that this can be accomplished requires these computer systems to extract meaning.

Autonomy's meaning-based computing platform, IDOL, is capable of processing any type of information from any source. IDOL can aggregate hundreds of file formats, including voice, video, document management systems, e-mail servers, web servers, relational database systems, and file systems.

Google's most recent plans for "augmented humanity" will most certainly give Autonomy.com something to think about. According to Google CEO Eric Schmidt, Google knows pretty much everything about us—i.e., "We know roughly who you are, roughly what you care about, roughly who your friends are." Schmidt sees a future where we simply don't forget anything because the computer (read that Google) remembers everything. Some of this already exists if you're using Google Tasks, Contacts, Calendar, and Docs. Your searches too are stored and accessible by Google. If you are using Google e-mail and chat, all of this data lives on Google servers as well. Google's plan is to be able to suggest what you should do based on what your interests or knowledge requirements are. It intends to use this knowledge to suggest ideas and come up with solutions that you might have come up if you did the analysis on your own. Some writers are comparing this eventuality as a clone, or "your own virtual you." Coupled with Google's new voice synthesizer, which can replicate your voice, it's not too much of a stretch to find that one day you will go on vacation and your clone will give your team a call to set up a project meeting on something you (or it) is working on.

SEMANTIC WEB

Google cloning is actually an extension of something that exists today. Tim Berners-Lee, who invented the World Wide Web as well as HTML,

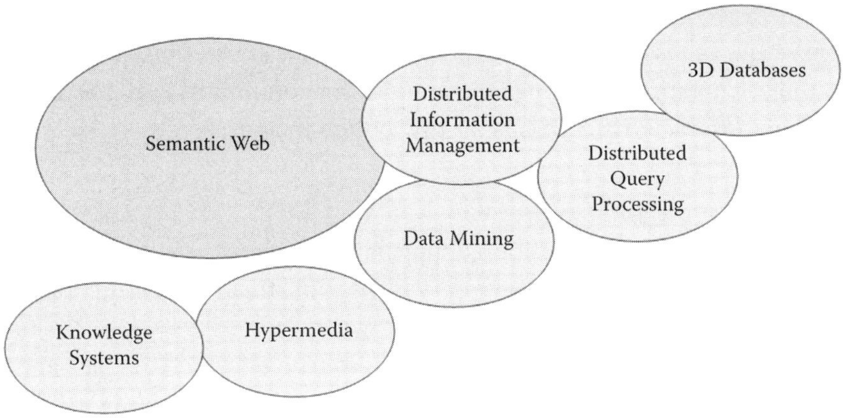

FIGURE 10.5
The Semantic Web.

also came up the idea of the Semantic Web, as shown in Figure 10.5. The Semantic Web is a synthesis of all corporate and external data, including results from data-mining activities, hypermedia, knowledge systems, and so on, which uses a common interface that makes data easily accessible by all (e.g., suppliers, customers, employees).

The Semantic Web is sometimes called the "Defined Web" and is the ultimate repository of all content and knowledge on the web. It uses XML (extensible markup language, a formalized version of HTML) to tag information on Intranets, Extranets, and the Internet.

Tim Berners-Lee explains the Semantic Web as follows:

> At the doctor's office, Lucy instructed her Semantic Web agent through her handheld web browser. The agent promptly retrieved information about Mom's ***prescribed treatment*** from the doctor's agent, looked up several lists of ***providers***, and checked for the ones ***in-plan*** for Mom's insurance within a ***20-mile radius*** of her ***home*** and with a ***rating*** of ***excellent*** or ***very good*** on trusted rating services. It then began trying to find a match between available ***appointment times*** (supplied by the agents of individual providers through their websites) and Pete's and Lucy's busy schedules.

Hewlett-Packard's Semantic Web research group frequently circulates items of interest such as news articles, software tools, and links to websites. They call these snippets, or information nuggets (Cayzer, 2004). Since e-mail is not the ideal medium for this type of content they needed to find a technique for decentralized, informal knowledge management. They began a research project to create a system that was capable of aggregating, annotating, indexing, and searching a community's snippets. The required characteristics of this for this system include:

1. Ease of use and capture
2. Decentralized aggregation. Snippets will be in a variety of locations and formats. It will be necessary to integrate them and perform some global search over the result.
3. Distributed knowledge. Information consumer should be able to add value by enriching snippets at the point of use by adding ratings, annotations, and so on.
4. Flexible data model. Snippets are polymorphic. The system should be able to handle e-mail, web pages, documents, text fragments, images, and so on.
5. Extensible. It should be possible to extend the snippet data schema to model the changing world.
6. Inferencing. It should be possible to infer new metadata from old. For example, a machine should "know" that a snippet about a particular HP Photosmart model is about a digital camera.

Some have suggested that blogs make the idea tool for this type of content and knowledge management. However, today's blogging tools offer only some of the capabilities mentioned. Traditional blogging has many limitations but the most important limitation is that metadata is used only for headline syndication in a blog. Metadata is not extensible, not linked to a risk-flexible data model, and not capable of supporting vocabulary mixing and inferencing.

The researchers, therefore, looked to the Semantic Web for a solution. As we've discussed, the premise of the Semantic Web is that data can be shared and reused across application, enterprise, and community boundaries. RSS1.0 (web.resource.org/rss/1.0) is a Semantic Web vocabulary that provides a way to express and integrate with rich information models. The Semantic Web standard Resource Description Framework (RDF) specifies a web-scale information modeling format (www.w3.org/RDF). Using these tools they came up with a prototype (http://www.semanticfocus.com/blog/) for creating what they called a Semantic Blog. The prototype has some interesting searching capabilities. For example, snippets can be searched for either through their own attributes (e.g., "I'm interested in snippets about HP") or through the attributes of their attached blog entry (e.g., "I'm interested in snippets captured by Bob").

VIRTUAL WORLDS

Perhaps the most interesting of all social-based community software is Linden Labs Second Life (http://www.secondlife.com). Though primarily used for such fun activities as fantasy role-playing (pirates, goths, sci-fi, and all that), Second Life does have a serious side.

In 2008, IBM's Academy of Technology held a virtual world conference and annual meeting in Second Life, as shown in Figure 10.6. The virtual meeting conference space had room for breakout sessions, a library, and various areas for community gathering. IBM estimates that the ROI for the virtual world conference was about $320,000 and that the annual meeting cost one-fifth that of a real-world event.

Just think of the possibilities. Project team members near and far can use Second Life to hold virtual, but tactile, team meetings and even work with clients.

FIGURE 10.6
Using Second Life to host a conference.

KNOWLEDGE MANAGEMENT TOOLS

Knowledge management (KM) has been defined as the identification and analysis of available and required knowledge, and the subsequent planning and control of actions, to develop these into "knowledge assets" that will enable a business to generate profits and/or increase its competitive position. The major focus of knowledge management is to identify and gather content from documents, reports and other sources and to be able to search that content for meaningful relationships. A variety of business intelligence, artificial intelligence, and content management methodologies and tools are the framework under which knowledge management operates.

Groups of individuals who share knowledge about a common work practice over a period of time, though they are not part of a formally constituted work team, are considered to be "communities of practice." Communities of practice generally cut across traditional organizational boundaries. They enable individuals to acquire new knowledge faster. They may also be called communities of interest if the people share an interest in something but do not necessarily perform the work on a daily basis. For example, in one government agency a group of employees who were actively involved in multi-party, multi-issue settlement negotiations began a monthly discussion group during which they explored process issues, discussed lessons learned, and shared tools and techniques. CoPs can be more or less structured depending on the needs of the membership.

Communities of practice provide a mechanism for sharing knowledge throughout one organization or across several organizations. They lead to an improved network of organizational contacts, supply opportunities for peer-group recognition, and support continuous learning, all of which reinforce knowledge transfer and contribute to better results. They are valuable for sharing tacit (implicit) knowledge.

To be successful, CoPs require support from the organization(s). However, if management closely controls their agendas and methods of operation, they are seldom successful. This is more of an issue for communities of practice within organizations.

Communities of practice can be used virtually anywhere within an organization: within one organizational unit or across organizational boundaries, with a small or large group of people, in one geographical location or multiple locations, and so on. They can also be used to bring together people from multiple companies, organized around a profession, shared roles, or common issues.

They create value when there is tacit information that, if shared, leads to better results for individuals and the organization. They are also valuable in situations where knowledge is being constantly gained and where sharing this knowledge is beneficial to the accomplishment of the organization's goals.

There are different kinds of CoPs. Some develop best practices, some create guidelines, and others meet to share common concerns, problems, and solutions. They can connect in different ways: face-to-face, in small or large meetings, or electronically. These virtual communities of practice called simply VCoPs.

VCoPs (as well as face-to-face CoPs) need a way to capture their collective experiences for online examination. Daimler AG does this using something they call the EBOK system. This is short for Engineering Book of Knowledge. It provides best practice information on pretty much everything related to the manufacture of cars. Tech CoPs share knowledge related across car processes and then consolidate this knowledge in the EBOK system.

CoPs provide a great degree of what academics refer to as "social capital." It is social capital that provides the motivation and commitment required to populate knowledge stores such as EBOK.

One of the more recent advances in CoP methodology is to take it from small-team interaction to large-group intervention, although some dispute whether this can be effectively done at all. There have been some experiments where up to 300 people were brought together within a CoP to work through organizational issues. There are a variety of CoP-based designs for groups of this size. The World Café is perhaps the most well known and popular of these designs, which also includes Open Space Technology, Participative Design, and Wisdom Circles.

The World Café (http://www.theworldcafe.com/) describes its process this way: it is an innovative yet simple methodology for hosting conversations. These conversations link and build on each other as people move between groups, cross-pollinate ideas, and discover new insights into the questions and issues raised. As a process, the World Café can evoke and make visible the collective intelligence of any group, thus increasing people's capacity for effective action in pursuit of common aim.

In a face-to-face environment, the way to do this is quite simple. Tables are provided where a series of conversational rounds, lasting from 20 to

45 minutes, are held tackling a specific question. Participants are encouraged to write, doodle, or draw key ideas and themes on the tablecloths, as shown in Figure 10.7. At the end of each round, one person remains at the table as the host, while the others travel to new tables. The hosts welcome the newcomers and share the table's conversation so far. The newcomers share what they discussed from the tables they've already visited. And so on. After the last round, participants return to their individual tables to integrate all of this information. At the end of the session, everyone shares and explores emerging themes, insights, and learning. This serves to capture the collective intelligence of the whole (Raelin, 2008).

Visiting the World Café's website demonstrates how they modified this construct to suit the online environment. One of the outputs of this sort of brainstorming session might be a tag cloud, which is a visual depiction of user-generated tags based on discussions. Tags are usually single words and are normally listed alphabetically, and the importance of a tag is shown with font size or colors as shown in Figure 10.8.

Tag clouds were popularized by websites such as Flickr and Technorati. They actually serve a very useful purpose for software engineers providing a way to classify, organize, and prioritize the results of any meetings. Since individual tags can be hyperlinks, it is possible to use this as a way to store

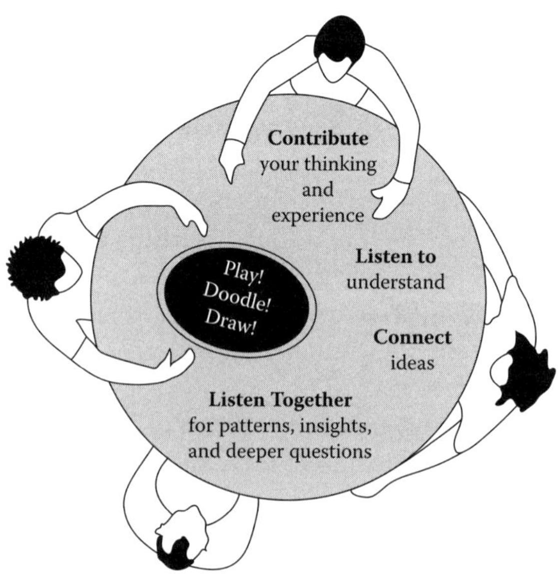

FIGURE 10.7
The World Café methodology.

FIGURE 10.8
Tag cloud.

increasingly granular levels of information. Perhaps the most well known of cloud tag generators is Wordle (http://www.wordle.net/create).

MASHUPS

Web developers have long been engaged in what is known as service composition. This is the practice of creating value-added services by re-using existing service components. Mashups are a new emerging paradigm of Web 2.0 that enables developers, and even more talented end-users, to create new web-based applications and services that address specific needs and interests.

The term *mashup* implies fast integration. This is done using open APIs and data sources to produce enriched results that were not necessarily the original reason for producing the raw source data. Mashup tools generally support visual wiring of GUI widgets, services, and components together.

Some tech leaders have since discontinued their mashup tool offerings (Microsoft Popfly in 2009 and Google Mashup Editor in 2009). However, Yahoo Pipes (http://pipes.yahoo.com/pipes/) is still being supported. As Yahoo describes it:

> Pipes is a free online service that lets you remix popular feed types and create data mashups using a visual editor. You can use Pipes to run your own web projects, or publish and share your own web services without ever having to write a line of code. You make a Pipe by dragging pre-configured modules onto a canvas and wiring them together in the Pipes Editor. Each Pipe consists of two or more modules, each of which performs a single, specific task. For example, the Fetch module will retrieve a feed URL, while the Sort module will re-order a feed based on criteria you provide (you can find a complete list of available modules in the documentation). You can wire modules together by clicking on one module's output terminal and dragging the wire to another module's input terminal. Once the terminals are wired together the output from the first module will serve as input to the second module. In addition to data feeds, Pipes also lets you add user input fields into your Pipe. These show up at runtime as form fields that users of your Pipe can fill in.

JackBe Corporation is a privately held software provider of enterprise mashup software. JackBe's flagship product is an Enterprise Mashup Platform called Presto (http://www.jackbe.com/products/), with support for Microsoft SharePoint. JackBe launched its Enterprise App Store product in July 2010 as a platform for creating internal enterprise application stores. The Enterprise App Store is primarily aimed at non-developers, allowing them to create new business applications and then share them with other users. JackBe is a founding member of the Open Mashup Alliance (OMA), which promotes enterprise mashup interoperability and portability. JackBe was the original contributor and continues to be a key supporter of the OMA's Enterprise Mashup Markup Language (EMML),

EMML, or Enterprise Mashup Markup Language, is an XML markup language for creating enterprise mashups. These are software applications that consume and mash data from variety of sources, often performing logical or mathematical operations as well as presenting data. Mashed data produced by enterprise mashups are presented in graphical user interfaces as mashlets, widgets, or gadgets. EMML is an open language specification that is promoted by the Open Mashup Alliance.

EMML is fairly easy to understand and use, as it is a derivative of the now familiar XML markup language. For example, the EMML code below joins Yahoo! News, Financial News, and Reuters feeds.

```
<merge inputvariables = "$YahooRSS, $FinancialNewsRss,
$ReutersRSS"
outputvariable = "$NewsAggregate"/>
```

Detailed documentation for EMML can be found on the Open Mashup Alliance website (http://www.openmashup.org/omadocs/v1.0/index.html).

As you can see, there are a wide variety of tools out there that can support social enterprising. There are three methodologies to choose from when making the platform decision: (1) off the shelf, (2) mashup, and (3) build your own. This chapter has provided information that will get you started moving in the direction that is the most suitable for your organization.

REFERENCES

Anderson, C. (2006). *The long tail.* New York: Hyperion.

Cayzer, S. (2004, December). Semantic blogging and decentralized knowledge management. *Communications of the ACM, 47*(12), 47–52.

Raelin, J.A. (2008). *Work-based learning: Bridging knowledge and action in the workplace.* San Francisco: Jossey-Bass.

Quick Start 1

Software-Based Authentication

Increased use of mobile technology by your personnel demands that businesses make the switch to safe, authenticated access to enterprise applications. If businesses encourage BYOD on a large scale, they must, according to a report by authentication specialist Encap, make the switch to software-based authentication platforms. Per Encap's survey, here are the whys.

PROCEDURES/ISSUES/POLICIES

1. Have 3,000 employees save $165,000 by switching to smart device–based software from hardware-based solutions.
2. Capital-based expenditure: Onset costs for hardware one-time passwords (OTP) is $202,000 versus smart device software at $9,000—a 95% decrease in expenditures (OTP replacement costs are over 95% more expensive. SMS OTP cost per user $35 vs. $15 for smart device.)
3. Report concluded: "Can't argue with the survey results. Hardware-based authentication is heading toward a demise...smart-device authentication protects your data at an excellent price point."

BIBLIOGRAPHY

CIOinsight. (2012, July 5). *Software-based authentication key to successful BYOD strategy.* Retrieved from http://www.enduserexperience.info/articles/share/366781/.

Quick Start 2

BYOD: Making It Work for Your Firm

They're ubiquitous. Everywhere you look—smartphones, tablets, laptops. But once they enter the office, they're hidden away in pockets, desk drawers, attaché cases—vanished, unutilized. But the hive is now buzzing that this shouldn't be. They want to bring their tools into sunlight—untether from your network. Should you allow it? Will it hurt or hinder your workflow? This Quick Start will provide some best practices that can help make BYOD go more smoothly in your organization.

PROCEDURES/ISSUES/POLICIES

1. Company should have users set passwords that are set to time out after so many minutes of inactivity.
2. Users must store highly sensitive documents on company servers—not device. But if they do store on device, put info in folders separate from personal information, thus making it easy if necessary (if users device is stolen or lost or if he/she leaves the company) for IT to remotely wipe just company data.
3. Reinforce to users that company rules pertaining to proprietary data on their device are still in force even when device is off-site. Make them very aware that there is no sharing of this device at home.
4. Store company data and applications virtually (setting up enterprise applications that can easily be accessed by mobile devices), on central servers, or on a secure network. Devices will then only be allowed to interface, retrieving what is vital for task, preventing information from being stored, opened to possible security breaches.

5. Work with telecommunication companies to make sure there are enough towers to handle this increased demand.
6. Big plus: Network runs faster, far less data flowing out from servers than there is in a client server setup. Also, less servers, less dollars spent.
7. Make sure users know that they, not IT, are responsible for all knowledge and upkeep of their device.
8. Make sure users check with IT before purchasing device, and make sure it can make a smooth connection to the network (and, if not, help in making it happen). Cooperation is the goal.
9. Say yes to your mobile staff—sales force, field managers, marketing personnel. Say no to people on a production factory line.
10. Before plugging in, users must be fully aware of your BYOD policies: what sites they can visit, what data can or cannot be stored on device.
11. Training should not be online (too easy to skim through important facts) but in person, either one-on-one or in small groups.
12. According to a recent survey, of the 131 companies that reported having BYOD programs, 4% covered the entire costs of the device, 36% said they provide some financial help—but 60% have employees pick up the whole tab.
13. Again, according to survey, 31% claimed savings on hardware and support, while 43% reported no great savings at all. But goodwill gained from listening to your employees may compensate for those companies not seeing profit improvement.

BIBLIOGRAPHY

Nash, K. S. (2011, October 1). The B.Y.O.T. buzz. *CIO Magazine*. Retrieved from http://www.cio.com/article/690504/Bring_Your_Own_Tech_9_Things_IT_Needs_To_Know.

Quick Start 3

Software Selection from Multiple Packages

Many projects can make use of package software to satisfy part or all of a functional requirement. In making this decision, the purchase cost of the package must be weighed against the development costs estimated as part of the planning step. The decision is further complicated when more than one software package is evaluated. This Quick Start provides a recommended evaluation procedure.

PROCEDURES/ISSUES/POLICIES

1. Cost—the real cost of vendor-supplied software (purchase price + cost to modify + cost to add + maintenance fee)
2. Service and support—based on other users with identical environments
3. Documentation—for users and local maintenance
4. Expandability/flexibility—to address future applications or changes in environment
5. Reputation—of the vendor and the vendor-supplied software
6. Stability—based on the age of the package and the number of releases over the past two years
7. Machine or operating system dependency—based on programming languages used, special features tied to special hardware
8. Completeness—of function and performance based on software scope

A Software Evaluation Matrix should be developed to evaluate software packages against each other. First, establish a weight factor, based on importance, for each characteristic. Grade each candidate package on a scale of 1 to 10 for each characteristic listed above. The final grade for each package is

$$\Sigma\ [(\text{characteristic})_k(\text{weighting factor})_k]$$

where $k = 1$ to 8.

BIBLIOGRAPHY

General Electric Company. (1986). *Software engineering handbook*. New York: McGraw-Hill.

Quick Start 4

The Make-Buy Decision

Many projects can make use of package software to satisfy part or all of a functional requirement. In making this decision, the purchase cost of the package must be weighed against the development costs estimated as part of the planning step. As part of this process the following questions in this Quick Start should be answered.

PROCEDURES/ISSUES/POLICIES

1. Does the vendor-supplied software meet all functional requirements defined in the scope of the plan? If not, what percentage of the function will have to be enhanced or added locally? What costs are associated with these enhancements?
2. Has the vendor-supplied software been developed using software engineering methods? Is it maintainable? Does a good documentation base exist? What documentation is supplied with the package?
3. Does the vendor-supplied software meet human interface requirements for the system to be developed?
4. Does the vendor-supplied software already have a user base? Are current users happy with the package? With vendor's support of the package? Is there a user group?
5. What is the vendor's policy on software maintenance? On error correction and reporting? What are the vendor's rates for future adaptation or enhancement of the software? Does a maintenance contract exist? Is the vendor the original developer of the package?
6. Will the vendor supply source code or will the source code be placed in escrow?

7. Have adequate benchmark and validation tests been conducted on the vendor's software?
8. Is there more than one candidate vendor package? Have all the candidates been evaluated? Have benchmark tests been conducted?
9. How are new releases of the package handled? How long are the older releases supported? What is the frequency (based on past performance) of new releases?
10. Is special training required to use the package? To operate the package? Is training conducted at the local site? Is there any cost associated with training?

BIBLIOGRAPHY

General Electric Company. (1986). *Software engineering handbook.* New York: McGraw-Hill.

Quick Start 5

Balanced Scorecard Metrics

All metrics are accompanied by targets. For the most part, these are percentages that will be ascertained via a calculation based on data entry of raw data. Some targets have the word *baseline* encoded. Baseline indicates that the metric is informational; in other words, only the raw value will be displayed (i.e., aggregated by the specified period—weekly, monthly, etc.). The targets should be set to default (or 0 in the case of baselined targets). The entirety of metrics provided is greater than the "norm" for a typical balanced scorecard, which usually has just a few key metrics per perspective. It should be noted that many of these metrics can be modified to measure systems developed using social software engineering methods. It should be noted that BYOD impacts each of these metrics in some way.

Financial Objectives	Measures	Targets	KPI
Optimize cost efficiency of purchasing	Cost to spend ratio [1] <1%	F1	
	Negotiated cost savings [2]	> = 20%	F2
	Costs avoided/total costs [3]	> = 10%	F3
	Percentage of goods and services obtained through competitive procurement practices [4]	> = 19%	F4
Control costs	Dollar amount under budget	Baseline	F5
	Dollar amount over budget	Baseline	F6
	Budget as a percentage of revenue	< = 30%	F7
	Expenses per employee	< = 35,000	F8
	Cost of acquired technology/technology developed in house	< = 50%	F9
	% new products/services where break-even point is within one year	80%	F10

Financial Objectives	Measures	Targets	KPI
	Total cost of ownership [5]	< = $6,000 per device per year	F11
	Overtime ratio [6]	< = 25%	F12
	Cost performance index [7]	> = 1	F13
	Average break-even point [8]	< = 1.5 years	F14
	Schedule performance index [9]	> = 1	F15
	Total cost reductions due to use of technology	> = 33%	F16
	Workforce reduction due to use of new products	> = 10%	F17
	Contractor utilization [10]	< = 35%	F18
Increase business value	Revenue from new products or services [11]	Baseline	F19
	Average ROI [12]	> = 1	F20
	% resources devoted to strategic projects	> = 55%	F21
	% favorable rating of project management by top management	> = 93%	F22
	Average cost/benefit ratio	> = 22%	F23
	Net present value [13]	> = 1	F24
	Assets per employee	Baseline	F25
	Revenues per employee	Baseline	F26
	Profits per employee	Baseline	F27
Improve technology acquisition process	Total expenditures	Baseline	F28
	Total expenditures/industry average Expenditures	> = 1	F29
	Amount of new technology acquired through M&A	Baseline	F30

[1] Operational costs/purchasing obligations (goods and services purchased).

[2] Cost savings compared to total costs.

[3] Costs avoided compared to total costs. You can avoid costs by re-using hardware/software, utilizing a partner, etc.

[4] Difference between average qualified bid and the cost of the successful bid. The sum of each calculation is aggregated into a new savings ratio for all transactions.

[5] Additional capital costs—software, IT support software and network infrastructure; technical support costs—hardware and software deployment, help desk staffing, system maintenance; administration costs—financing, procurement, vendor management, user training, asset management; end-user operations costs—the costs incurred from downtime and in some cases, end-users supporting other end-users as opposed to help desk technicians supporting them.

[6] Overtime hours/regular hours worked.

[7] Ratio of earned value to actual cost. EV, often called the budgeted cost of work performed, is an estimate of the value of work actually completed. It is based on the original planned costs of a project.

[8] Break-even analysis. All projects have associated costs. All projects will also have associated benefits. At the outset of a project costs will far exceed benefits. However, at some point the benefits will start outweighing the costs. This is called the break-even point. The analysis that is done to figure out when this break-even point will occur is called break-even analysis.

[9] SPI is the ratio of earned value to planned value and is used to determine whether the project is on target. (See Cost Performance Index for a definition of earned value, EV.)

[10] Cost of external contractors/cost of internal resources.

[11] Use real dollars if systems are external customer facing. Use internal budget dollars if these are internal customer facing systems.

[12] Return on Investment. Most organizations select projects that have a positive return on investment. The return on investment, or ROI as it is most commonly known, is the additional amount earned after costs are earned back.

The formula for ROI is

$$\mathrm{ROI} = \frac{(\mathrm{Benefit} - \mathrm{Cost})}{\mathrm{Cost}}$$

Organizations want ROI to be positive.

[13] NPV is a method of calculating the expected monetary gain or loss by discounting all expected future cash inflows and outflows to the present point in time. If financial value is a key criterion organizations should only consider projects with a positive NPV. This is because the positive NPV means the return from the project exceeds the cost of capital—the return available by investing elsewhere. Higher NPVs are more desirable than lower NPVs.

Formula for NPV:

$$\mathrm{NPV} = -II + (\text{sum of})\ [OCF/(1+R(r))t] + [\mathrm{TCF}/(1+R(r))n]$$

where

II = initial investment

OFC = operating cash flows in year t

t = year

n = life span (in years) of the project

$R(r)$ = project required rate of return

(From http://www.mtholyoke.edu/~aahirsch/howvalueproject.html.)

[14] Use research from a company such as http://www.infotech.com/.

Customer Objectives	Measures	Targets	KPI
Increase customer satisfaction	% of customers satisfied with system timeliness (speed)	> = 92%	C1
	% of customers satisfied with responsiveness to questions	> = 92%	C2
	% of customers satisfied with quality	> = 92%	C3
	% of customers satisfied with sales/ customer service representatives	> = 92%	C4
	Length of time to resolve disputes	< = 4 hours	C5
Conformance with customer requests	% of baselined projects with a plan	> = 90%	C6
	% customer requests satisfied	> = 90%	C7
Increase customer base	Customer lifetime value ($)	Baseline	C8
	Share of wallet (%) [1]	> = 25%	C9
	Retention %	> = 80%	C10
	Win-back percent	> = 85%	C11
	New acquisitions/current number of customers	> = 10%	C12
	Rate of defection	< = 3%	C13
Enhance customer-facing systems	Average number of searches per order/ query	Baseline	C14
	Average number of support calls per order/query	Baseline	C15
	Average elapsed time to select product and select an order	Baseline	C16
	Average elapsed time to search website	Baseline	C17
	Number of steps required to select and purchase	Baseline	C18
	Average time to answer incoming phone call	Baseline	C19
	% availability of customer facing applications	> = 98%	C20
	Average cost to service each customer's transaction	Baseline	C21
Support internal customers	% better decisions	> = 90%	C22
	% time reduction in making decisions	> = 90%	C23
	Average time to answer a support phone call	Baseline	C24

[1] Compare to competition using service such as http://www.lexisnexis.com/marketintelligence/.

Internal Business Processes Objectives	Measures	Targets	KPI
Improve data quality	Forms inputted	Baseline	I1
	Data entry error rate	< = 3%	I2
	Age of current data	Baseline	I3
	% of employees who have up-to-date data	> = 98%	I4
Improve balance between technical and strategic activities	% of time devoted to maintenance	< = 20	I5
	Strategic project counts	Baseline	I6
	% of time devoted to ad-hoc activities	< = 15%	I7
Increase product quality and reliability	% reduction in demand for customer support	> = 25%	I8
	Number of end-user queries handled	Baseline	I9
	Average time to address an end-user problem	< = 4 hours	I10
	Equipment downtime	< = 1%	I11
	Mean time to failure	< = 1,000 hours	I12
	% remaining known product faults	< = 5%	I13
	% of projects with lessons learned in database	> = 95%	I14
	Fault density [1]	< = 3%	I15
	Defect density [2]	< = 3%	I16
	Cumulative failure [3]	Baseline	I17
	Fault days number [4]	< = 1	I18
	Functional test coverage [5]	> = 95%	I19
	Requirements traceability [6]	> = 98%	I20
	Maturity index [7]	> = 1	I21
	% of conflicting requirements	< = 5%	I22
	Test coverage [8]	> = 92%	I23
	Cyclomatic complexity [9]	< = 20	I24
	% of project time allocated to quality testing	> = 15%	I25
Reduce risk	% definitional uncertainty risk [10]	< = 10%	I26
	% technological risk [11]	< = 45%	I27
	% developmental risk [12]	<10%	I28
	% non-alignment risk [13]	< = 4%	I29
	% Service delivery risk [14]	< = 5%	I30

Internal Business Processes Objectives	Measures	Targets	KPI
	Number of fraudulent transactions	< = 1%	I31
	% of systems that have risk contingency plans	> = 95%	I32
	% of systems that have been assessed for security breaches	> = 95%	I33
Improve processes	% resources devoted to planning and review of product development activities	> = 25%	I34
	% resources devoted to R&D	Baseline	I35
	Average time required to develop a new product/service	Baseline	I36
	Person-months of effort/project	Baseline	I37
	% requirements fulfilled	> = 90%	I38
	Pages of documentation	Baseline	I39
	% of on-time implementations	> = 97%	I40
	% expected features delivered	>98%	I41
	Average time to provide feedback to the project team	< = 1 day	I42
	Project development time	> = 50%	I43
	% project backlog	< = 10%	I44
	% project cancellation rate	< = 20%	I45
	Support personnel to development personnel ratio	> = 35%	I56
Enhance resource planning	Number of supplier relationships	Baseline	I47
	Decision speed	<5 days	I48
	Paper work reduction	> = 10%	I49
Monitor change management	Number of change requests per month	Baseline	I50
	% change to customer environment	Baseline	I51
	Changes released per month	Baseline	I52
Enhance applications portfolio	Age distribution of projects	Baseline	I53
	Technical performance of project portfolio [15]	Baseline	I54
	Rate of product acceptance	> = 95%	I55

[1] Faults of a specific severity/thousand.
[2] Total number of unique defects detected.

[3] Failures per period.

[4] Number of days that faults spend in the system from their creation to their removal.

[5] Number of requirements for which test cases have been completed/total number of functional requirements.

[6] Number of requirements met/number of original requirements.

[7] Number of functions in current delivery – (adds + changes + deletes)/number of functions in current delivery.

[8] (implemented capabilities/required capabilities)*(capabilities tested)/total capabilities)*100%.

[9] Cyclomatic complexity equals the number of decisions plus one. Cyclomatic complexity, also known as V(G) or the graph theoretic number, is calculated by simply counting the number of decision statements. A high cyclomatic complexity denotes a complex procedure that's hard to understand, test, and maintain. There's a relationship between cyclomatic complexity and the "risk" in a procedure.

[10] Low degree of project specification. Rate risk probability from 0 to 100%.

[11] Use of bleeding edge technology. Rate risk probability from 0 to 100%.

[12] Lack of development skill sets.

[13] Resistance of employees or end-users to change. Rate probability of risk from 0 to 100%.

[14] Problems with delivering system—e.g., interface difficulties. Rate risk probability from 0 to 100%.

[15] Rate on a scale of 1 to 2 with 1 being unsatisfactory and 2 being satisfactory.

Learning & Growth Objectives	Measures	Targets	KPI
Create a quality workforce	% of employees meeting mandatory qualification standards	> = 95%	L1
	% of voluntary separations	> = 98%	L2
	% of leaders' time devoted to mentoring	> = 45%	L3
	% of employees with certifications	> = 54%	L4
	% of employees with degrees	> = 75%	L5
	% of employees with three or more years of experience	> = 75%	L6
	Average appraisal rating	Baseline	L7
	Number of employee suggestions	Baseline	L8
	% expert in currently used technologies	> = 95%	L9
	Rookie ratio [1]	< = 10%	L10
	% expert in emerging technologies	> = 75%	L11
	Proportion of support staff	> = 35%	L12
	Availability of strategic information	> = 100%	L13
	Intranet searches	Baseline	L14
	Average years of experience with team	Baseline	L15
	Average years of experience with language	Baseline	L16
	Average years of experience with software	Baseline	L17
	% of employees whose performance evaluation plans are aligned with organizational goals and objectives	> = 98%	L18
	% conformity with HR roadmap as a basis for resource allocation	> = 95%	L19
	% of critical positions with current competency profiles and succession plans in place	> = 98%	L20
	% number of net meetings	> = 20%	L21
	Number of new templates, procedures tools to increase productivity	Baseline	L22
Increase employee satisfaction	% of employees satisfied with the work environment	> = 98%	L23
	% of employees satisfied with the professionalism, culture, values, and empowerment	> = 98%	L24
	Employee overtime	Baseline	L25
	Employee absenteeism	Baseline	L26
	Discrimination charges	Baseline	L27
	Employee grievances	Baseline	L28

Learning & Growth Objectives	Measures	Targets	KPI
	Tardiness	Baseline	L29
	Number of employee suggestions implemented	Baseline	L30
	% in-house promotions	> = 90%	L31
Enhance employee training	% of technical training goals met	> = 90%	L32
	Number of training sessions attended per employee	Baseline	L33
	Training budget as a percentage of overall budget	> = 20%	L34
	Frequency of use of new skills	> = 85%	L35
Enhance R&D	Research budget as a percentage of budget	> = 35%	L36
	Number of quality improvements	Baseline	L37
	Number of innovative processes deployed	Baseline	L38
	% of R&D directly in line with business strategy	> = 98%	L39
	Number of technologies owned or possessed by company	Baseline	L40
	Number of new patents generated by R&D	Baseline	L41
	Number of patentable innovations not yet patented	Baseline	L42
	Number of patents protecting the core of a specific technology or business area	Baseline	L43
	Number of entrepreneurs in company [2]	Baseline	L44
	% of workforce that is currently dedicated to innovation projects	> = 5%	L45
	Number of new products, services, and businesses launched	Baseline	L46
	% of employees who have received training in innovation	> = 5%	L47
Social software engineering	Number of wikis	Baseline	L48
	Number of blogs	Baseline	L49
	Number of group workspaces	Baseline	L50
	Number of collaborative project plans	Baseline	L51
	Number of collaborative spreadsheets	Baseline	L52
	Number of teams using social software engineering	Baseline	L53

Learning & Growth Objectives	Measures	Targets	KPI
	Number of team members using social software engineering	Baseline	L54
	Maturity of collaboration	Baseline	L55
	Degree of communication efficiency	Baseline	L56
	Collaborative lessons learned	Baseline	L57

[1] Rookie means new, inexperienced, or untrained personnel.
[2] Number of individuals who previously started a business.

Quick Start 6

Common BYOD Mistakes

An ill-conceived BYOD strategy could result in a company being held legally accountable for mishandled "protected" information. To prevent this occurrence, a CIO must avoid these mistakes when bringing BYOD into the company.

PROCEDURES/ISSUES/POLICIES

1. It's the apps. What users value most in their mobile technology, but what might inadvertently prove lethal to your organization are the apps themselves. Viruses! Malware! They could lurk within the friendliest, most relied upon apps. Don't trust that if the problem hasn't been discovered, it doesn't exist.

   IT must manage every and all apps—especially those that allow access to corporate info or e-mail. Restrict any apps that you sense might be dangerous. Utilize mobile device management (MDM) solutions that allow IT to have control over apps (the ability to push out mandatory corporate apps) and the ability to restrict the use of designated categories of apps.
2. Unless IT says a strong "yes-yes," users will say a strong "no-no" to password controls on their mobile devices. The enterprise device management platform should make available to IT the ability to (1) require passwords; (2) determine their appropriate levels of complexity; and (3) support automatic oversight of the enterprise-defined life cycle for passwords—forcing their regular changing at a company's discretion. The plus for users: If anyone forgets a password, MDM

solutions support remote clearing of passwords, without requiring that the entire device be wiped.

3. As many firms offer some sort of financial assistance for the purchase of and monthly payment plans for mobile devices, keeping abreast of data usage is a must. Knowing when a user is about to reach their monthly allotment will allow IT to keep its costs down. It is also important to monitor and control the use of expensive roaming services. Selecting a platform that integrates basic device control with advanced expense management could control security as well as costs.
4. Avoiding unnecessary reimbursements requires keeping "eyes-on" all financially supported devices. How is this accomplished? An MDM solution would allow IT to centrally administer BYOD devices, generating monthly reports of active devices and automatic reconciliation of reimbursements with device and employee status.

BIBLIOGRAPHY

Gupta, P. J. (2012, March 27). Developing a BYOD strategy: The 5 mistakes to avoid. *Forbes Magazine*. Retrieved from http://www.forbes.com/sites/ciocentral/2012/03/27/developing-a-byod-strategy-the-5-mistakes-to-avoid/.

Quick Start 7

BYOD Corporate Policy

Ninety-five percent! According to a survey by Cisco IBSG Horizons of 600 U.S. IT and business leaders, that's how many that are now allowing employee-owned devices in the workplace. Additionally, of these 95%, 84% provide support for these devices. And, surprisingly, despite security concerns, the overwhelmingly majority consider BYOD a positive upgrade for their companies. But it could be less of a plus if your company device policy is not adapted for the BYOD environment. Most policies have these gaps and they must be confronted.

PROCEDURES/ISSUES/POLICIES

1. A user-owned device can't be treated the same as company-purchased devices for their workers. Policies need to be adapted to be as close as possible to standard mobile device agreements but need to not ignore users' interests as well.
2. Don't gum it up with complicated legalese. Make it as easy to read and understand as possible. A page that summarizes the workers' responsibilities and your rules would work best—the employee initials each point of the summary or checks a box.
3. A successful BYOD policy means giving workers assurances that your company won't be going "drone" on their devices: won't be reading their texts, eavesdropping on their calls, reading their e-mails, and so on. If a device is lost, the company would do a wipe, but only of company-related data.

4. When workers use their own devices for both work and play, overages of both phone and data usage can easily occur, and who pays for what must be clearly spelled out. Precisely define which categories your business will cover and reimburse. The workers will then contribute their share (to be worked out in the agreement) via payroll deduction. This will also indemnify the employer from any potential fringe benefit tax issues. (This could be a problem if you allowed an employee unlimited use of your mobile connection.)
5. Getting it right means bringing IT, HR, finance, legal, and, not to be forgotten, the user together. All voices must be clearly heard and all issues confronted before the final new policy is updated and ready for signature.
6. IT—not the user—must lead. A fair-and-balanced BYOD policy (one that addresses all issues of privacy, security, and costs) will create the perfect environment for BYOD success.

BIBLIOGRAPHY

Pearce, R. (2012, May 3). BYOD 101: Creating a BYOD policy for users. *CIO Magazine*. Retrieved from http://www.cio.com.au/article/426081/byod_101_creating_byod_policy_users/.

Quick Start 8

Mobile Device Management Functionality Guide

Collaboration is key for successful project management. If you decide to utilize BYOD, it is now IT's task to ensure that things are protected. Here's what IT should consider when selecting a mobile content security solution.

PROCEDURES/ISSUES/POLICIES

1. A secure mobile file-sharing service should support any and all platforms of mobile devices.
2. Encrypt. The solution should impose strict access controls for individual files and for shared workspaces. At rest, in transmit over SSL, and even if left open on device that's not in use, files should be encrypted. Set expiration dates for files. Solution should ensure that mobile access never puts at risk data security or regulatory compliance.
3. Making sure data is secured, solution should allow information to be shared across corporate boundaries with external users—that is, partners and customers. Secure communication should not be strictly limited to users within the organization.
4. Secure workspaces so that workers on the go can easily track discussions, revisions, and other activities on important files. Productivity is thus increased, eliminating the need for long e-mail threads.
5. Included in the list of IT-approved apps, a mobile app specifically supported (whitelisted) by the enterprise app store (MDM) solution

vendor. Whitelisted apps limit the risk of infection and also give IT management of software updates and data tracking.

6. It is important for both business and personal data to each be stored separately. Prying eyes should be limited on both ends, restricting administrator access to view-only and the ability to wipe devices that have been lost or stolen.
7. Much utilized content management solutions, such as SharePoint, Autonomy iManage, and File Net, should be cleared and set up for mobile access offering plug-in components and permissions granted through admin controls that extend the already established data infrastructure to authorized internal and external mobile users.
8. With rich media files (videos, medical images, etc.) becoming more and more the norm, the solution should be designed to support large files.
9. A vital component of a fully deployed content mobility solution has to be administrative dashboards and logging. Complete visibility and control to enact immediate changes to content access per project and as changes occur in the enterprises.
10. Audit controls that support compliance with industry regulations such as GLBA, HIPAA, and SOX demand super-strength security. Businesses need to stay compliant while serving their mobile workforce—ease of use can never come at the expense of these regulations.

BIBLIOGRAPHY

Information Week. BYOD requires mobile device management. Retrieved from http://www.informationweek.com/news/mobility/business/229402912.

Quick Start 9

Legal Issues with BYOD

Your company has decided to allow employees to use their own devices. What are the next steps? How do you make sure that no conflicts arise from a device that will now be available both for personal and business use?

PROCEDURES/ISSUES/POLICIES

1. **Performance management**. What constitutes work, and what constitutes personal times? The lines do tend to get blurred. This definitely creates challenges with regard to work conduct versus personal off-work freedoms.
2. **Discrimination**. Employers might find themselves aware of personal medical info (via apps on the device). To avoid potential liability for disability discrimination, this is information that should never get into your hands.
3. **Harassment**. Will you ultimately be held responsible? With the ease of a tweet, worker-worker harassment could quickly develop. You're responsible for a harassment-free workplace. How do you ensure such bullying doesn't occur?
4. **Overtime liability.** If an off-the-clock nonexempt worker checks his e-mail and responds with the appropriate action, can you be held responsible for overtime payments?
5. **Payroll.** Employers, under the FLSA's minimum wage provisions, may be held accountable to reimburse employees for the personal costs of their own devices—that is, monthly phone bill—if they can be interpreted as employer business expenses, and the cost, factored

into their wage rate, results in their pay falling below the statutory minimum wage.

6. **Privacy: Know the laws.** Federal laws (e.g., Computer Fraud and Abuse Act, Stored Communications Act) put very strong restrictions on unauthorized access to computers and e-mail. Walls must be set up between business and personal data.
7. **Workplace safety.** A company might find itself paying worker's comp costs or involved in a lawsuit, if a worker suffers injuries while texting and driving.

THE FIXES: HOW TO INOCULATE YOUR COMPANY AGAINST POTENTIAL LEGAL TROUBLE

1. Plan. What devices will you permit, and what policies will you enact?
2. Amend or create employee agreements in which you clearly state the consequences of improperly using their own devices.
3. Get written consent from employees to allow company access to data on devices.
4. If your workforce is unionized, go over the bargaining agreement for potential restrictions.
5. If your workforce is unionized, any new BYOD policy would be subject to collective bargaining.
6. Company executives, legal, HR, and any employees who have access to highly confidential company information should not be allowed to use their own devices. Protect your data.
7. Carefully evaluate which employees would be allowed to BYOD—for instance, sales force personnel (when they leave your company it will be their mobile number your customers will have, not your company's).
8. Install MDM (mobile device management) software. These are applications that will allow companies, for example, to issue remote wipe commands, or prevent the usage of designated apps on their devices.
9. Restrict the usage of cloud-based apps, cloud-based backup, or synchronizing with home computers for work-connected data.
10. Make very clear that if an employee's personal device is to be used for work, never should it be used by their friends or family members.

11. When an employee leaves, how will you preserve data on devices for which there is no company reimbursement? Text messages, if a policy is not spelled out in an agreement, could become a point of major contention.

BIBLIOGRAPHY

McGuire, M. J. (2012). The data security, privacy, and eDiscovery challenges posed by Bring Your Own Device (BYOD) policies. A presentation before the Minnesota CLE's 2012 Upper Midwest Employment Law Institute, May 21–22, St. Paul, MN. Retrieved from http://www.employmentlawdaily.com/index.php/2012/07/29/littler-mendelson-attorney-warns-of-pitfalls-of-byod/.

Quick Start 10

Managing Online Content Checklist

PROCEDURES/ISSUES/POLICIES

General

1. Consider what type of content needs to be managed.
2. Review how content is currently managed and the adequacy of these processes.
3. Consider whether existing processes will be adequate in the foreseeable future.
4. Evaluate the particular challenges the organization may have in managing content.
5. Ensure that the organization has clearly documented and up-to-date processes for managing all types of content.
6. Consider the challenges in managing Intranets/Extranets.

Content Management Issues

1. Identify information and services to be provided.
2. Determine end-user information needs.
3. Allocate roles and responsibilities.
4. Maintain a list of content owners.
5. Focus on establishing viable content management processes.
6. Assist content creators to create suitable resources for delivery.
7. Establish testing processes.
8. Review and remove or amend content as necessary.
9. Meet archiving and storage requirements.
10. Assess and manage any legal implications of content.
11. Track content approval.

12. Manage user feedback.
13. Select appropriate content management tools.

BIBLIOGRAPHY

Managing Online Content. (2004). Retrieved from http://www.agimo.gov.au/__data/assets/file/33918/BPC8.pdf.

Quick Start 11

Selecting a Content Management System Checklist

PROCEDURES/ISSUES/POLICIES

Before You Start

1. Consider the time required to select an appropriate product.
2. Consider the range of products available in the marketplace.
3. Build content management knowledge.
4. Consider risks and risk mitigation strategies.
5. Redesign the site if necessary.

Determining Project Goals and Targets

1. Focus on business outcomes.
2. Specify targets and how their achievement will be measured.

Determining and Documenting Business Requirements

1. Focus on business needs rather than technical solutions.
2. Address compliance needs.
3. Provide descriptions and examples to clarify meaning.
4. Avoid specifying too many requirements.
5. Make use of existing resources.
6. Consider gaining an external review of requirements.
7. Consider the use of scenarios to help document requirements.

Producing Documentation

1. Include background information.
2. Include any new site design.
3. Specify technical infrastructure.

Evaluating and Selecting a CMS

1. Use scenarios during demonstrations.
2. Visit reference sites.
3. Focus on usability and simplicity.
4. Assess the vendor's implementation methodology.
5. Consider the total cost of ownership.

BIBLIOGRAPHY

Australian Government. (2005). Selecting a content management system. Retrieved from http://www.agimo.gov.au/practice/delivery/checklists/select_cms.

Quick Start 12

BYOD Lessons Learned

As with online dating you should be cautious. Though MDM (mobile device management) may appear to be an easy adaptable solution, it is not a panacea; it cannot alleviate all your anxieties about allowing your workers to use their own devices. Don't deceive yourself into believing it will simply make bring your own technology (BYOT) safe and stress-free for both you and your workers. A Forrester report, culled from conversations with four I&O (infrastructure and operations) employees who "friended" MDMs, should provide valuable advice for those new to BYOD.

PROCEDURES/ISSUES/POLICIES

Each Unique

1. Each mobile device is reflective of its owner (each one contains particular apps and programs that work for them). Thus one MDM solution for all will never work. Different employees will require distinct kinds of mobile support from IT. IT will have to have at the ready solutions for different platforms, applications, and devices personally purchased or corporate provided.

Survey...Survey...Survey

1. Stay up-to-the-minute on your employees' mobile software and hardware needs. What will best help them perform their tasks at hand? This awareness will enable IT to procure and employ the appropriate tech solutions to those who need it most.

Clarity

1. There should be no guesswork. Policy should be clear as to what your company will or will not allow regarding mobile devices, be they company provided or privately owned. First and foremost should be the apps and programs that are allowable and will be supported by IT.
2. IT should leave no doubt that not all devices and services are supported. They should also consider having staffers with mobile devices sign an official mobile device policy form that states that IT has the right to wipe corporate devices at any time, if such situations arise.

Each and Every Platform Should Be IT's BFF

1. Employees will circumvent you; they will find a way to complete tasks on devices that employ iOS and Android platforms. Since you cannot stop this use, your IT department must truly get to know these platforms, discover their security and management weakness, and rectify to the best of their ability.

The App Store Problem

1. Practically non-existent are MDM vendors who offer application delivery methods, or "stores," that truly meet enterprise management and security requirements while delivering software to various devices and platforms. As this is a huge obstacle in delivering the apps they require, IT should work with suppliers to develop and test application delivery methods that can deliver complex applications to a variety of device types.

Virtualization: Might It Be a Temporary Savior?

1. How do you bring critical Windows apps to non-Windows devices? Until vendors are set up to offer "mature" application stores that cater to a wider variety of mobile platforms, companies should consider virtualization products. Citrix is a supplier of such products.

BIBLIOGRAPHY

Sacco, A. (n.d.). Managing mobile devices: 10 lessons learned, via Forrester. *CIO Magazine*. Retrieved from http://www.cio.com/article/690281/Managing_Mobile_Devices_10_Lessons_Learned_via_Forrester.

Quick Start 13

BYOD Risks

Traditional security technologies that rely on endpoint security, configuration management, or establishing and controlling a network perimeter will no longer be sufficient for companies that are greeting BYOD with open arms. This ultimately means that CIOs will have to seek out innovative, data-centric approaches as they come to terms with losing control of sensitive data. What follows is a "GPS" to secure your data in the BYOD era.

PROCEDURES/ISSUES/POLICIES

1. As recent security issues with Dropbox and legal issues with Megaupload have revealed, the consumer cloud is not the safest place for sensitive corporate documents. Thus as users quickly turn to these consumer-grade file-sharing services, it is up to IT to provide a secure enterprise alternative that controls the documents themselves.
2. There are many regulations a company can easily run afoul of. For example, a spreadsheet loaded with consumers' credit card info takes a quick trip down the "information superhighway" to the mobile device of a marketing executive (a payment card industry violation) or confidential not-yet-published financial results are sent by a corporate secretary to a CFO's iPad in a consumer cloud story service (a Sarbanes–Oxley Act issue). These are just a sample of some of the non-compliance mines that lay in wait for a misstep—a matter that could be compounded if the data is not encrypted and the device is lost or stolen. Since supporting BYOD means acknowledging that corporate data will be transmitted to and stored by devices

you cannot fully trust, IT must consider protecting documents with digital rights or other permissions to actively remain always in compliance.

3. When the lawyers come a-calling, electronically stored information (ESI) can present problems for both discovery (e-discovery) and retention. The confusion arises when mobile workers use consumer-type file-syncing applications.
4. Mobile devices can and will go missing. With sensitive data stored on these machines, this is definitely headache-inducing for CIOs. For most companies who deal globally, unless the data is encrypted, breach notification laws will apply. For partially managed devices or "sandboxed" applications, organizations may be able to remotely destroy corporate data, unless they run afoul of a different issue: employee privacy.
5. Think before you wipe. If your company has a global presence, know other countries' laws. EU privacy laws state that enterprises are prohibited from remotely wiping smartphones and tablets that contain employees' personal data along with corporate data.
6. Be advised, that adoption of mobile device management (MDM) solutions will further stress your IT department. They will now be responsible for a larger number of devices not previously in their sphere of responsibility. But it is unavoidable as these solutions are necessary tools to protect your data and your workers' privacy.
7. Not all containerization solutions work on all platforms, leading to problems when adopting BYOD.
8. Android and IT help desks: Running enterprise applications and handling corporate documents on those devices present both usability and access issues.
9. In the rush to quickly allow BYOD in the workplace, most companies have failed to update their policies to reflect BYOD issues. Policies should be updated immediately as soon as BYOD is given the go-ahead.

BIBLIOGRAPHY

Preimesberger, C. (2012, April 17). Data security in the BYOD era: 10 big risks facing enterprises. *EWeek*. Retrieved from http://www.eweek.com/c/a/Enterprise-Networking/Data-Security-in-the-BYOD-Era-10-Big-Risks-Facing-Enterprises-211991/.

Quick Start 14

Getting Started with BYOD

These 13 guidelines should put your company on a successful BYOD path. They should ensure the creation of a peaceful, secure, and productive mobile environment.

PROCEDURES/ISSUES/POLICIES

1. As it will affect more than IT (any department that uses mobile devices will be affected as well), policies need to be quickly enacted. Here are some questions to consider:
   a. Devices: Will the company give the worker free choice, or will only certain devices be allowed?
   b. Data plans: Will the company pay at all...or only a stipend...or allow the worker to expense out?
   c. Compliance: What data under law must be protected (encrypted)—for example, HIPAA requires native encryption on any device that holds data subject to the act.
   d. Security: What security measures need to be put in place (e.g., passcode protection, jailbroken/rooted devices, anti-malware apps, device restrictions, iCloud backup)?
   e. Applications: What apps are barred? IP scanning, data sharing, Dropbox?
   f. Agreements: Have you put in place an Acceptable Usage Agreement (AUA) for employee devices with corporate data?
   g. Services: What will be accessible? E-mail? Certain wireless networks or VPNs? CRM?

h. Privacy: What data will be accessed from employee-owned devices…what personal data is never collected?

2. Know exactly what devices will be in use (exactly how many devices, and who owns what, is vital for a successful MDM strategy). To succeed in this task, you'll need a tool that can communicate in real-time with your e-mail environment and detect all the devices connected to your corporate network. Keep in mind that once ActiveSync is activated for a mailbox, there are usually no barriers to syncing multiple devices without IT's knowledge. All devices need to be incorporated and immediate notification has to be given to the owners that security policies are being enacted.
3. If locating and completing the paperwork is complex and difficult, it will bring forth a worker's desire not to comply. To ensure that all workers and their devices are enrolled, make sure, leveraging the proper technology, that the process is simple and secure and will configure their device at the same time. The simplest solution would be to allow users to follow an e-mail link or text that leads to an MDM profile being created on their device.
4. A definite nonstarter would be a BYOD policy and MDM solution that increases IT's workload—bringing more, not less, users to the help desk. All devices should be configured over-the-air, maximizing the efficiency for both IT and business users alike.
5. Once the AU is accepted, your platform should deliver all the profiles, credentials, and settings the employee needs to access: e-mail, contacts, and calendar; VPN, corporate documents, and content; internal and public apps. At the same time, you will be creating profiles to restrict access to certain applications and generate warnings when users goes over their data usage or stipend limit for the month.
6. Users clamor for, and you should give them, a robust self-service platform. This platform would allow them to directly perform tasks such as reset pins and passwords; geo-locate a lost device from a web portal, using mapping integration; and wipe a device remotely, removing all sensitive corporate data. Additionally, a self-service portal would help employees understand why they may be out of compliance, ensuring their cooperation in data protection and security—a task you will be unable to perform without their cooperation.
7. A well-conceived BYOD program holds employee data just as sacred and secure as your businesses'. Make it crystal clear to employees what data you can and cannot collect from their devices. A MDM

solution should be equipped to parse what information it can access and what it cannot (e.g., personal e-mails, contacts, and calendars; application data and text messages; call history and voice mails). But do make it clear what you will collect, how it will be used, and how it will be to their benefit. An advanced MDM solution can, for example, disable app inventory reporting to restrict administrators from seeing personal applications and deactivate location services to prevent access to location indicators such as physical address, geographical coordinates, IP address, and Wi-Fi SSID.

8. Make sure corporate apps, documents, and other material reside in a separate sphere on a user's device—totally segregated from their own personal stuff (photos, e-mails, etc.). Thus, if a worker leaves your employ, IT will have no difficulty wiping the device of just your sensitive data. Their own private info will be unreachable, untouchable by you.
9. Automated policies should be put in place to continuously monitor for certain scenarios: Is the user trying to disable device management? Does the device comply with security protocol? Are adjustments forthcoming based on the data you are viewing? This should give you a sense if you need to establish any additional policies or rules. Here are a few common issues.
    a. Getting to the "root" of jailbreaking: Getting around that annoying payment "thingy," employees sometimes "jailbreak" or "root" a phone, to get access to paid apps for free. As this could open the door to data-stealing malware, your MDM solution should be able to take immediate action, at blink-speed wiping corporate data from the "jailbroken" device.
    b. Spare the wipe, send an SMS: Sometimes less drastic action is called for. An MDM solution should be able to enforce policies based on the offense. If it is just time-wasting games, MDM can message the users, allowing them time to remove the app before IT hits the wipe button.
    c. New operating system available: To keep your BYOD efficiently tuned, users need a simple way to be alerted when a new OS is ready for installation. The perfect MDM solution allows OS upgrades to become a self-service function.
10. You should be able to track in-network and roaming data usage on devices, generating alerts if a user crosses a threshold of data usage.
11. Set roaming and in-network megabit limits, customizing the billing day to create notifications based on percentage uses. Also

recommended is educating users on the benefits of using Wi-Fi when available. Automatic Wi-Fi configuration helps ensure that devices automatically connect to Wi-Fi while in corporate locations.

12. If the stipend plan covers only a certain amount, being aware of when they reach that moment when they will have to pay will definitely be appreciated by your workers.
13. When drafting the BYOD policy, carefully consider how said policy will affect ROI. One size never fits all; compare approaches between company-owned devices and BYOD. Which will keep the most dollars in your coffers? Will you be saving by supplying a device versus subsidizing a data plan on an employee-owned device? Allowing more employees to work free of broadband tethers (not every employee is eligible for a company-granted mobile device) will definitely increase productivity.

BIBLIOGRAPHY

Fiberlink (n.d.). *The Ten Commandments of BYOD*. White Paper. http://www.maas360.com.

Quick Start 15

BYOD Security Tips

It is becoming clear that allowing workers to use their smart devices for work-related activities is reaping positive benefits for those companies who have said yes to BYOD. They have definitely been seeing a strong uptick in worker satisfaction (not to mention saving dollars by not having to purchase corporate-issued devices). But it can't be entered into willy-nilly. For those companies ill-prepared there is a very strong negative: The fortress for your data security could easily be breached. What follows are methods for securing against mobile malware and other risks.

PROCEDURES/ISSUES/POLICIES

1. The security option exists, but how many users really password protect their devices—making them unusable until they enter the password or pin? Your BYOD policy has to strongly state and enforce this if the device is being used to access and work with corporate data. A password or pin has to be created and used routinely. This is step that will protect your data if the device is lost or stolen.
2. There should be put into effect a set time that the device will lock and users will have to re-enter pin or password to gain reentry.
3. Keeping it simple is never a good idea when it comes to passwords. Your policy should state that all passwords must contain both letters and numbers.

4. As security products exist that allow companies to remotely wipe lost or stolen devices, users must agree to this option if you allow them to use their device for work.
5. Also available is technology that will allow companies to remotely disable work accounts from users who leave or are fired from your firm. This must be included in your BYOD policy.
6. If a device is rooted or jailbroken, immediate suspension of rights to access to corporate networks and data should be enacted.
7. If a phone has third-party apps, its owners' ready and free access to your corporate network and data should be immediately denied. It's these type of apps that have been known to give IT a security migraine.
8. Employees should be prompted to create new passwords every 90 days.

BIBLIOGRAPHY

Burt, J. (2012, June 8). BYOD security: 8 steps enterprises can take to limit risks to company data. *eWeek*. Retrieved from http://www.eweek.com/c/a/Security/BYOD-Security-8-Steps-Enterprises-Can-Take-to-Limit-Risks-to-Company-Data-608974/.

Quick Start 16

Cloud Migration Tips

Cloud migration is the current trend that needs to be adequately assessed before implementation. Here are some guidelines to do so.

PROCEDURES/ISSUES/POLICIES

1. Paying software licensing and support fees, cloud provider fees, cloud system administration fees, and data communication fees... they're known, probably accounted for...but don't be surprised by lesser known migration fees such as the costs of re-coding apps to work in a virtualized environment; reformatting data to sync with SaaS provider formats; organizing identity and access management; and developing processes to manage the cloud.
2. Stricter privacy rules and mandated more rigorous compliance could make utilizing the cloud impractical. It could possibly force a firm to take back data from the cloud and account for its accuracy; cleanse cloud storage data; configure in-house systems to take the place of cloud services; pay early termination penalties; re-apportion IT resources to support services being reverted; or even buy physical resources to host services being returned.
3. The cloud is an environment rich with possible risks. These risks mean your firm has to be on guard. This translates to purchasing data encryption tools, planning and testing mitigation strategies, and maintaining backups and auditing logs off-line.

4. Don't get locked in with only one provider. This course of action may hinder future adoption of open standards-based services as they arise. Make sure you can make the switch without incurring large outlays of capital.

BIBLIOGRAPHY

McCarthy, J. (2012, August 6). *5 hidden costs of cloud migration*. CRN. Retrieved from http://www.crn.com/slideshows/cloud/240004991/5-hidden-costs-of-cloud-migration.htm.

Quick Start 17

Hitching Your Network to BYOD

According to the Aberdeen research group, companies now spend an extra $170,000 a year per 1,000 mobile devices deployed in a BYOD environment—a budget-busting 33% more than the traditional corporate-wireless model. So even though you gain a more productive workforce, the monies spent on software installation and security maintenance definitely add up. What follows is a discussion on hidden networking costs and how to overcome them.

PROCEDURES/ISSUES/POLICIES

1. Don't be reactive...be proactive. Be aware, even if your company has yet to give an official OK, your employees ***will be*** using their personal devices on your network. This desire to increase their productivity could have the unplanned result of leaving your enterprise vulnerable to possible financial and emotional stresses down the line. This will require increased spending and the need to invest in tools that will gain you the proper visibility, governance, and control.
2. If your firm is not mindful, if the proper steps aren't taken, very costly data breaches can occur. Wise companies know such monies must be spent now or much more will be spent later in cleanup (the average cost of a data breach in 2011 was $5.5 million). Yes, it's easy to find yourself tumbling down a very expensive hole created by BYOD.
3. IT may be spending considerably more man-hours sourcing out which rogue devices are a threat and which, though unknown to the network, are benign. The companies with the most smarts will

create the ability to exclude who isn't a threat, thus streamlining the monitoring of suspicious network access.

4. Once you go BYOD, make sure IT has the funding and resources necessary to service the multiple devices and software platforms that will be coming their way.
5. Do you know and do you have ready access to who accesses your networks—when and where via wireless? Historical data accumulation has never been more important. Compliance and security make it vital to capture real-time data as well as log user behavior over time.
6. Any place with a Wi-Fi connection can now be an office, and since these public networks could do potential harm to your data and network, make sure you have the resources and guidelines in place to govern and oversee your mobile workers.
7. Now that devices are mobile, network managers will have to make crystal clear to workers their new responsibilities under BYOD… another task for an already tasked-out IT department.
8. Securing networks by isolating mobile access to a separate VLAN outside the corporate network and using an existing network management system (NMS) without adding any mobile-device management capabilities may appear to save you dollars but could prove costly in the end. Without the ability to track individual users, data vulnerability will be the result.
9. Invest the man-hours necessary to discover who is already using personal devices during work and off hours. This knowledge will definitely help you better plan forthcoming yearly budgets.
10. Make sure substantial wireless bandwidth is available so that no employee's task is hindered by slow networks.

BIBLIOGRAPHY

Preimesberger, C. (2012, July 30). IT security & network security news & reviews: BYOD environments: 10 hidden networking costs and how to overcome them. *EWeek*. Retrieved from http://www.eweek.com/c/a/Security/BYOD-Environments-10-Hidden-Networking-Costs-and-How-to-Overcome-Them-407533/.

Appendix A: Security Glossary

Term	Definition
Acceptable Level of Risk	A judicious, carefully considered, and fully documented assessment by the appropriate Designated Approving Authority (AO) that an AIS meets the minimum requirements of applicable security directives. The assessment should take into account and carefully document the sensitivity and criticality of information, threats, vulnerabilities, and countermeasures and their effectiveness in compensating for vulnerabilities, and operational requirements.
Acceptable Risk	A concern that is deemed acceptable to responsible management, due to the cost and magnitude of implementing countermeasures to mitigate the risk.
Accountability	Accountability is (1) The quality or state that enables violations or attempted violations of IT security to be traced to individuals who may then be held responsible. (2) The security goal that generates the requirement for actions of an entity to be traced uniquely to that entity. This supports non-repudiation, deterrence, fault isolation, intrusion detection and prevention, after-action recovery and legal action.
Accreditation	(1) The procedure for accepting an information technology (IT) system to process sensitive information within a particular operational environment. (2) Formal declaration by a Designated Approving Authority (AO) that an information system is approved to operate in a particular security configuration using a prescribed set of safeguards. (3) The managerial authorization and approval granted to a system or network to process sensitive data in an operational environment. This authorization is made on the basis of a certification recommendation by designated technical personnel with extensive security expertise and direct knowledge of the system. This authorization is granted only if the design and implementation of the system meet pre-specified technical requirements for achieving adequate data security. (4) A formal declaration by the AO, based on the recommendation of the certifier, that the information system is approved to operate in a particular security mode using a prescribed set of safeguards. Accreditation is the official management authorization for operation of an AIS and is based on the certification process, the assessment and analysis of the certifier, and other management considerations. The accreditation statement affixes security responsibility to the AO and shows that due care for security has been taken.

Term	Definition
Accreditation Package	The evidence provided to the authorizing official to be used in the security accreditation decision process. Evidence includes, but is not limited to, (1) the system security plan; (2) the assessment results from the security certification; and (3) the plan of action and milestones.
Active Content	Active content refers to electronic documents that can carry out or trigger actions automatically on a computer platform without the intervention of a user. Active content technologies allow mobile code associated with a document to execute as the document is rendered. Examples of active content include PostScript documents, web pages containing Java applets and JavaScript instructions, proprietary desktop-application formatted files containing macros, spreadsheet formulas, or other interpretable content, interpreted electronic mail formats having embedded code or bearing executable attachments, and ActiveX technology. Active content is also frequently, but not necessarily, associated with Mobile Code.
Adequate Security	Security commensurate with the risk and the magnitude of harm resulting from the loss, misuse, or unauthorized access to, or modification of, information.
Application	The use of information resources (information and information technology) to satisfy a specific set of users requirements (See Major Application).
Assurance	Grounds for confidence that the other four security goals (integrity, availability, confidentiality, and accountability) have been adequately met by a specific implementation. "Adequately met" includes (1) functionality that performs correctly, (2) sufficient protection against unintentional errors (by users or software), and (3) sufficient resistance to intentional penetration or bypass.
Audit Log	A chronological record of system activities that enables the reconstruction and examination of the sequence of events and activities surrounding or leading to an operation, a procedure or an event in a transaction from its inception to final results. The audit log also serves as the chain of custody for the history of use of a record. This term is synonymous with Audit Records and Audit Trails.
Authentication	The process of determining the identity of a user, device, or other entity in a computer system, as a prerequisite to allowing access to resources in a system. Verification of a user's identity ensures that the person requesting access to the network is, in fact, the person to whom entry is authorized.

Term	Definition
Authorized User	A member of the public, employee, contractor, or subcontractor with assigned, approved permissions and privileges to access the network. An authorized user has access to specific activities and resources on the network. Use beyond those authorized is a violation of policy and of the law.
Automated Information System (AIS)	A combination of functional users, information technology personnel, business processes and procedures, application software, system software, documentation, commercial off-the-shelf software, computer, networking, and other information technology resources that collect, record, process, store, communicate, retrieve, display, and disseminate information.
Availability	Assurance that information, services, and AIS resources are accessible to authorized users and/or system-related processes on a timely and reliable basis and are protected from denial of service.
Certification	The technical evaluation that establishes the extent to which a computer system, application, or network design and implementation meet a specified set of security requirements. See also Accreditation.
Chief Information Security Officer	See Senior Agency Information Security Officer.
Common Criteria	A multi-part standard (ISO/IEC 15408) that defines criteria to be used as the basis for evaluating security properties of information technology products and systems. By establishing such a common criteria base, the results of an information technology security evaluation are meaningful to a wider audience.
Common Security Control	Security control that can be applied to one or more agency information systems and has the following properties: (1) the development, implementation, and assessment of the control can be assigned to a responsible official or organizational element (other than the information system owner); and (2) the results from the assessment of the control can be used to support the security certification and accreditation processes of an agency information system where that control has been applied.
Confidentiality	Assurance that information in an IT system is not disclosed to unauthorized persons, processes, or devices.
Configuration Control	Process for controlling modifications to hardware, firmware, software, and documentation to ensure the information system is protected against improper modifications prior to, during, and after system implementation.
Configuration Management	The management of security features and assurances through the control of changes made to hardware, software, firmware, documentation, test, test fixtures, and test documentation throughout the life cycle of an automated information system (AIS).

Term	Definition
Contingency Plan	A plan maintained for emergency response, backup operations, and post-disaster recovery for an IS, to ensure the availability of critical resources and to facilitate the continuity of operations in an emergency situation.
Countermeasures	Actions, devices, procedures, techniques, or other measures that reduce the vulnerability of an information system. Synonymous with security controls and safeguards.
Defense in Depth	An approach for establishing an adequate computer security posture that integrates people, technology, and operations. In the Defense in Depth approach, security solutions are layered within and among IT assets to minimize single points of failure, and security solutions are selected based on their relative level of robustness in view of the value of the asset protected. Implementation of this approach recognizes that the highly interactive nature of information systems and enclaves creates a shared risk environment; therefore, the adequate assurance of any single asset is dependent upon the adequate assurance of all interconnecting assets.
Executable Content	Executable content is a subset of mobile code that is largely invisible to the user and operates without a user decision. Executable content is automatically activated upon retrieval without user interaction.
Firewall	A firewall system can be a router, a personal computer, a host, or a collection of hosts, set up specifically to shield a site or subnet from malicious hosts outside the site or subnet. A firewall system is usually located at a higher-level gateway, such as a site's connection to the Internet; however, firewall systems can be located at lower-level gateways to provide protection for some smaller collections of hosts or subnets. A firewall forces all network connections to pass through the gateway where they can be examined and evaluated, and provides other services such as advanced authentication measures to replace simple passwords. The firewall may then restrict access to or from selected systems, block certain Transmission Control Protocol/Internet Protocol (TCP/IP) services, or provide other security features.
General Support System	An interconnected information resource under the same direct management control that shares common functionality. It normally includes hardware, software, information, data, applications, communications, facilities, and people, and provides support for a variety of users and/or applications. Individual applications support different mission-related functions. Users may be from the same or different organizations.

Term	Definition
High-Impact System	An information system in which at least one security objective (i.e., confidentiality, integrity, or availability) is assigned a FIPS 199 potential impact value of high.
Host-Based Security	The technique of securing an individual system from attack; host-based security is operating system and version dependent.
Identification and Authentication (I&A)	Identity of an entity with some level of assurance.
Impact	The cumulative effect upon an organization or its customers if a critical business process cannot be performed.
Individual Accountability	Requires individual users to be held accountable for their actions after being notified of the rules of behavior in using the system and the penalties associated with the violation of those rules.
Information Resources	Information and related resources, such as personnel, equipment, funds, and information technology.
Information Security	The protection of information and information systems from unauthorized access, use, disclosure, disruption, modification, or destruction in order to provide confidentiality, integrity, and availability.
Information System	A discrete set of information resources organized for the collection, processing, maintenance, use, sharing, dissemination, or disposition of information.
Information Technology	Any equipment or interconnected system or subsystem of equipment that is used in the automatic acquisition, storage, manipulation, management, movement, control, display, switching, interchange, transmission, or reception of data or information by the executive agency. For purposes of the preceding sentence, equipment is used by an executive agency if the equipment is used by the executive agency directly or is used by a contractor under a contract with the executive agency that (1) requires the use of such equipment; or (2) requires the use, to a significant extent, of such equipment in the performance of a service or the furnishing of a product. The term information technology includes computers, ancillary equipment, software, firmware, and similar procedures, services (including support services), and related resources.
Integrity	Assurance that information in an IT system is protected from unauthorized, unanticipated, or unintentional modification or destruction. System integrity also addresses the quality of an IT system reflecting the logical correctness and reliability of the operating system; the logical completeness of the hardware and software implementing the protection mechanisms; and the consistency of the data structures and occurrence of the stored data.

Term	Definition
Intrusion Detection	Intrusion detection refers to the process of identifying attempts to penetrate a system and gain unauthorized access.
Key Management Infrastructure (KMI)	Framework established to issue, maintain, and revoke keys accommodating a variety of security technologies, including the use of software; the supporting infrastructure for a public key infrastructure (PKI).
Least Privilege	Limiting permissions or privileges to those necessary to perform a specific job. This principle is implemented by assigning appropriate rights or privileges, as determined by the job performed and the permissions requested and approved by a supervisor, to each user ID/password combination. Also see Need to Know.
Low-Impact System	An information system in which all three security objectives (i.e., confidentiality, integrity, and availability) are assigned a FIPS 199 potential impact value of low.
Major Application	An application that requires special attention to security due to the risk and magnitude of harm resulting from the loss, misuse, or unauthorized access to or modification of the information in the application. Note: All applications require some level of protection. Certain applications, because of the information in them, however, require special management oversight and should be treated as major. Adequate security for other applications should be provided by security of the systems in which they operate. Major applications include applications that meet the above definition, but at a minimum include applications that meet any one of the following criteria: (1) are mission critical; (2) are reviewed under the annual IT Investment review process.
Management Controls	Controls that address management of the security aspects of the IT system and the management of risk for the system. Management controls include risk management, review of security controls, system life cycle controls, processing authorization controls, and system security plan controls.
Material Weakness	A deficiency that the agency head determines to be significant enough to be reported outside the agency (i.e., included in the annual Integrity Act report to the President and the Congress) shall be considered a "material weakness." This designation requires a judgment by agency managers as to the relative risk and significance of deficiencies. Agencies may wish to use a different term to describe less significant deficiencies, which are reported only internally in an agency. In identifying and assessing the relative importance of deficiencies, particular attention should be paid to the views of the agency's IG.

Term	Definition
Mobile Code	The term for code obtained from remote systems, transmitted across a network, and executed on a local system. Mobile code also refers to web-based code downloaded and run by the user's browser. Mobile code refers to programs (e.g., script, macro, or other portable instruction) that can be shipped unchanged to a heterogeneous collection of platforms and executed with identical semantics. The term also applies to situations involving a large homogeneous collection of platforms (e.g., Microsoft Windows). Also see Active Content.
Moderate-Impact System	An information system in which at least one security objective (i.e., confidentiality, integrity, or availability) is assigned a potential impact value of moderate and no security objective is assigned a potential impact value of high.
Need to Know	The concept of limiting access to information to those people who have a need to see or use it in performing their jobs. Also see Least Privilege.
Non-repudiation	Assurance that the sender of information is provided with proof of delivery and the recipient is provided with proof of the sender's identity, so neither can later deny having processed the information.
Operational Controls	Address security methods that focus on mechanisms primarily implemented and executed by people (as opposed to systems).
Operating System	An organized collection of techniques, procedures, programs, or routines for operating an information system.
Plan of Action and Milestones (POA&M)	A document that identifies tasks needing to be accomplished. It details resources required to accomplish the elements of the plan, any milestones in meeting the tasks, and scheduled completion dates for the milestones.
Potential Impact	The loss of confidentiality, integrity, or availability could be expected to have (1) a limited adverse effect (low), (2) a serious adverse effect (moderate), or (3) a severe or catastrophic adverse effect (high) on organizational operations, organizational assets, or individuals.
Privacy Impact Assessment	An analysis of how information is handled: (1) to ensure handling conforms to applicable legal, regulatory, and policy requirements regarding privacy; (2) to determine the risks and effects of collecting, maintaining, and disseminating information in identifiable form in an electronic information system; and (3) to examine and evaluate protections and alternative processes for handling information to mitigate potential privacy risks.
Protection Needs Elicitation	The process of determining or eliciting from customers their information protection needs.

Term	Definition
Public Key Infrastructure (PKI)	A set of policies, processes, server platforms, software, and workstations used for the purpose of administering certificates and public-private key pairs, including the ability to issue, maintain, and revoke public key certificates.
Residual Information	Data left in storage after processing operations are complete, but before degaussing or rewriting has taken place.
Residual Risk	The potential for the occurrence of an adverse event, after adjusting for the impact of all in-place safeguards. (See Acceptable Risk.)
Risk	The possibility of harm or loss to any software, information, hardware, administrative, physical, communications, or personnel resource within an automated information system or activity. Risk is a measure of the likelihood and the consequence of events or acts that could cause a system compromise, including the unauthorized disclosure, destruction, removal, modification, or interruption of system assets.
Risk Analysis	An analysis of system assets and vulnerabilities to establish an expected loss from certain events, based on estimated probabilities of occurrence.
Risk Assessment	The process of identifying the risks to system security. This assessment includes determining the probability of occurrence, the resulting impact, and additional safeguards that would mitigate this impact. Part of Risk Management and synonymous with Risk Analysis.
Risk Management	(1) The ongoing process of assessing the risk to automated information resources and information, as part of a risk-based approach used to determine adequate security for a system by analyzing the threats and vulnerabilities and selecting appropriate, cost-effective controls to achieve and maintain an acceptable level of risk. (2) The total process of identifying, controlling, and mitigating information system–related risks. It includes risk assessment; cost-benefit analysis; and the selection, implementation, test, and security evaluation of safeguards. This overall system security review considers both effectiveness and efficiency, including impact on the mission and constraints due to policy, regulations, and laws.
Rules of Behavior	Established, implemented rules concerning use of, security in, and acceptable level of risk for the system. Rules will clearly delineate responsibilities and expected behavior of all individuals with access to the system. Rules should cover such matters as work at home, dial-in access, connection to the Internet, use of copyrighted works, unofficial use of equipment, the assignment and limitation of system privileges, and individual accountability.

Term	Definition
Safeguards	Protective measures prescribed to meet the security requirements (i.e., confidentiality, integrity, and availability) specified for an information system. Safeguards may include security features, management constraints, personnel security, and security of physical structures, areas, and devices. Synonymous with security controls and countermeasures.
Security Assurance	Security assurance is the degree of confidence that all security controls perform as intended to protect the system and the processed information.
Security Category [FIPS 199]	The characterization of information or an information system based on an assessment of the potential impact that a loss of confidentiality, integrity, or availability of such information or information system would have on organizational operations, organizational assets, or individuals.
Security Controls [FIPS 199]	The management, operational, and technical controls (i.e., safeguards or countermeasures) prescribed for an information system to protect the confidentiality, integrity, and availability of the system and its information.
Security Impact Analysis	The analysis conducted by an agency official, often during the continuous monitoring phase of the security certification and accreditation process, to determine the extent to which changes to the information system have affected the security posture of the system.
Security Objective	Confidentiality, integrity, or availability.
Security Policy	What security means to the user; a statement of what is meant when claims of security are made. More formally, it is the set of rules and conditions governing the access and use of information. Typically, a security policy will refer to the conventional security services, such as confidentiality, integrity, availability, etc., and perhaps their underlying mechanisms and functions.
Security Violation	Any loss, misuse, unauthorized modification, disclosure of or access to information, applications, systems, networks, and information technology infrastructure and resources.
Sensitive Information	Refers to information that requires protection due to the risk and magnitude of loss or harm that could result from inadvertent or deliberate disclosure, alteration, or destruction of the information. The term includes information whose improper use or disclosure could adversely affect the ability of an agency to accomplish its mission; proprietary information; records about individuals requiring protection under the Privacy Act; and information not releasable under the Freedom of Information Act.
Signature (Digital, Electronic)	A process that operates on a message to ensure message source authenticity and integrity, and may be required for source non-repudiation.

Term	Definition
System Security Plan (SSP)	A document that identifies the information system components; operational environment; sensitivity and risks; and detailed, cost-effective measures to protect a system or group of systems. The SSP documents the system security requirements and how they are met throughout the life cycle of the system.
Target of Evaluation (TOE)	A Common Criteria term for an IT product or system and its associated administrator and user guidance documentation that is the subject of a security evaluation.
Technical Controls	Consist of hardware and software controls used to provide automated protection to the system or applications. Technical controls operate within the IT system and applications. Sometimes called Technical Countermeasures.
Threat	An activity, deliberate or unintentional, with potential for causing harm to an automated information system or activity.
Token	A token is an object that represents something else, such as another object (either physical or virtual). A security token is a physical device, such as a special smart card, that together with something that a user knows, such as a PIN, will enable authorized access to a computer system or network.
User	Individual or (system) process authorized to access an information system.
Vulnerability	A flaw or weakness in system security procedures, design, implementation, or internal controls that could be exercised (accidentally triggered or intentionally exploited) and result in a security breach or a violation of the system's security policy.
Workstation	Any computer connected to a Local Area Network (LAN). This includes personal computers, desktops, and information resources used or shared by one user.

Appendix B: Employee Mobile Device Agreement

This is a legally binding and enforceable agreement. In exchange for allowing you to use your personal device in our corporate environment, you agree as follows:

Acceptance of this agreement is a condition to your being allowed to use your personal device in our corporate environment, and you agree to abide by the Company's Mobile Device Policy (URL TBD) and any amendments from time to time. The Mobile Device Policy forms part of this contract.

If your device is lost or stolen, you must notify (TBD) immediately by e-mail (TBD) or telephone (TBD) to report the loss.

Things you should know:

1. The Company may access all information, applications, and data stored on your personal device while it is enrolled.
2. You irrevocably consent to such access in accordance with the Company's Privacy Policy until your personal device is de-enrolled from the program.
3. The Company has the authority to remotely wipe data on personal devices (and personal data if necessary) should the need arise, including for security reasons or if employment is terminated by either party.
4. In case of violation of the Company's Mobile Device Policy, the organization may take any or all of the following steps, among others:

    - Special training to help you understand security measures
    - Loss of mobile device privileges
    - Surrender of device and/or remote wiping of the device
    - Termination of employment

This device must remain compliant with the Company's Mobile Device Policy to continue to be allowed access to the corporate network, e-mail, contacts, and other corporate information.

If you wish to no longer use your personal device in our corporate environment, you must contact (TBD) to have the device removed. The company may delete all information on your personal device prior to removing your personal device from the program.

(Agree) I have read and understood the Company's Mobile Device Policy. I agree to these terms and wish to proceed with the enrollment of my personal device.

Signature ____

Appendix C: Mobile Device Security Checklist

Laptop computers and mobile devices offer the convenience of mobility, but the risk of lost or stolen machines and of wrongful access to sensitive data is high. The use of laptops and other mobile devices demands attention to security precautions. Users must follow the following requirements:

Laptops and mobile devices are a prime target for theft everywhere. So given the risk of theft and the potential losses that theft can cause, there are some security measures that individuals can take to protect the device and the information on it.

Mobile users must take reasonable steps to mitigate the vulnerabilities and risks associated with mobile computing. The following Quick Start provides a comprehensive set of guidelines.

1. Never set the login dialog box to remember the password.
2. Keep antivirus protection up to date, as well as the operating system and application security patches.
3. Password-protect all devices, such as removable drives and compact disks (CDs).
4. Do not store unencrypted sensitive information on mobile devices.
5. Incorporate a time-out function that requires re-authentication after 30 minutes of inactivity.
6. Back up your data to a location separate from the device.
7. Include both hardware/device-based authorization and application-based authorization for access control mechanisms.
8. Do not keep mobile devices online when not in use. Either shut them off or physically disconnect them from the Internet connection.
9. Lost or misplaced devices must be immediately reported.
10. Use a login password that is not easily guessed.
11. Never keep passwords or account numbers on the machine or in the case.
12. Keep the device out of sight when not in use, preferably in a locked drawer or cabinet.
13. Never let the device out of your sight in an airport or other public area.

14. When traveling by plane or rail, never place the device in checked baggage.
15. Never put the device on the conveyor belt at a security checkpoint until the person in front of you has successfully passed through the metal detector.
16. Never leave the device visible in a vehicle. If you must, cover it with something or put it in the trunk.
17. Avoid leaving the device in a hotel room, but if you must do so, use a cable lock or at least lower the risk of theft by keeping it out of sight. Locking it securely in another piece of luggage or room safe should make it secure from theft.
18. Store all sensitive data files in encrypted form will prevent disclosure of the data even if the laptop is stolen.
19. Back up sensitive data to a location other than the laptop hard drive. Keep CDs and diskettes and carry them separately from the laptop.

Appendix D: Security Configuration Recommendations for Apple iOS 5 Devices*

1 INTRODUCTION

1.1 How to Use This Guide

1.1.1 Read Sections Completely and in Order

Each section tends to build on information discussed in prior sections. Each section should be read and understood completely. Instructions should never be blindly applied. Relevant discussion may occur immediately after instructions for an action, so be sure to read the whole section before beginning implementation. Careful consideration is essential for deploying iOS devices in an enterprise environment where multiple supporting devices and software components may need to be configured properly in order to function.

1.1.2 Understand the Purpose of This Guidance

The purpose of the guidance is to provide security-relevant configuration recommendations. It does not imply the suitability or unsuitability of any product for any particular situation, which entails a risk decision.

1.1.3 Limitations

This guide is limited in its scope to security-related issues. This guide does not claim to offer comprehensive configuration guidance. For general

* Reprinted from The National Security Agency (NSA) (March 2012).The Mitigations Group of the Information Assurance Directorate. http://www.nsa.gov/ia/_files/os/applemac/Apple_iOS_5_Guide.pdf

configuration and implementation guidance refer to other sources such as Apple [1].

1.1.4 Test in Non-production Environment

To the extent possible, guidance should be tested in a non-production environment before deployment. Ensure that any test environment simulates the configuration in which the devices will be deployed as closely as possible.

1.1.5 Formatting Conventions

Commands intended for shell execution, file paths, and configuration file text, are featured in a monospace font. Menu options and GUI elements will be set in a bold, sans serif font. Settings appropriate to the device itself will be typeset in-line (i.e., Settings Airplane Mode). Actionable instructions are typically embedded in a box.

1.2 General Principles

The following general principles motivate much of the advice in this guide and should also influence any configuration decisions that are not explicitly addressed.

1.2.1 Encrypt Transmitted Data Whenever Possible

Data transmitted over a network, whether via wire or wirelessly, is susceptible to passive monitoring. Whenever practical mechanisms exist for encrypting this data-in-transit, they should be applied. Even if data is expected to be transmitted only over a local network, it should still be encrypted if possible. Encrypting authentication data, such as passwords, is particularly important. iOS's support for SSL, WPA2, and VPN protocols demonstrates its capabilities, when such features are activated, to adhere to this principle.

1.2.2 Encrypt Stored Data Whenever Possible

Data on mobile devices is particularly susceptible to compromise due to loss of physical control. Whenever practical solutions exist, they should be employed to protect this data. The Data Protection API on iOS devices is used by some applications, and demonstrates the devices' capability to provide such protection. Drawing on applications that use this capability (and ensuring that internally developed enterprise applications also use it), and setting an appropriately complex passcode, follow this principle.

1.2.3 Minimize Software to Minimize Vulnerability

The easiest and simplest way to avoid the vulnerabilities in a particular piece of software is to avoid installing the software altogether. Hundreds of thousands of third-party applications, or "apps," written by thousands of different developers are available for iOS devices. These developers may have willfully or accidentally introduced vulnerabilities. For some environments, a particular app may fulfill a mission-critical need. In other cases an app might needlessly introduce additional risk to the system. Certain risk scenarios may call for minimizing apps. BYOD scenarios, on the other hand, generally imply the consideration and acceptance of such risks.

1.2.4 Leverage Security Features, Never Disable Them

Security features should be effectively used to improve a system's resistance to attacks. These features can improve a system's robustness against attack for only the cost of a little effort spent doing configuration. For example, iOS's enforcement of code signing of apps provides assurance of integrity both during installation and at runtime. Disabling this feature through the use of "jailbreaking" tools provided by the hacker community significantly decreases an iOS device's resistance to attack.

1.2.5 Grant Least Privilege

Grant the least privilege necessary for users to perform tasks. The more privileges (or capabilities) that a user has, the more opportunities he or she will have to enable the compromise of the system (and be a victim of such a compromise). For example, a configuration profile can disallow use of the Safari web browser and the camera. Disabling the camera prevents a malicious or careless user from photographing sensitive areas, while disabling Safari helps ensure the user is protected from any web-based attacks (albeit at significant loss of capability). Similarly, it is possible to restrict the installation of third-party apps, and this may be the right balance between security and functionality for some environments.

1.3 Risks, Mitigations, and Consequences

Understanding the risks—and available mitigations—involved in the deployment of smartphone platforms such as iOS provides a background for certain risk decisions. An attacker who has compromised any mobile device, and can remotely maintain control of that device, can use this access to gather a great deal of information about the user of the device and his or her environment. As described by NIST Special Publication 800-124 [7], the consequences of such attacks include the following

- Collecting audio ("hot-microphone" eavesdropping)
- Using the cameras
- Geolocation of the device (and presumably the user)
- Collecting all data, including credentials stored on the device or accessed by it
- Acting as the user on any network to which the device later connects

The following table describes risks (with attack vector) along with applicable mitigations that are either built into the iOS platform or can be employed by administrators or users. The following table is provided as a summary for risk decision makers—and to motivate administrators to apply mitigations whenever practical. It should not be used to draw comparisons between iOS and other platforms.

Risk	Mitigation
Data Compromise Due to Lost Device (still reachable over any network interface—cellular or Wi-Fi)	Enabling a passcode provides protection for apps that leverage the data protection API, such as Apple's Mail app and third-party apps, as well as for credential storage in keychains. Using the latest hardware currently prevents usage of public jailbreak tools to access other data on a lost device. Activating a remote wipe can be performed via ActiveSync, MDM, or iCloud. Find My iPhone or other geolocation could permit the lost device to be located.
Data Compromise Due to Lost Device (not reachable over any network interface)	Enabling a passcode encrypts some data on the device. Using the latest hardware currently prevents usage of public jailbreak tools to access other data on a lost device.

Risk	Mitigation
Data Compromise Due to Casual Access Attempt	Enabling a passcode prevents a casual snoop from accessing the device. Provide user training to stress importance of physical control at all times.
Data Compromise via Host Computer Backup/Sync	Ensure proper hygiene and configuration of systems used for backup/sync. This may entail enterprise rollout of iTunes, to ensure protection of backup data. Train users not to connect their device to any untrusted computers/devices and provide additional AC outlet chargers. Encrypting iOS device backups in iTunes can mitigate data loss if the host computer is later compromised or lost.
Exploitation of Device via Malicious App	The sandboxing feature prevents apps from carrying out certain malicious activities. The App Store's app vetting process provides accountability for developers, which discourages creation of malicious apps. Disabling the App Store, or permitting only installation of enterprise-created apps, further mitigates any threat from third-party app developers (at significant cost to capability).
Exploitation of Device via Malicious Wi-Fi Network	Apply software updates. Provide user training on connecting only to trusted networks. Provide user training to encourage use of the VPN.
Exploitation of Device via Bluetooth Communications	Apply software updates. Monitor compliance with MDM software. iOS only implements a small subset of the available Bluetooth profiles, which decreases its likelihood to contain vulnerabilities that would give rise to exploitation.
Exploitation of Device via Cellular Network (e.g., SMS/MMS, baseband communications)	Apply software updates. Monitor compliance with MDM software. Provide user training to ensure awareness during travel.
Exploitation of Device via Malicious E-mail or Web Page	Apply software updates, with particular vigilance after public release of jailbreak tools. Monitor compliance with MDM software.

2 CONFIGURATION DEPLOYMENT

This section presents information about creating and deploying settings to iOS devices, which are generally contained in configuration profiles. Configuration profiles are simply XML files that conform to Apple's XML DTD and the plist format. Additional information is available at http://www.apple.com/iphone/business/resources/. The settings contained in configuration policies are discussed in Section 3.

2.1 Nature of Configuration Profiles

Understand that a user who controls an iOS device can opt to erase the device, which erases all data from the device including any configuration profiles. Understand also that users can typically append further restrictive settings, as well as services, onto the device, even in the presence of a configuration profile. Configuration profile settings enforcement on the iOS devices are cumulative indicating that they can further restrict existing settings when applied.

iOS configuration profiles specify a collection of settings that can control some security-relevant behavior of an iOS device, but are not designed to provide an enterprise with total, arbitrary control over the user's device.

A "carrot and stick" approach can be employed to avoid tempting users to remove a configuration profile (either directly or via device reset). Bind "carrots" (such as credentials needed for enterprise access) to "sticks" (such as a passcode policy) in a single configuration profile. Removing a configuration profile implies that credentials necessary for accessing enterprise services (such as VPN certificates or e-mail accounts) would also be lost, and thus deny the user such services. Also in this case, MDM software would become unable to query the device and the enterprise would be alerted as to the device's unmanaged status.

2.2 Mobile Device Management Software

Third-party MDM products, as well as Apple's own OS X Lion Server, can automate the deployment of configuration profiles and carry out the operational management of devices. Configuration profiles can also be provided via secure web-based services. Configuration profiles can also be created using Apple's iPhone Configuration Utility ("iPCU") as described in Section 2.3.2, but it does not provide mechanisms for automated deployment or reporting. iPCU provides a convenient means of surveying the settings which can be deployed to devices, although there is no guarantee that a particular MDM product will support all settings.

2.2.1 Select Mobile Device Management (MDM) Software

Select an MDM product which uses Apple's MDM API, unless enterprise management of the devices is not needed.

Apple's MDM API provides the supported mechanism for enterprise device management, and various third-party vendors have built products upon it. For more information, see http://www.apple.com/iphone/business/integration/mdm/.

2.2.2 Understand Capabilities of MDM Software

Mobile device management software may also include features that are not part of the supported Apple MDM API:

- "Jailbreak detection" can determine if a user has chosen to jailbreak his or her device, which is a useful feature for enterprises who monitor compliance. However, it does not provide high assurance that a device has not been maliciously jailbroken by a sophisticated attacker. The situation is analogous to "root detection" on another mobile platform. It is also analogous to the historical and difficult problem of rootkit detection on desktop or server operating systems. In all these cases, the operating system itself becomes compromised. Since it alone operates at the most privileged levels, there are limits to the extent to which any add-on software can "ask a liar if he is lying."
  - The system's cryptographically verified boot process, runtime enforcement of code signatures, app sandboxing mechanism, controlled software distribution model via "app stores," and rapid software update capability very strongly address the problem of jailbreak-based attacks by themselves. Using add-on software to query for signs of jailbreak may provide an additional layer of defense.
- "Secure containers" can provide data-at-rest protection and data-in-transit protection. These are typically software libraries included by third-party apps, which then make use of their functionality instead of that provided by the system's software libraries. These "containers"

can be useful if the system's capable, built-in mechanisms that already provide these features do not meet particular requirements or certifications. Note, however, that they cannot protect their contents against privileged code running on the device, such as would result from a sophisticated, malicious jailbreak attack during system operation.

- They should also not be confused with the sandboxing feature of the iOS kernel as described in Blazakis [4]. Rather, the sandboxing feature strongly addresses the problem of malicious or co-opted apps trying to perform undesirable activities on the system (such as elevating their privileges) in the first place. Sandboxing constitutes a significant obstacle to attackers, but it does not allow apps to (rather inconceivably) protect themselves if the underlying operating system is compromised. App sandboxing may serve as a means of jailbreak detection as discussed above, in that an app which can access beyond its sandbox may infer that it is running on a compromised device.

2.3 Deploying Configuration Profiles

After a configuration profile is created—typically in an MDM console—it must be deployed to devices. This section discusses methods available for installing a configuration profile onto an iOS device, along with their security implications.

Customizing profiles to individual users implies embedding sensitive authentication information within transmitted profiles. This introduces a need for confidentiality during transmission of such files.

2.3.1 Deploy Over-the-Air with Encryption and Authentication

If configuration profiles will be deployed over-the-air, ensure use of authentication and encryption.

If the iPhone can authenticate a configuration profile during its installation, the Settings General Profile screen will display Verified.

Over-the-air deployment that is authenticated and encrypted requires the support of enterprise infrastructure, such as directory services, an enterprise certificate trusted by iPhone, an SCEP server, and a web server. The server component of MDM products may provide some of this infrastructure.

Deploying configuration profiles to a device over-the-air consists of three major steps:

- Authentication of the user, typically leveraging existing directory services.
- Enrollment, which involves the device transmitting device-specific information to the enterprise, and receiving a device certificate in return.
- Installation of an encrypted, authenticated configuration profile onto the device.

Some MDM products include a server component that provides a web-based service for users to initiate this process, while others initiate the process by requiring users to download a particular MDM client app from the App Store; which can facilitate the process.

Transmission and data formats used by the MDM protocol are thoroughly standards-based. Detailed, authoritative description of the transactions between the device and the enterprise are available to Apple-registered developers at http://developer.apple.com.

Additional description and security analysis is available in https://github.com/intrepidusgroup/imdmtools/blob/master/Presentations/InsideAppleMDM_ShmooCon_2012.pdf, linked from http://intrepidusgroup.com/insight/2012/01/changes-to-apple-mdm-for-ios-5-x/.

2.3.2 Manual Deployment with iPhone Configuration Utility

Manually using the iPhone Configuration Utility (iPCU) is the safest means of deploying configuration profiles to devices, but does not scale well as it depends on administrators' manual intervention. It also implies that an MDM server will not be used to remotely monitor device status. Nevertheless, transferring the profile to a device that is directly connected via USB cable avoids threats to confidentiality and integrity inherent in network transfers.

iPCU is available at http://www.apple.com/support/iphone/enterprise/ (cryptographic checksum unavailable). Documentation is available at http://help.apple.com/iosdeployment-ipcu/.

2.3.3 Avoid Unauthenticated, Unencrypted Deployment Methods

Avoid deployment of configuration profiles through methods that do not provide encryption and authentication. E-mail is especially discouraged.

It is possible to distribute configuration profiles to individual devices by e-mailing the profile to the user of the device or providing a link via SMS. Once the profile is accepted by the end user, the iOS device facilitates its installation. These methods are not recommended because they do not generally provide authentication of the sender of the configuration profile, or encryption of the profile itself during transmission. Users should generally be taught not to have confidence about the origin of e-mail attachments or SMS messages.

E-mailing configuration profiles also presupposes that the user has configured an e-mail account on the iPhone. Furthermore, once the configuration profile is in the receiver's mailbox, it will remain there until it is manually deleted. If the mobile profile contains sensitive information, its prolonged existence in an unmanaged mailbox poses additional risk.

3 DEVICE CONFIGURATION

This chapter makes recommendations for security-relevant settings that reside on the iOS device itself. Section D.3.1 presents settings that can be administratively deployed to an iOS device via a configuration profile. Deploying configuration profiles in a layered approach—with each profile containing payloads targeted for specific services—e.g., Exchange Access/requirements/access identity, is highly recommended so that an individual profile can be removed along with all the data for that one service without negatively affecting the rest of the devices and profiles. This approach involves creating one configuration profile for baseline services/devices, and then adding profiles for specific services. Many of the recommended settings can also be set manually on individual devices and provide value even if the device is not managed by an enterprise. Section D.3.2 presents recommended settings that can only be applied manually.

3.1 Deployable Device Settings

The following subsections correspond to the types of configuration payloads, which can be surveyed via the iPhone Configuration Utility.

3.1.1 General

Apply the following general settings to identify the profile being deployed and to prevent users from removing the profile:

- Enter Name, Identifier, and Description as appropriate.
- Set Security to Never if practical, as it controls when and how the profile can be removed from the device. Letting end-users remove configuration profiles allows them to easily remove security settings contained in the profile. At the same time, this may not be practical for organizations implementing bring-your-own-device (BYOD) schemes that may allow for users to opt in or out at any time.

Note that Never ties a configuration profile to the device, and cannot be removed unless the device is wiped. However, configuration profiles containing MDM payloads cannot be set to Never. The user always has the ability to opt out of MDM, but all configuration profiles, accounts, and data associated with those configuration profiles (delivered under MDM) would also be wiped from the device.

3.1.2 Passcode

The remarkable attention paid to passcode quality requirements represents misplaced priorities in the current network environment, as passcodes do not protect against many contemporary threats. However, setting a passcode enables cryptographic features that can protect data on the device if it is lost, stolen or temporarily out of possession. Hardware and software cryptographic features of iOS devices—not present on typical desktop or server systems—provide significant protections against the password-guessing threat when the passcode feature is enabled. Furthermore, iOS devices are likely to store only a single user's credentials, while complex passcode policies are designed to protect against the compromise of large numbers of credentials when they are stored on a single system that becomes compromised (such as a directory server). Onerous passcode policies may also drive users to attempt to subvert the settings. For these reasons, IT decision makers should understand that onerous passcode policies on iOS devices provide little value (in the best case), and may end up being counterproductive. See Section 3.1.2.2 for discussion of which data is protected by enabling the passcode.

The following publicly available research provides rationale for these recommendations:

- Apple iOS 4 Security Evaluation by Dino Dai Zovi at http://trailofbits.com/2011/08/10/ios-4-security-evaluation/. The slides' section "Attacking Passcode" provides highly relevant platform-specific discussion for iOS devices.
- NIST Special Publication 800-118 DRAFT Guide to Enterprise Password Management at http://csrc.nist.gov/publications/PubsDrafts.html#SP-800-118 provides discussion about factors that should be considered in order to create effective password strength recommendations.

3.1.2.1 Enable Passcode

The following passcode settings are recommended, and can be deployed via a configuration profile.

3.1.2.1.1 Disable Simple Value for Passcode

> Set Allow simple value to Unchecked.

This will enable display of the entire keyboard for passcode entry, instead of only a numeric keypad (and setting other requirements will also enable this).

3.1.2.1.2 Require Alphanumeric Value for Passcode

> Set Require alphanumeric value to Checked.

Requiring alphanumeric values should increase the search space in a password-guessing attack.

3.1.2.1.3 Set Minimum Passcode Length

> Set Minimum passcode length to 6.

Setting a minimum length should increase the search space in a password-guessing attack. A passcode length of 6 may be a reasonable balance between user experience and security for many deployment scenarios.

3.1.2.1.4 Set Minimum Number of Complex Characters

> Set Minimum number of complex characters to 1.

Requiring complex characters should increase the search space in a password-guessing attack.

3.1.2.1.5 Set Maximum Passcode Age

> Set Maximum passcode age to 120 days, if there is a need for such rotation.

Changing passcodes regularly prevents an attacker who has compromised the password from re-using it to regain access. This is an unlikely scenario, but is addressed by setting a password expiration.

3.1.2.1.6 Set Auto-Lock Time

> Set Auto-Lock (in minutes) to 5 minutes, or less.

This ensures that the device will require passcode entry if lost or left unattended.

3.1.2.1.7 Set Passcode History

> Set Passcode History to 3.

This ensures that users cannot trivially alternate between passcodes.

3.1.2.1.8 Set Grace Period for Device Lock

> Set Grace period for device lock to 5 minutes, or less.

This permits unlock of the device after a certain period of time has passed since the last device lock. Allowing a grace period enhances usability and makes users more likely to tolerate passcode requirements.

3.1.2.1.9 Set Maximum Number of Failed Attempts

> Set Maximum number of failed attempts to 10 attempts, or fewer.

Setting the device to automatically erase after a number of failed attempts can protect against witless password guessing attacks conducted through the unlock screen. (However, it does not protect against those conducted by processes running on the device; see Section 3.1.2.2 for more discussion.)

3.1.2.2 Understand Which Files Are Protected by Encryption

Enabling a passcode activates the Data Protection feature of iOS. The Data Protection feature encrypts items with a key whose availability depends on entry of the passcode. Currently, the following items are protected:

- E-mail messages stored by the built-in Mail app
- Inactive apps' screenshots displayed at app re-launch to create impression of "instant resume"
- Some keychain items such as e-mail passwords and iTunes backup password
- Data stored by third-party apps which use the Data Protection API

In fact, the rest of the files on the device are encrypted, but they are still available to an attacker who can get privileged code to execute on the device. This is because the encryption key for these files is available even without the passcode (unlike the files above).

For older hardware models such as iPhone 3GS, iPad, and iPhone 4, this remains possible using publicly available tools that provide the ability to execute privileged code on any device in physical possession. Examples of such tools include The iPhone Dev Team's redsn0w, which itself leverages a collection of exploits including limera1n by George Hotz (geohot). No tools have been released by the hacker community which allow for exploiting the boot ROM in this manner for iPhone 4S and iPad 2, however.

Note also that even if privileged code can be run by an attacker on a lost or stolen iPhone, a password-guessing attack against the protected files must be executed on the device itself. This is because the key that encrypts the items listed above is derived from the passcode as well as a key that is bound to the hardware of the device (and not considered extricable from it).

The following references provide detailed explanation:

- iPhone data protection in depth by Jean-Baptiste B′edrune and Jean Sigwald (Sogeti ESEC) available at http://esec-lab.sogeti.com/dotclear/public/publications/11-hitbamsterdam-iphonedataprotection.pdflinked from http://esec-lab.sogeti.com/post/iOS-5-data-protection-updates.
- Apple iOS 4 Security Evaluation by Dino Dai Zovi (Trail of Bits) available at http://trailofbits. files.wordpress.com/2011/08/apple-ios-4-security-evaluation-whitepaper.pdf linked from http://trailofbits.com/2011/08/10/ios-4-security-evaluation/.

3.1.3 Restrictions

Some security-relevant restrictions can be placed upon the user of the iOS device.

3.1.3.1 Disable Installation of Third-Party Apps

Unless necessary, disable Allow installing apps. This is unusual for a general-purpose device.

While iOS includes features such as sandboxing that are designed to prevent third-party apps from influencing the integrity of the operating system, they do have the ability to access data stored on the device such as Address Book (until recently), Location Data, or the Photo Library and have the ability to transmit this information.

3.1.3.2 Disable Camera

Disable Allow use of camera, if concerns exist about capturing sensitive images.

3.1.3.3 Disable Screen Capture

Disable Allow screen capture, if concerns exist about storing screen contents in the Photo Library.

While unlikely, this feature could accidentally (or intentionally) be triggered (by simultaneously pressing the Home and Sleep buttons) and lead to storage of sensitive information outside the intended storage area.

3.1.3.4 Disable or Configure Safari

> If Safari can be disabled, uncheck Allow use of Safari. This is very unusual for a general-purpose device.

If Safari is needed, security-relevant Safari settings can be configured as follows.

3.1.3.4.1 Disable Safari Autofill

> Set Enable autofill to Unchecked. This prevents storage of some potentially sensitive information by Safari.

3.1.3.4.2 Enable Safari Fraud Warning

> Set Force fraud warning to Checked. This ensures users are warned when visiting known-fraudulent web sites.

3.1.3.4.3 Enable Safari Pop-up Blocking

> Set Block pop-ups to Checked.

3.1.3.4.4 Accept Cookies from Visited Sites Only

> Set Accept cookies to From visited sites.

3.1.3.5 iCloud configuration

Policies regarding the usage of "cloud" storage services continue to evolve, as do the assurances of safety by cloud providers. In general, if there is a need to store potentially sensitive information on the iOS device, then the following restrictions are recommended.

3.1.3.5.1 Disable iCloud Backups

Set Allow backup to Unchecked.

3.1.3.5.2 Disable iCloud Document Sync

Set Allow document sync to Unchecked.

3.1.3.5.3 Disable iCloud Photo Stream

Set Allow Photo Stream to Unchecked.

3.1.3.6 Security and Privacy

The Security and Privacy restrictions can control whether the device will send diagnostic data to Apple, whether the device will require the user to encrypt backups, and whether the user can decide to accept untrusted TLS certificates.

3.1.3.6.1 Disable Sending Diagnostic Data to Apple

Set Allow diagnostic data to be sent to Apple to Unchecked, if this presents concerns about inadvertent transmission of sensitive data.

3.1.3.6.2 Disable User's Acceptance of Untrusted TLS Certificates

Set Allow user to accept untrusted TLS certificates to Unchecked.

Root CAs trusted by iOS are available at http://support.apple.com/kb/HT5012.

3.1.3.6.3 Force Encrypted Backups

Set Force encrypted backups to Checked, to protect device backups if the host later becomes compromised.

3.1.4 Wi-Fi

iOS devices support 802.1X authentication for WPA2 Enterprise networks, and this is strongly recommended. A RADIUS server is required for 802.1X authentication and typically involves the use of public key infrastructure. User education and training is also important, since the user has control over the device's network settings. Section 4.2.4 contains information for users.

DoD Instruction 8420.01, available at http://www.dtic.mil/whs/directives/corres/pdf/842001p.pdf, provides information for DoD entities regarding the configuration and deployment of Wi-Fi networks.

3.1.4.1 Use WPA /WPA2 Enterprise for Wi-Fi Encryption

Using WPA/WPA2 Enterprise with TLS for authentication is recommended. If TLS support is not available, PEAP is the next best choice for authentication. All other authentication protocols are not recommended.

Use WPA/WPA2 if authentication support is not available. Proxy servers can be configured with Wi-Fi as another layer for providing control of the connection.

3.1.4.2 Disable Auto Join for Wi-Fi

Ensure that Auto Join is disabled for Wi-Fi networks.

Disabling auto join ensures that users are aware of when connections to Wi-Fi networks are being made.

3.1.5 VPN

VPN connectivity obviously depends on an enterprise's available infrastructure, but VPNs that use IPsec are preferred.

Several SSL VPNs are also supported by iOS. Actual VPNs are preferred over SSL VPNs as they are designed to protect system-wide network communications. Note, however, that at this time iOS VPNs cannot be configured to route all traffic through a VPN, and operate in split tunnel mode.

This behavior occurs even if Send All Traffic is selected as part of any VPN's configuration.

3.1.5.1 Select IPsec (Cisco) or L2TP for Use as VPN

Select IPsec (Cisco) or L2TP (which also uses IPsec) for use as the Connection Type if possible. Use of hardware tokens is generally preferred over passwords for user authentication.

Apple provides documentation regarding iOS VPN capabilities in the following documents:

- VPN server configuration for iOS devices, available at http://help.apple.com/iosdeployment-vpn/
- iOS: Supported protocols for VPN, available at http://support.apple.com/kb/HT1288

The following documents provide recommendations for configuring VPNs in an enterprise infrastructure:

- Guide to IPSec VPNs (NIST SP 800-77), available at http://csrc.nist.gov/publications/nistpubs/800-77/sp800-77.pdf.
- Guide to SSL VPNs (NIST SP 800-113), available at http://csrc.nist.gov/publications/nistpubs/800-113/SP800-113.pdf.

3.1.6 E-mail

Permitting users to access only enterprise-supported e-mail accounts decreases the risk posed by e-mail-based attacks. It ensures that enterprise-provided countermeasures against e-mail attacks (such as content filters or anti-virus software) can scan e-mail transmitted to the device.

3.1.6.1 Prevent Moving Messages between Mail Accounts

Disable Allow Move for all e-mail accounts.

3.1.6.2 Enable SSL for Mail Connections

Ensure Use SSL is enabled for all incoming and outgoing e-mail accounts.

3.1.6.3 Enable S/MIME Support for Mail If Needed

Set Enable S/MIME to Checked, if encrypted and authenticated e-mail support is needed.

Ensure that transmission of configuration profiles to devices is encrypted and authenticated if S/MIME certificates containing private keys are embedded. The iOS device can also be configured to use an SCEP server to retrieve S/MIME certificates for use with Mail.

3.1.7 Exchange ActiveSync

If your organization employs Microsoft Exchange to manage user accounts and maintain device policies, configuring Exchange ActiveSync will bind the device to the user's Microsoft Exchange account, syncing e-mail, calendars, and contacts with the device.

3.1.8 Prevent Moving Messages between ActiveSync Accounts

Disable Allow Move for all Exchange ActiveSync accounts.

3.1.9 Allow Mail from This Account Only from the Mail App

Enable Use Only in Mail for all Exchange ActiveSync accounts.

3.1.10 Enable SSL for ActiveSync Communications

Ensure Use SSL is Checked for all Exchange ActiveSync accounts.

3.1.10.1 Enable S/MIME Support for ActiveSync If Needed

Set Enable S/MIME to Checked, if encrypted and authenticated e-mail support is needed.

Ensure that transmission of configuration profiles to devices is encrypted and authenticated if S/MIME certificates containing private keys are embedded. The iOS device can also be configured to use an SCEP server to retrieve S/MIME certificates for use with Mail.

3.1.11 LDAP

3.1.11.1 Enable SSL for LDAP Connections

Ensure Use SSL is enabled if using an LDAP service.

3.1.12 CalDav

3.1.12.1 Enable SSL for CalDav Connections

Ensure Use SSL is enabled if using a CalDav service.

3.1.13 Subscribed Calendars

3.1.13.1 Enable SSL for Subscribed Calendar Connections

Ensure Use SSL is enabled if connecting to calendar subscriptions.

3.1.14 Credentials

If your organization employs any self-signed certificates, embed them in the configuration profile or use SCEP (see Section 3.1.15) to distribute. Note that embedding any credentials into the configuration profile introduces the need for encryption during profile deployment as discussed in Section D.2.3.1.

3.1.15 SCEP

If your organization will use the Simple Certificate Enrollment Protocol to distribute certificates and configuration profiles, include its settings with the configuration profile. These settings may be handled by MDM products in a manner that is automated, and not tied to individual users.

3.1.15.1 Set a Challenge Password

In the Challenge field, enter a strong passphrase to be used as a preshared secret for automatic enrollment.

3.1.16 Mobile Device Management

Some behavior of mobile device management (MDM) software can be configured inside a configuration profile. This includes how much information an MDM server can retrieve from a device, whether an MDM server can update profiles remotely, whether an MDM server can remotely wipe a device, and whether an MDM server can reset a device's password. These settings allow for more fine-grained adjustment between enterprise control versus user control of a device. Some MDM products may not permit administrators to disable some of their capability for querying devices.

3.1.16.1 Sign Messages

Set Sign messages to Checked.

This setting causes responses generated by the device (in response to commands from the MDM server) to be signed with the device's identity certificate.

3.1.16.2 Check Out When Removed

Set Check out when removed to Checked.

This causes the device to send a message to the MDM server whenever the configuration profile is removed.

3.1.16.3 Access Rights for Remote Administrators

The following settings control what an MDM server is permitted to query from an iOS device. For an enterprise-owned, enterprise-controlled device, permitting the enterprise administrator to query as much information as possible is appropriate. Some MDM products may simply include these access rights by default and offer options to retrieve less information from the device.

At the same time, querying all of these types of information may not be appropriate even for some enterprise users, and for enterprises that support BYOD scenarios. The terms of any individual organization's "BYOD Contract" with their users is beyond the scope of this document.

3.1.16.3.1 Allow Remote Query of General Settings

In the Query device for section, set General settings to Checked.

3.1.16.3.2 Allow Remote Query of Network Settings

In the Query device for section, set Network settings to Checked.

3.1.16.3.3 Allow Remote Query of Security Settings

In the Query device for section, set Security settings to Checked.

3.1.16.3.4 Allow Remote Query of Restrictions

In the Query device for section, set Restriction to Checked.

3.1.16.3.5 Allow Remote Query of Configuration Profiles

In the Query device for section, set Configuration Profiles to Checked.

3.1.16.3.6 Allow Remote Query of Provisioning Profiles

In the Query device for section, set Provisioning Profiles to Checked.

3.1.16.3.7 Allow Remote Query of Applications

In the Query device for section, set Applications to Checked.

3.1.16.3.8 Allow Remote Addition/Removal of Configuration Profiles

In the Add/Remove section, set Configuration Profiles to Checked.

3.1.16.3.9 Allow Remote Addition/Removal of Provisioning Profiles

In the Add/Remove section, set Provisioning Profiles to Checked.

This allows an MDM to be able to update profiles remotely.

3.1.16.3.10 Allow or Disallow Remote Change of Device Password

In the Security section, set Change device password to Unchecked or Checked. This entails a risk decision, though Checked is likely to be appropriate for most scenarios.

Most enterprises are likely well served by permitting the MDM administrator to remotely send a change password command, in order to allow users with forgotten passcodes to maintain access to their devices. This would also permit an enterprise with appropriate authority, and which needed to overcome the Data Protection feature (such as for forensics purposes) the ability to do so.

At the same time, an attacker who has compromised communications between the device and its MDM server (or the MDM server itself), could maliciously send a password-change command to defeat the data-at-rest protection on the devices. This would depend upon an attacker's physical compromise of the device as well as compromise of TLS communications (or the MDM server itself). This unlikely scenario is described in Schuetz [9].

3.1.16.3.11 Allow Remote Wipe

> Set Remote wipe to Checked.

This permits an MDM server administrator to remotely wipe an iOS device in the event that it is lost.

Note also that a layered configuration profile approach, which involves specific configuration profiles permitting access to specific services (which can be removed by an MDM server), effectively permits selective removal of access to services (and their local data). This can provide a form of remote wipe that is more appropriate with BYOD scenarios that are incompatible with IT staff wiping entire devices.

3.2 Manually Configured Device Settings

The following security-relevant settings can be manually applied. These settings depend on the user's control of the device, and thus training users can help them make appropriate choices.

3.2.1 Disable Loading of Remote Images, If Practical

> To disable the automatic loading of images in e-mail, set Settings Mail, Contacts, Calendars Load Remote Images Off, if this is practical.

Automatically loading images in e-mail messages can leak usage information to authors of fraudulent e-mail. It can also provide an opportunity for malicious images to exploit any implementation flaws in complex graphics libraries. At the same time, this may also inhibit viewing of images that are useful.

3.2.2 Disable Bluetooth Manually, If Practical

> To disable Bluetooth, set Settings General Bluetooth Off when practical.

Leaving Bluetooth enabled can expose the presence of an iOS device, although the device provides visual cues when it is in the Bluetooth "discoverable" mode, which allows it to pair with other devices. The Bluetooth profiles supported by iOS are described at http://support.apple.com/kb/HT3647.

3.2.3 Disable Wi-Fi, If Practical

> If the iOS device is not to be connected to a Wi-Fi network, disable Wi-Fi. Set Settings General Network Wi-Fi Wi-Fi Off.

Disabling Ask to Join Networks will prevent the phone from automatically associating with previously known (but potentially spoofed) access points without user interaction, and should be disabled whenever possible. Users should be instructed to use only trusted Wi-Fi networks, as discussed in Section 4.2.4.

3.2.4 Disable Ping Manually

> If Ping could spread potentially sensitive information, disable it by setting Settings General Restrictions Ping Off.

Ping is Apple's social network for music.

3.2.5 Disable Location Services, If Practical

> If the ability of apps and web pages to determine the location of the device poses an unacceptable risk, disable Location Services. Set Settings General Location Services Off. Note also that usage of Location Service can be controlled on a per-app basis, at the user's discretion. Given the utility of location information for some apps (such as Maps), user-determined settings may be most practical.

If an application (such as Maps) wishes to use Location Services while being disabled, the user will be prompted to return to Settings to enable it.

4 DEVICE USAGE AND HANDLING

This chapter provides recommendations on device usage and handling, for both administrators and users. Section D.4.1 provides handling and usage guidance for administrators. These topics include issuing devices, managing and accounting for devices once in users' hands, and effectively educating users on secure device usage.

Section 4.2 provides handling and usage guidance for users, which must be effectively communicated by administrators. These topics include important recommendations such as maintaining physical control of the device, not jailbreaking the device, and preventing connections to untrusted networks. This section closes with suggested usage statements that could be provided to users.

4.1 Handling Guidance for Administrators

If the enterprise is planning to procure and distribute devices to users, administrators should establish procedures for this activity. Some items from this section may not apply to BYOD scenarios, however, such as inventory management and prompt retirement of unsupported devices.

4.1.1 Establish a User Training Program

Create or make available training resources to educate users about device security issues and organization policies. Ensure that all device users are aware of risks and properly trained to mitigate them.

Security and policy awareness training reduces the risk of user-originated security compromise. This relates closely to any agreements between the user and enterprise regarding device handling, which should be verified for each user prior to their being issued a device, as described in Section 4.1.2.4.

4.1.2 Issuing Devices

This section provides recommendations for enterprises issuing iOS devices.

4.1.2.1 Issue Only Supported Devices

Ensure that only supported hardware versions are issued. Supported hardware versions are defined as those that can run the latest version of iOS and receive all updates. To determine this, administrators will need to manually note which systems can be updated whenever security updates are provided.

Sometimes only the current version and the previous version of the iPhone or iPad hardware can run all updates. This suggests that IT planners should anticipate a 2-year (or 3-year, at most) refresh cycle for enterprise-purchased devices.

4.1.2.2 Erase and Reset Devices, If Re-issuing

If re-issuing devices, erase them before distributing them to users.

Use the command Settings General Reset Erase All Content and Settings to erase a device. Clearing content and settings returns the device to a stable state and prevents accidental exposure of the prior user's data.

4.1.2.3 Update Device-to-User Registration

Establish a system for attributing individual devices to users prior to issuance. This information must be updated every time a device is issued or transferred. Existing inventory tracking systems or MDM software can enable automation of this process.

The following pieces of information from each device can be useful:

- UDID (Unique Device Identifier)
- Serial Number
- IMEI (if equipped with a cellular connectivity)
- Model Number
- Wi-Fi MAC Address
- Bluetooth MAC Address

MDM products may also report this information. This information should be protected accordingly.

4.1.2.4 Verify User Training History

Ensure that users are familiar with the training before receiving a new device, and at regular intervals afterward.

4.1.2.5 Provide Recharging Hardware with Device

Distribute AC power adapters to users when issuing devices and warn users not to connect their devices to unauthorized systems. It may be prudent to distribute additional AC power adapters to remove the temptation to connect the devices to unknown PCs.

Connecting iOS devices to unauthorized systems, even if only intending to recharge the device, presents a security risk. Providing a power adapter, and easy access to replacements and additional adapters, will help combat temptation to connect to other systems. Users should never be left with connecting to a computer as their only option to recharge their device.

4.1.3 Dealing with a Lost or Stolen iOS Device

If an iOS device is reported as lost or stolen, the device should be immediately disabled to prevent unauthorized use or access. The system administrator can issue a remote "Wipe" command to erase all media, data, and settings from the device, restoring it to factory settings. Be aware of the circumstances under which issuing a wipe may not be possible, such as keeping a device in Airplane Mode or simply lacking network connectivity.

4.1.3.1 Establish Procedure for Lost or Stolen iOS Devices

> Establish and test a procedure to issue a wipe command to erase data from a lost or stolen iOS device. Ensure that users are also aware of their responsibilities to report lost or stolen devices, as documented in Section 4.2.1.2.

Wipe commands can be issued by an MDM server or by Exchange ActiveSync. Users can also initiate remote wipe using iCloud, if the device is enrolled.

4.1.4 Retire Devices That Cannot Run Latest iOS Version

> Immediately retire any devices that cannot run the latest iOS version. This requires vigilance on the part of administrators, to monitor when an update is issued but is not supported on older devices.

iOS updates include both security patches as well as new functionality. Ensure that all iOS device hardware provided and managed by the enterprise can always run the latest iOS. For example, all iPhone 3G devices should be immediately retired, because they cannot run iOS 5.

4.1.5 Monitor Devices Using MDM, Especially for Updates

As discussed in Section 2.2, MDM products enable enterprise integration and reporting for iOS devices. Regularly monitor the status of devices using MDM software and respond accordingly. Particularly important is ensuring that the version of iOS is kept up to date, which implies that all available security updates are installed. Some MDM products include the ability to disable access to enterprise resources if devices are not kept up to date or are otherwise not compliant.

4.2 Handling Guidance for Users

User education is one of the strongest tools an organization can use to minimize the risk of security issues. Educating users helps raise awareness of their actions and helps them understand the reasoning behind policy decisions.

This section details physical handling guidance and security policy topics to be reinforced to users through an organization-developed user education program.

4.2.1 Physical Control

Maintain physical control of your iOS device at all times.

All guidance contained in this document depends upon uninterrupted physical control of your iOS device. It is your responsibility to maintain possession of the device.

Never leave your iOS device unattended in an insecure location. An unattended device is at high risk for loss, theft, and other forms of compromise that could violate the confidentiality, integrity, or availability of the device and the information contained therein.

4.2.1.1 Surrendering Physical Control

Learn the proper procedure for relinquishing control of the iOS device to another entity.

There are times when physical control of the iOS device must be surrendered, such as when passing through security or customs inspections. The following are possible methods of mitigating potential loss of personal, financial, or company information.

- Before entering security or customs checkpoints, power down the iOS device, remove its SIM card using the SIM eject tool or an unwound paper clip, and place the SIM card in a physically separate location such as a bag or your coat pocket.
- Place the device in a clear, tamper evident bag.
- Ensure passcode is enabled.

Organizations may elect to require all of these steps based on their security policy.

4.2.1.2 Notify Security or Administrative Personnel upon Loss of Physical Control

Obtain the contact information of your System Security Officer (SSO) for use in reporting the loss of physical control of your iOS device and learn which scenarios require SSO notification.

If there is any suspicion that a device has been accessed by an unauthorized user, report the incident immediately to the appropriate SSO or administrative personnel.

If a device is lost or stolen, the administrator or SSO should be contacted immediately to execute the remote wipe procedure through Microsoft Exchange as described in Section 4.1.3 and to create a detailed incident report describing the event.

Even if you lose control of your iOS device for a period of time but regain it later, it should be inspected for signs of physical compromise by system administration or security personnel. If a compromise is suspected, actions should be taken to sanitize or destroy the device, depending on the sensitivity of the data and severity of the situation in which it was compromised.

4.2.1.3 Be Aware of Your Surroundings

Be aware of the danger of "shoulder surfing," which refers to the ability of others to see your entry or viewing of sensitive information on the phone.

Because anyone nearby can potentially view any information displayed on the device, be wary of your environment when viewing any sensitive information, and particularly wary when entering passwords. Due to obvious physical and user interface constraints, password entry is susceptible to shoulder surfing, whether by observation of finger position or brief display of each character on-screen. Some third-party products may be available to mitigate this risk.

4.2.1.4 Follow Procedures for Secure Areas

Learn the proper procedure for handling your iOS device in a secure area.

If your organization has a secure area for talking about confidential information, you should be educated about the risks of bringing your iOS device into those areas. The following policies may be implemented for device security in secure areas:

- Leave iOS devices outside conference rooms.
- Applications that record audio or video must be removed or their use restricted.
- Ensure the camera on the back of the iOS device is blocked (e.g., opaque tape) to prevent photo or video recording.
- Ensure that all iOS devices, if present, are in airplane mode with Wi-Fi turned off. Refer to Section 3 for more information.

4.2.2 Do Not Jailbreak or Unlock Your iOS Device

Jailbreaking is a term that describes the process of modifying the iOS device's operating system, often with the goal of running unsigned code or performing unsupported customizations to the operating system.

Unlocking allows users to operate an iOS device on a cellular network it is not authorized to connect to. Unlocking an iOS device requires a jailbroken iOS device first.

Do not jailbreak or unlock your iOS device. Doing so makes it much easier for attackers to introduce malicious code onto the device.

Jailbreaking significantly increases the iOS device's susceptibility to compromise. It disables the enforcement of code signatures, a critical security feature. This enables access to a wide range of software with little accountability and minimal vetting. Jailbreaking tools also typically install and activate services that make the device easier to remotely access, such as SSH.

4.2.3 Install Software Updates When Available

> Install software updates as quickly as possible. Updates can be applied over-the-air, and are indicated by a red circle on the Settings app. Apply by following Settings General Software Update.

Software updates for iOS devices can contain fixes for security vulnerabilities. As these vulnerabilities often become public knowledge when the updates are released, installing updates as soon as they are available is strongly recommended. Supported third-party software should not be broken by updates.

Prior to iOS 5, applying iOS updates always required the use of iTunes. Migrating from iOS 4 to iOS 5 also requires the use of iTunes.

4.2.4 Connect Only to Trusted Networks

> Do not connect your iOS device to untrusted wireless networks.

Connections to untrusted Wi-Fi networks introduce some risks. Attacks on the iOS device, or eavesdropping on the data it transmits, can occur due to use of such networks. Because the user controls the Wi-Fi settings, he or she must understand the risks associated with untrusted wireless networks and behave responsibly. Some organizations have policies that forbid connection to non-enterprise controlled networks. Other organizations forbid or prevent the use of personal devices on enterprise networks.

4.2.5 E-mail Accounts

4.2.5.1 Consider Risks of Using Personal E-mail Accounts

> Do not add personal e-mail accounts to your iOS device, unless you are comfortable with (or approved for) the additional risk.

Adding personal e-mail accounts implies that personal, non-company data will be transferred to and stored on the device. This likely violates organizational policy with regard to use of company resources for personal use, but it also increases risk. It increases the risk of your personal information being compromised as a result of an attack against the device, and also increases the risks of company information being compromised as a result of an attack carried out against your personal e-mail account. See the next section for more information about phishing attacks and the motivation for segregating e-mail accounts between different systems.

4.2.5.2 Be Aware of Phishing

> Be aware of phishing attempts, including receiving mobile profiles from attackers.

Phishing is a term referring to a fraudulent communication (usually e-mail) pretending to be from a reputable source asking for personal, financial, or company information. Adding personal e-mail accounts to your iOS device greatly increases your availability to receive phishing e-mails, which may accidentally release important information about yourself or your organization. By removing personal e-mail accounts from the device, you are protecting your organization from divulging information through your device to these malicious actors.

4.2.6 Disable Bluetooth If Practical

Disable Bluetooth communication if not necessary.

Disabling Bluetooth reduces the possible attack surface for exploitation, although such vulnerabilities are rare and the iOS over-the-air update process enables rapid patching upon any public disclosure. Bluetooth also permits wireless device discovery and can be used to reveal a limited amount of information from the device. If practical, it is safest to keep Bluetooth disabled. The Bluetooth profiles available on iOS devices are documented at http://support.apple.com/kb/HT3647.

4.2.7 Recharge Device Only through Approved Methods

Recharge your device by either connecting to an organization-approved system or by using the AC power adapter you received when you were issued your device.

Connecting your iOS device to unknown systems exposes the device to unnecessary risks, including the loss of personal or company information. Syncing only with trusted systems also helps maintain the integrity of your iOS device.

5 SUPPORTING INFRASTRUCTURE

This section contains recommendations for infrastructure elements that support iOS device deployment.

5.1 iTunes

With iOS 5, use of iTunes is no longer a prerequisite for deployment of iOS devices. However, iTunes supports the ability to back up data from iOS devices. If a backup capability is necessary, iTunes deployment in the enterprise may be necessary. Alternatively, data could be backed up in "cloud" services or users could be expected to back up iOS devices on personally owned systems (as in a BYOD scenario). However, legal concerns may arise regarding the presence of enterprise data on personally owned systems.

If enterprise deployment of iTunes is planned in order to support the ability to back up iOS devices, it can be configured to improve its security posture. A small number of items are also presented that are of negligible security concern, but may be of interest to administrators who have network bandwidth or deployment concerns.

Apple provides guidance for iTunes deployment in support of iOS at http://help.apple.com/iosdeployment-itunes/.

- Settings for Mac OS X systems, and mechanisms for deploying them, are described at http://support.apple.com/kb/HT2653 and http://support.apple.com/kb/HT3490.
- Settings for Windows systems are described at http://support.apple.com/kb/HT2102.

The following sections reference specific settings but do not provide implementation instructions, which vary by host platform and systems management mechanism. Most settings here also correspond to settings in the GUI, which become "grayed-out" if administratively disabled.

5.1.1 Disable Music Sharing

> To prevent the system from sharing music (and potentially other files) over the local network when iTunes is running, set the disable SharedMusic key to true.

5.1.2 Disable Ping

> To prevent users from using Ping to potentially share sensitive information, set the disable Ping key to true.

5.1.3 Disable iTunes Store (If Bandwidth Constrained)

If using the iTunes store is not appropriate due to limited bandwidth, set the disable MusicStore key to YES.

5.1.4 Disable Radio (If Bandwidth Constrained)

If using streaming audio is not appropriate due to limited bandwidth, set the disable Radio key to YES.

5.1.5 Use Activation-Only Mode (If Direct Connectivity Unavailable)

iOS 5 permits device activation if network connectivity is available. However, if cellular or trusted Wi-Fi network connectivity is not available to support device activation, iTunes can be put into a special mode to support rapid activation of multiple devices. This is described in http://support.apple.com/kb/HT4335.

6 DEPLOYMENT CHECKLIST

Configuration Creation and Deployment Items

Section	Action	Result	Notes
2.1	Understand the enforceability of configuration profiles		
2.2.1	Select mobile device management (MDM) software		
2.2.2	Understand capabilities of MDM software		
2.3.1	Ensure configuration profiles are deployed with encryption and authentication, if deploying over-the-air		
2.3.2	Manually deploy configuration profiles using iPCU (unusual)		
2.3.3	Avoid deploying configuration profiles via unauthenticated, unencrypted methods such as e-mail		

Configuration Profile Items

Section	Action	Result	Notes
3.1.1	Disallow removal of configuration profiles, if practical		
3.1.2	Enable passcode on device		
3.1.2	Disallow simple values for passcode		
3.1.2	Set passcode minimum length to 6		
3.1.2	Set complex character minimum length to 1		
3.1.2	Set maximum passcode age to 120 days or longer		
3.1.2	Set passcode auto-lock to 5 minutes or less		
3.1.2	Set passcode grace period to 5 minutes or less		
3.1.2	Set passcode number of failed attempts permitted to 10, or fewer		
3.1.2.2	Understand which files are protected by encryption		
3.1.3.1	Disable installation of third-party apps if possible		
3.1.3.2	Disable camera if appropriate		
3.1.3.3	Disable screen capture if appropriate		

Section	Action	Result	Notes
3.1.3.4	Disable (unusual) or configure Safari		
3.1.3.4.1	Configure Safari restriction: disable autofill		
3.1.3.4.2	Configure Safari restriction: enable fraud warning		
3.1.3.4.3	Configure Safari restriction: block pop-ups		
3.1.3.4.4	Configure Safari restrictions: accept cookies from visited sites only		
3.1.3.5.1	Disable iCloud backups unless needed		
3.1.3.5.2	Disable iCloud document sync unless needed		
3.1.3.5.3	Disable iCloud photo stream unless needed		
3.1.3.6.1	Disable sending diagnostic data to Apple		
3.1.3.6.2	Disable user's acceptance of untrusted TLS certificates		
3.1.3.6.3	Force encrypted backups of device data		
3.1.4.1	Use WPA/WPA2 Enterprise with TLS for Wi-Fi encryption		
3.1.4.2	Disable auto-join for Wi-Fi networks		
3.1.5.1	Select IPsec (Cisco) or L2TP for use as VPN		
3.1.6.1	Disable allow move for e-mail accounts		
3.1.6.2	Enable SSL for all incoming e-mail accounts		
3.1.6.2	Enable SSL for all outgoing e-mail accounts		
3.1.6.3	Enable S/MIME support and add certificates, if needed		
3.1.8	Disable allow move for ActiveSync accounts		
3.1.9	Prevent outgoing mail from being sent outside of Mail app for Exchange Accounts		
3.1.10	Enable SSL for ActiveSync communications		
3.1.10.1	Enable S/MIME support and add certificates, if needed		
3.1.11.1	Enable SSL for LDAP connections		
3.1.12.1	Enable SSL for any CalDav connections		
3.1.13.1	Enable SSL for subscribed calendar connections		
3.1.16.1	For MDM, enable message signing		
3.1.16.2	For MDM, check out when profile is removed		
3.1.16.3.1	For MDM, allow remote query of general settings		
3.1.16.3.2	For MDM, allow remote query of network settings		

Section	Action	Result	Notes
3.1.16.3.3	For MDM, allow remote query of security settings		
3.1.16.3.4	For MDM, allow remote query of restrictions		
3.1.16.3.5	For MDM, allow remote query of configuration profiles		
3.1.16.3.6	For MDM, allow remote query of provisioning profiles		
3.1.16.3.7	For MDM, allow remote query of applications		
3.1.16.3.8	For MDM, allow remote addition/removal of configuration profiles		
3.1.16.3.9	For MDM, allow remote addition/removal of provisioning profiles		
3.1.16.3.10	For MDM, allow or disallow remote activation of device password change		
3.1.16.3.11	Allow remote wipe		

Usage and Handling Items

Section	Action	Result	Notes
4.1.1	Establish a user training program		
4.1.2.1	Issue only supported devices		
4.1.2.2	Reset devices prior to any re-issuance		
4.1.2.3	Establish device-to-user registration prior to issuance		
4.1.2.4	Verify user compliance with training programs before issuance		
4.1.2.5	Provide recharging hardware with device and warn users not to connect to unauthorized systems		
4.1.3.1	Establish procedure for lost or stolen devices		
4.1.4	Retire devices that cannot run latest iOS version		
4.1.5	Monitor devices using MDM software, especially for updates		

Supporting Infrastructure Items

Section	Action	Result	Notes
5.1	Determine whether to support backup via iTunes deployment		
5.1.1	If deploying iTunes, disable music sharing		
5.1.2	If deploying iTunes, disable Ping		
5.1.3	If deploying iTunes and bandwidth-constrained, disable iTunes Store		
5.1.4	If deploying iTunes and bandwidth-constrained, disable Radio		
5.1.5	If devices cannot be wirelessly activated, use iTunes in activation-only mode		

REFERENCE

The Mitigations Group of the Information Assurance Directorate. National Security Agency. http://www.nsa.gov/ia/_files/os/applemac/Apple_iOS_5_Guide.pdf

BIBLIOGRAPHY

1. Apple, Inc. *iOS Deployment Guides*, Dec. 2008. http://www.apple.com/iphone/business/resources/.
2. Apple, Inc. *iPhone User Guide* (for iOS 5.0 Software), Oct. 2011. http://manuals.info.apple.com/en_US/iphone_user_guide.pdf.
3. Bédrune, J.-B., and Sigwald, J. *iPhone Data Protection in Depth*, May 2011. http://esec-lab. sogeti.com/dotclear/public/publications/11-hitbamsterdam-iphonedataprotection.pdf.
4. Blazakis, D. *The Apple Sandbox*, Jan. 2011. http://securityevaluators.com/files/papers/apple-sandbox.pdf.
5. Dai Zovi, D. *iOS 4 Security Evaluation*, Aug. 2011. http://trailofbits.files.wordpress.com/2011/08/apple-ios-4-security-evaluation-whitepaper.pdf.
6. Defence Signals Directorate. *iOS Hardening Configuration Guide*, Jun. 2011. http://www.dsd. gov.au/publications/iOS_Hardening_Guide.pdf.
7. National Institute of Standards and Technology. *Guidelines on Cell Phone and PDA Security*, Oct. 2008. http://csrc.nist.gov/publications/nistpubs/800-124/SP800-124.pdf.
8. National Security Agency. *Information Assurance Mitigations Guidance*, Jan. 2012. http://www. nsa.gov/ia/mitigation_guidance/index.shtml.
9. Schuetz, D. *Inside Apple's MDM Black Box*, Jan. 2012. https://github.com/intrepidusgroup/imdmtools/blob/master/Presentations/InsideAppleMDM_ShmooCon_2012.pdf.

Appendix E: Traditional IT Metrics Reference*

Why should we care about productivity and quality? There are several reasons. The first and foremost reason is that our customers and end-users require a working, quality product. Measuring the process as well as the product tells us whether we've achieved our goal. However, there are other more subtle reasons why we need to measure productivity and quality

The development of systems is becoming increasing complex, particularly since we moved in the more mobile technologies. Unless we measure we will never know whether our efforts have been successful.

On occasion, technology is used just for the sake of using a new technology. This is not an effective use of a technology. Measuring the effectiveness of an implementation assures us that our decision has been cost-effective.

We measure productivity and quality to quantify the project's progress as well as to quantify the attributes of the product. A metric enables us to understand and manage the process as well as to measure the impact of change to the process (e.g., new methods, training). The use of metrics also enables us to know when we've met our goals (e.g., usability, performance, test coverage).

In measuring software systems we can create metrics based on the different parts of a system (e.g., requirements, specifications, code, documentation, tests, training). For each of these components we can measure its attributes, which include usability, maintainability, extendibility, size, defect level, performance, and completeness.

While the majority of organizations will use metrics found in books such as this one, it is possible to generate metrics specific to a particular task. Characteristics of metrics dictate that they should be

1. Collectable
2. Reproducible
3. Pertinent
4. System independent

* Reprinted from IEEE Std 982.1-1988, IEEE Standard Dictionary of Measures to Produce Reliable Software. Copyright 1988 IEEE.

1 TYPICAL IT METRICS

Sample product metrics include the following:

1. Size: lines of code, pages of documentation, number and size of test, token count, function count
2. Complexity: decision count, variable count, number of modules, size/volume, depth of nesting
3. Reliability: count of changes required by phase, count of discovered defects, defect density = number of defects/size, count of changed lines of code

Sample process metrics include the following:

1. Complexity: time to design, code and test, defect discovery rate by phase, cost to develop, number of external interfaces, defect fix rate
2. Methods and tool use: number of tools used and why, project infrastructure tools, tools not used and why
3. Resource metrics: years experience with team, years experience with language, years experience with type of software, MIPS per person, support personnel to engineering personnel ratio, non-project time to project time ratio, variance of schedule, variance of effort. Productivity: % time to redesign, % time to redo, variance of schedule, variance of effort

Once the organization determines the slate of metrics to be implemented, it must develop a methodology for reviewing the results of the metrics program. Metrics are useless if they don't result in improved quality and/or productivity. At a minimum, the organization should do the following:

1. Determine the metric and measuring technique
2. Measure to understand where you are
3. Establish worst, best, planned cases
4. Modify the process or product depending on results of measurement
5. Re-measure to see what's changed
6. Reiterate

2 DEVELOPING AN IT ASSESSMENT PROGRAM

A four-stepped procedure (Linkman and Walker, 1991) is outlined for establishing targets and means for IT system development assessment. The procedure is not focused on any particular set of metrics; rather it believes that metrics should be selected on the basis of goals. This procedure is suitable for setting up goals for either the entire project deliverables or for any partial product created in the software life cycle.

1. Define measurable goals: The project goals establishment process is similar to the development process for project deliverables. Software projects usually start with abstract problem concepts and the final project deliverables are obtained by continuously partitioning and refining the problem into tangible and manageable pieces. Final Quantified goals can be transformed from initial intangible goals by following the same divide-and-conquer method for software deliverables. Three sources of information are helpful to establishing the targets:
   a. Historical data under the assumptions that data are available, development environment is stable, and projects are similar in terms of type, size, and complexity.
   b. Synthetic data such as modeling results are useful if models used are calibrated to specific development environment.
   c. Expert opinions
2. Maintain balanced goals: The measurable goals are usually established on the basis of the following four factors: cost, schedule, effort, and quality. It is feasible to achieve just a single goal, but it is always a challenge to deliver a project with the minimum staff and resource, on time, and within budget. It needs to be kept in mind that trade-off is always involved and all issues should be addressed to reach a set of balanced goals.
3. Set up intermediate goals: A project should never be measured only at its end point. Checkpoints should be set up to provide confidence that the project is running on course. The common practice involves, setting up quantifiable targets for each phase, measuring the actual values against the targets, establishing a plan to make corrections for any deviations. All four aforementioned factors should be broken down into phase or activity for setting up intermediate targets. Measurements for cost and effort can be divided into machine and

human resources according to software life cycle phase so that expenditures can be monitored to ensure project is running within budget. Schedule should always be defined in terms of milestones or check points to ensure intermediate products can be evaluated and final product will be delivered on time. Quality of intermediate products should always be measured to guarantee the final deliverable will meet its target goal.

4. Establish means of assessment: Two aspects are involved in this activity:
   a. Data collection: Based on the project characteristics such as size, complexity, level of control, and so on, a decision should be made in terms of whether a manual data collection process or an automated data collection process should be used. If non-automated way is applied, then the availability of the collection medium at the right time should be emphasized.
   b. Data analysis: The following two types of analyses should be considered:
      1. Project analysis—This type of analysis consists of checkpoint analysis and continuous analysis (trend analysis) and is concerned with verifying the intermediate targets are met to ensure that the project is on the right track.
      2. Component analysis—This type of analysis concentrates on the finer level of details of the end product and is concerned with identifying those components in the product that may require special attention and action. The complete process includes deciding on the set of measures to be analyzed, identifying the components detected as anomalous using measured data, finding out the root cause of the anomalies, and taking actions to make correction.

3 TRADITIONAL CONFIGURATION MANAGEMENT METRICS

The following metrics are typically used by those measuring the CM process:

1. Average rate of variance from scheduled time
2. Rate of first pass approvals

3. Volume of deviation requests by cause
4. The number of scheduled, performed, and completed configuration management audits by each phase of the life cycle.
5. The rate of new changes being released and the rate that changes are being verified as completed. History compiled from successive deliveries is used to refine the scope of the expected rate.
6. The number of completed versus scheduled (stratified by type and priority) actions.
7. Man-hours per project
8. Schedule variances
9. Tests per requirement
10. Change category count
11. Changes by source
12. Cost variances
13. Errors per thousand lines of code (KSLOC)
14. Requirements volatility

4 IEEE PROCESS FOR MEASUREMENT

Using the IEEE methodology (IEEE, 1989) the measurement process can be described in nine stages. These stages may overlap or occur in different sequences depending on organization needs. Each of these stages in the measurement process influences the production of a delivered product with the potential for high reliability. Other factors influencing the measurement process include the following:

1. A firm management commitment to continually assess product and process maturity, or stability or both during the project
2. Use of trained personnel in applying measures to the project in a useful way
3. Software support tools
4. A clear understanding of the distinctions among errors, faults, and failures

Product measures include the following:

1. Errors, faults, and failures is the count of defects with respect to human cause, program bugs, and observed system malfunctions.
2. Mean time to failure, failure rate is a derivative measure of defect occurrence and time.
3. Reliability growth and projection is the assessment of change in failure-freeness of the product under testing or operation.
4. Remaining product faults is the assessment of fault-freeness of the product in development, test, or maintenance.
5. Completeness and consistency is the assessment of the presence and agreement of all necessary software system parts.
6. Complexity is the assessment of complicating factors in a system.

Process measures include the following:

1. Management control measures address the quantity and distribution of error and faults and the trend of cost necessary for defect removal.
2. Coverage measures allow one to monitor the ability of developers and managers to guarantee the required completeness in all the activities of the life cycle and support the definition of corrective actions.
3. Risk, benefit, cost evaluation measures support delivery decisions based both on technical and cost criteria.
4. Risk can be assessed based on residual faults present in the product at delivery and the cost with the resulting support activity.

The nine stages are as follows:

- Stage 1: Plan organizational strategy. Initiate a planning process. Form a planning group and review reliability constraints and objectives, giving consideration to user needs and requirements. Identify the reliability characteristics of a software product necessary to achieve these objectives. Establish a strategy for measuring and managing software reliability. Document practices for conducting measurements.
- Stage 2: Determine software reliability goals. Define the reliability goals for the software being developed to optimize reliability in light of realistic assessments of project constraints, including size, scope, cost, and schedule.

- Review the requirements for the specific development effort, in order to determine the desired characteristics of the delivered software. For each characteristic, identify specific reliability goals that can be demonstrated by the software or measured against a particular value or condition. Establish an acceptable range of values. Consideration should be given to user needs and requirements.
- Establish intermediate reliability goals at various points in the development effort.

- Stage 3: Implement measurement process. Establish a software reliability measurement process that best fits an organization's needs. Review the rest of the process and select those stages that best lead to optimum reliability. Add to or enhance these stages as needed. Consider the following suggestions:

    1. Select appropriate data collection and measurement practices designed to optimize software reliability.
    2. Document the measures required, the intermediate and final milestones when measurements are taken, the data collection requirements, and the acceptable values for each measure.
    3. Assign responsibilities for performing and monitoring measurements, and provide necessary support for these activities from across the internal organization.
    4. Initiate a measure selection and evaluation process.
    5. Prepare educational material for training personnel in concepts, principles, and practices of software reliability and reliability measures.

- Stage 4: Select potential measures. Identify potential measures that would be helpful in achieving the reliability goals established in Stage 2.
- Stage 5: Prepare data collection and measurement plan. Prepare a data collection and measurement plan for the development and support effort. For each potential measure, determine the primitives needed to perform the measurement. Data should be organized so that information related to events during the development effort can be properly recorded in a database and retained for historical purposes.
    - For each intermediate reliability goal identified in Stage 2 identify the measures needed to achieve this goal. Identify the points during development when the measurements are to be taken.

Establish acceptable values or a range of values to assess whether the intermediate reliability goals are achieved.

- Include in the plan an approach for monitoring the measurement effort itself. The responsibility for collecting and reporting data, verifying its accuracy, computing measures, and interpreting the results should be described.

- Stage 6: Monitor the measurements. Once the data collection and reporting begins, monitor the measurements and the progress made during development, so as to manage the reliability and thereby achieve the goals for the delivered product. The measurements assist in determining whether the intermediate reliability goals are achieved and whether the final goal is achievable. Analyze the measure and determine if the results are sufficient to satisfy the reliability goals. Decide whether a measure results assists in affirming the reliability of the product or process being measured. Take corrective action.
- Stage 7: Assess reliability. Analyze measurements to ensure that reliability of the delivered software satisfies the reliability objectives and that the reliability as measured, is acceptable.
    - Identify assessment steps that are consistent with the reliability objectives documented in the data collection and measurement plan. Check the consistency of acceptance criteria and the sufficiency of tests to satisfactorily demonstrate that the reliability objectives have been achieved. Identify the organization responsible for determining final acceptance of the reliability of the software. Document the steps in assessing the reliability of the software.
- Stage 8: Use software. Assess the effectiveness of the measurement effort and perform necessary correction action. Conduct a follow-up analysis of the measurement effort to evaluate reliability assessment and development practices, record lessons learned and evaluate user satisfaction with the software's reliability.
- Stage 9: Retain software measurement data. Retain measurement data on the software throughout the development and operation phases for use by future projects. This data provides a baseline for reliability improvement and an opportunity to compare the same measures across completed projects. This information can assist in development future guidelines and standards.

5 METRICS AS A COMPONENT OF THE PROCESS MATURITY FRAMEWORK

Pfleeger (1990) has suggested a set of metrics for which data are to be collected and analyzed for the improvement of software engineering productivity. This set of metrics is based on a process maturity framework developed at the Software Engineering Institute at Carnegie Mellon University. The SEI framework divides organizations into five levels based on how mature (e.g., organized, professional, aligned to software tenets) the organization is. The five levels range from initial, or ad hoc, to an optimizing environment. Pfleeger recommends that metrics be divided into five levels as well. Each level is based on the amount of information made available to the development process. As the development process matures and improves, additional metrics can be collected and analyzed.

- Level 1: Initial Process. This level is characterized by an ad hoc approach to software development. Inputs to the process are not well defined but the outputs are as expected. Preliminary baseline project metrics should be gathered at this level to form a basis for comparison as improvements are made and maturity increases. This can be accomplished by comparing new project measurements with the baseline ones.
- Level 2: Repeatable Process. At this level the process is repeatable in much the same way that a subroutine is repeatable. The requirements act as input, the code as output, and constraints are such things as budget and schedule. Even though proper inputs produce proper outputs, there is no means to discern easily how the outputs are actually produced. Only project-related metrics make sense at this level since the activities within the actual transitions from input to output are not available to be measured. Measures are this level can include the following:

    1. Amount of effort needed to develop the system
    2. Overall project cost
    3. Software size: non-commented lines of code, function points, object and method count
    4. Personnel effort: actual person-months of effort, report
    5. Person months of effort

6. Requirements volatility: requirements changes

- Level 3: Defined Process. At this level the activities of the process are clearly defined. This additional structure means that the input to and output from each well-defined functional activity can be examined, which permits a measurement of the intermediate products. Measures include the following:
  1. Requirements complexity: number of distinct objects and actions addressed in requirements
  2. Design complexity: number of design modules, cyclomatic complexity, McCabe design complexity
  3. Code complexity: number of code modules, cyclomatic complexity
  4. Test complexity: number of paths to test, of object-oriented development then number of object interfaces to test
  5. Quality metrics: defects discovered, defects discovered per unit size (defect density), requirements faults discovered, design faults discovered, fault density for each product
  6. Pages of documentation

- Level 4: Managed Process. At this level, feedback from early project activities are used to set priorities for later project activities. At this level, activities are readily compared and contrasted, the effects of changes in one activity can be tracked in the others. At this level measurements can be made across activities and are used to control and stabilize the process so that productivity and quality can match expectation. The following types of data are recommended to be collected. Metrics at this stage, although derived from the following data, are tailored to the individual organization.
  1. Process type: What process model is used and how is it correlating to positive or negative consequences.
  2. Amount of producer reuse: How much of the system is designed for reuse. This includes reuse of requirements, design modules, test plans, and code.
  3. Amount of consumer reuse: How much does the project reuse components from other projects. This includes reuse of requirements, design modules, test plans, and code. (By reusing tested, proven components effort can be minimized and quality can be improved.)

4. Defect identification: How and when are defects discovered? Knowing this will indicate whether those process activities are effective.
5. Use of defect density model for testing: To what extent does the number of defects determine when testing is complete? This controls and focuses testing as well as increases the quality of the final product.
6. Use of configuration management: Is a configuration management scheme imposed on the development process? This permits traceability, which can be used to assess the impact of alterations.
7. Module completion over time: At what rates are modules being completed? This reflects the degree to which the process and development environment facilitate implementation and testing.

- Level 5: Optimizing Process. At this level measures from activities are used to change and improve the process. This process change can affect the organization and the project as well. Studies by SEI report that 85% of organizations are at level 1, 14% at level 2, 1% at level 3. None of the firms surveyed had reached levels 4 or 5. Therefore, the authors have not recommended a set of metrics for level 5.

5.1 Steps to Take in Using Metrics

1. Assess the process: determine the level of process maturity
2. Determine the appropriate metrics to collect
3. Recommend metrics, tools, and techniques
4. Estimate project cost and schedule
5. Collect appropriate level of metrics
6. Construct project database of metrics data that can be used for analysis and to track value of metrics over time
7. Cost and schedule evaluation: when the project is complete evaluate the initial estimates of cost and schedule for accuracy. Determine which of the factors may account for discrepancies between predicted and actual values.
8. Form a basis for future estimates

6 IEEE DEFINED METRICS

The IEEE standards (1988) were written with the objective to provide the software community with defined measures currently used as indicators of reliability. By emphasizing early reliability assessment, this standard supports methods through measurement to improve product reliability.

This section presents a sub-set of the IEEE standard easily adaptable by the general IT community.

6.1 Fault Density

This measure can be used to predict remaining faults by comparison with expected fault density, determine if sufficient testing has been completed, and establish standard fault densities for comparison and prediction.

$$F_d = F/KSLOC$$

where

F = total number of unique faults found in a given interval resulting in failures of a specified severity level

$KSLOC$ = number of source lines of executable code and nonexecutable data declarations in thousands

6.2 Defect Density

This measure can be used after design and code inspections of new development or large block modifications. If the defect density is outside the norm after several inspections, it is an indication of a problem.

$$DD = \frac{\sum_{i=1}^{I} D_i}{KSLOD}$$

where

D_i = total number of unique defects detected during the ith design or code inspection process

I = total number of inspections

$KSLOD$ = in the design phase this is the number of source lines of executable code and nonexecutable data declarations in thousands

6.3 Cumulative Failure Profile

This is a graphical method used to predict reliability, estimate additional testing time to reach an acceptable reliable system, and identify modules and subsystems that require additional testing. A plot is drawn of cumulative failures versus a suitable time base.

6.4 Fault-Days Number

This measure represents the number of days that faults spend in the system from their creation to their removal. For each fault detected and removed, during any phase, the number of days from its creation to its removal is determined (fault-days). The fault-days are then summed for all faults detected and removed, to get the fault-days number at system level, including all faults detected and removed up to the delivery date. In those cases where the creation date of the fault is not known, the fault is assumed to have been created at the middle of the phase in which it was introduced.

6.5 Functional or Modular Test Coverage

This measure is used to quantify a software test coverage index for a software delivery. From the system's functional requirements a cross-reference listing of associated modules must first be created.

$$\text{Functional (Modular) Test Coverage Index} = \frac{FE}{FT}$$

where

FE = number of the software functional (modular) requirements for which all test cases have been satisfactorily completed

FT = total number of software functional (modular) requirements

6.6 Requirements Traceability

This measure aids in identifying requirements that are either missing from, or in addition to, the original requirements.

$$\text{TM} = \frac{R1}{R2} \times 100\%$$

where

$R1$ = number of requirements met by the architecture

$R2$ = number of original requirements

6.7 Software Maturity Index

This measure is used to quantify the readiness of a software product. Changes from previous baselines to the current baselines are an indication of the current product stability.

$$SMI = \frac{M_T - (F_a + F_c + F_{\text{del}})}{M_T}$$

where

SMI = Maturity index

M_T = Number of software functions (modules) in the current delivery

F_a = Number of software functions (modules) in the current delivery that are additions to the previous delivery

F_c = Number of software functions (modules) in the current delivery that include internal changes from a previous delivery

F_{del} = number of software functions (modules) in the previous delivery that are deleted in the current delivery

The Software Maturity Index may be estimated as

$$SMI = \frac{M_T - F_c}{M_T}$$

6.8 Number of Conflicting Requirements

This measure is used to determine the reliability of a software system resulting from the software architecture under consideration, as represented by a specification based on the entity-relationship-attributed model. What is required is a list of the system's inputs, its outputs, and a list of the functions performed by each program. The mappings from the software architecture to the requirements are identified. Mappings from the same specification item to more than one differing requirement are examined for requirements inconsistency. Additionally, mappings from more than one spec item to a single requirement are examined for spec inconsistency.

6.9 Cyclomatic Complexity

This measure is used to determine the structured complexity of a coded module. The use of this measure is designed to limit the complexity of the module, thereby promoting understandability of the module.

$$C = E - N + 1$$

where

C = complexity

N = number of nodes (sequential groups of program statements)

E = number of edges (program flows between nodes)

6.10 Design Structure

This measure is used to determine the simplicity of the detailed design of a software program. The values determined can be used to identify problem areas within the software design.

$$DSM = \sum_{i=1}^{6} W_i D_i$$

where

DSM = Design structure measure

P1 = total number of modules in program

P2 = number of modules dependent on input or output

P3 = number of modules dependent on prior processing (state)
P4 = number of database elements
P5 = number of nonunique database elements
P6 = number of database segments
P7 = number of modules not single entrance/single exit

The design structure is the weighted sum of six derivatives determined by using the primitives given above.

D1 = designed organized top down
D2 = module dependence (P2/P1)
D3 = module dependent on prior processing (P3/P1)
D4 = database size (P5/P4)
D5 = database compartmentalization (P6/P4)
D6 = module single entrance/exit (P7/P1)

The weights (W_i) are assigned by the user based on the priority of each associated derivative. Each W_i has a value between 0 and 1.

6.11 Test Coverage

This is a measure of the completeness of the testing process from both a developer and user perspective. The measure relates directly to the development, integration, and operational test stages of product development.

$$TC\left(\%\right)=\frac{(implemented\ capabilities)}{(required\ capabilities)}\times\frac{(program\ primitives\ tested)}{(total\ program\ primitives)}\times 100\%$$

where

program functional primitives are either modules, segments, statements, branches, or paths
data functional primitives are classes of data
requirement primitives are test cases or functional capabilities

6.12 Data or Information Flow Complexity

This is a structural complexity or procedural complexity measure that can be used to evaluate the information flow structure of large-scale systems, the procedure and module information flow structure, the complexity of the interconnections between modules, and the degree of simplicity of relationships between subsystems and to correlate total observed failures and software reliability with data complexity.

$$\text{weighted IFC} = \text{length} \times (\text{fanin} \times \text{fanout})^2$$

where

IFC = Information flow complexity

fanin = local flows into a procedure + number of data structures form which the procedures retrieves data

fanout = local flows from a procedure + number of data structures that the procedure updates

length = number of source statements in a procedure (excluding comments)

The flow of information between modules and/or subsystems needs to be determined either through the use of automated techniques or charting mechanisms. A local flow from module A to B exists if one of the following occurs:

1. A calls B.
2. B calls A and A returns a value to B that is passed by B.
3. Both A and B are called by another module that passes a value from A to B.

6.13 Mean Time to Failure

This measure is the basic parameter required by most software reliability models. Detailed record keeping of failure occurrences that accurately track time (calendar or execution) at which the faults manifest themselves is essential.

6.14 Software Documentation and Source Listings

The objective of this measure is to collect information to identify the parts of the software maintenance products that may be inadequate for use in a software maintenance environment. Questionnaires are used to examine the format and content of the documentation and source code attributes from a maintainability perspective.

The questionnaires examine the following product characteristics:

1. Modularity
2. Descriptiveness
3. Consistency
4. Simplicity
5. Expandability
6. Testability

Two questionnaires, the Software Documentation Questionnaire and the Software Source Listing Questionnaire, are used to evaluate the software products in a desk audit.

For the software documentation evaluation the resource documents should include those that contain the program design specifications, program testing information and procedures, program maintenance information, and guidelines used in preparation of the documentation. Typical statements from the questionnaire include the following:

1. The documentation indicates that data storage locations are not used for more than one type of data structure.
2. Parameter inputs and outputs for each module are explained in the documentation.
3. Programming conventions for I/O processing have been established and followed.
4. The documentation indicates the resource (storage, timing, tape drives, disks, etc.) allocation is fixed throughout program execution.
5. The documentation indicates that there is a reasonable time margin for each major time critical program function.
6. The documentation indicates that the program has been designed to accommodate software test probes to aid in identifying processing performance.

The software source listings evaluation reviews either high order language or assembler source code. Multiple evaluations using the questionnaire are conducted for the unit level of the program (module). The modules selected should represent a sample size of at least 10% of the total source code. Typical instructions include the following:

1. Each function of this module is an easily recognizable block of code.
2. The quantity of comments does not detract from the legibility of the source listings.
3. Mathematical models as described/derived in the documentation correspond to the mathematical equations used in the source listing.
4. Esoteric (clever) programming is avoided in this module.
5. The size of any data structure that affects the processing logic of this module is parameterized.
6. Intermediate results within this module can be selectively collected for display without code modification.

7 IT DEVELOPER'S LIST OF METRICS

7.1 McCabe's Complexity Metric (1976)

McCabe's proposal for a cyclomatic complexity number was the first attempt to objectively quantify the "flow of control" complexity of software.

The metric is computed by decomposing the program into a directed graph that represents its flow of control. The cyclomatic complexity number is then calculated using this formula:

$$V(g) = \text{edges} - \text{nodes} + 2$$

In its shortened form, the cyclomatic complexity number is a count of decision points within a program with a single entry and a single exit plus one.

7.2 Halstead Effort Metric (1976)

In the 1970s Maurice Halstead developed a theory regarding the behavior of software. Some of his findings evolved into software metrics. One of these is referred to as *Effort* or just *E*, and is a well-known complexity metric.

The Effort measure is calculated as follows:

$$E = \text{Volume}/\text{Level}$$

where Volume is a measure of the size of a piece of code and Level is a measure of how "abstract" the program is. The level of abstracting varies from almost zero for programs with low abstraction to almost one for programs that are highly abstract.

REFERENCES

Halstead, M. (1977). *Elements of Software Science*. New York: Elsevier.

IEEE Guide for the Use of IEEE Standard Dictionary of Measures to Produce Reliable Software. (1989, June 12). Standard 982.2-1988. IEEE Standards Department. Piscatawy, NJ.

IEEE Standard of Measures to Produce Reliable Software. Standard 982.1-1988. IEEE Standards Department. Piscataway, NJ.

Linkman, S. G., and Walker, J. G. (1991). Controlling programs through measurement. *Information and Software Technology, 33*(1), pp. 93–102.

McCabe, T. (1976, December). A complexity measure. *IEEE Transactions on Software Engineering*, pp. 308–320.

Pfleeger, S. L., and McGowan, C. (1990). Software Metrics in the Process Maturity Framework. *Journal of Systems Software, 12*, pp. 255–261.

NOTE

The information contained within the IEEE standards metrics section is copyrighted information of the IEEE, extracted from IEEE Std. 982.1-1988, IEEE Standard Dictionary of Measures to Produce Reliable Software. This information was written within the context of IEEE Std 982.1-1988 and the IEEE takes no responsibility for or liability for damages resulting from the reader's misinterpretation of said information resulting from the placement and context of this publication.

Appendix F: Cloud Procurement Questions

SUGGESTED PROCUREMENT PREPARATION QUESTIONS

The questions below highlight several topics to consider when procuring cloud services. This is not an exhaustive list of all considerations, merely an informal guide.

General Questions

1. Who is actively involved in negotiating and reviewing the contract and ancillary Service Level Agreement for cloud services?
   a. Contracting officer/Procurement? Chief information officer? General counsel? Records officer? Privacy officer? E-discovery counsel? Cybersecurity personnel?
   b. What is the process for developing the organization's needs criteria and evaluating the cloud provider proposal and post-award performance?
2. Are the unique operational aspects of the cloud computing environment addressed in the acquisition plan? In particular, how are technical, schedule, and cost risks addressed?
3. Based on market research conducted, does the acquisition plan contemplate use of a system integrator in addition to a Cloud Service Provider (CSP)? Will the CSP be a subcontractor to the system integrator, or will the CSP have a direct contractual relationship with the organization?
4. Is there a clear statement in the contract for cloud services that all data is owned by the organization?
5. Can the cloud provider access or use the organization's information in the cloud?
6. How is the organization's data handled both at rest and in motion in the cloud?

7. Who has access to the organization's data, both in its live and backup state?
8. In the cloud, what geographic boundaries apply to data at rest and what boundaries are traversed by data in motion?
9. Where are the cloud servers that will store organization data physically located?
    a. Can the provider certify where the data is located at any one point in time?
10. How will the cloud provider meet applicable regulatory compliance requirements?
11. What is the potential termination liability?
12. How is the migration of data upon contract termination or completion addressed?
13. How is data destroyed? (e.g., upon request? Periodically?)
    a. Methodology used? (e.g., remove data pointer or overwritten in accordance with security standards)
    b. How does the cloud provider segregate data? If encryption schemes are used, have the design of those schemes been tested for efficacy?
14. If the cloud provider or reseller agreement incorporates URLs into the terms, which policies and terms are being incorporated into the agreement? (URLs are not static and change over time)
    a. What notice is provided to the organization if URLs/policies change? Remedies for organization if new policies or URLs are not acceptable?
15. What remedies are being agreed to for breach or violations of the agreement? Litigation? Mediation? Waiver of right to sue?
    a. Are choice of law and jurisdiction provisions in the agreement appropriate?
16. What rights are the organization waiving, if any?
17. Can the organization manage content in the cloud with its own tools or only through contractor resources?
18. How are upgrades and maintenance (hardware and software) handled? (e.g., who conducts these activities? How often?
19. How are asset availability, compatibility, software updates, and hardware refreshes addressed?
    a. What does the agreement say about estimated outage time the cloud provider foresees for standard hardware and software

updates and the cloud provider's estimated response time should an emergency take the system off line?

20. What responsibility does the cloud provider have for assuring proper patching and versioning control?
    a. What language is in the agreement specifically requiring the cloud provider to take on this responsibility?
21. Is there a discussion of how the cloud provider will continue to maintain or otherwise support the organization's data in a designated format to ensure that the data remains accessible/readable over the life of the data?
22. Did the organization discuss with the cloud provider additional services that may be provided in the cloud, for example e-discovery tools?
23. Does the contract support IPv6 ?
24. If there is confidential statistical information at issue, does the organization agreement ensure proper confidentiality?
25. If there is confidential statistical information at issue, does the organization agreement contain provisions to ensure that either organization staff created and provided appropriate confidential statistical information training guidelines or actually delivered confidential statistical information training to the cloud providers?

Service Level Agreement

1. Does the SLA have clearly defined terms, definitions, and performance parameters?
2. Does the SLA define who is responsible for measuring SLA performance?
3. What enforcement mechanisms are in the SLA (i.e., what penalties does a cloud service provider have for not meeting the SLA performance measures)?

CSP and End-User Agreements

1. Before signing the contract, consider if the organization bound by the cloud provider's Terms of Service (TOS) provisions, in addition to the contract terms and conditions?
    a. If so, how do those terms deal with privacy, cybersecurity, data disclosure/access, etc.?

   b. Is the TOS document proposed by the CSP the standard for industry practice or is it proprietary to that offeror? Can the TOS proposed be revised through negotiation?

E-Discovery Questions

1. How does the organization or CSP halt the routine destruction of organization information in the cloud when a litigation hold has been implemented?
2. Does the organization or the cloud provider's document retention/management plan apply to the organization's data stored in the cloud? Is it understood whose plan has priority in cases when they conflict?
3. Is the metadata preserved when organization data is migrated into, out of, and within the cloud? (i.e., are transfers forensically sound?)
   a. Will the organization be able to search the data in the cloud by metadata field? For example, will the organization be able to batch search for all organization data in the cloud by original date created, file type, or author?
   b. Does the cloud provider ensure that metadata remains linked to records during data migration?
4. Pursuant to the agreement, does the organization itself have the ability to search, retrieve, and review organization data in the cloud? Using the organization's own tools? Organization's e-discovery contractor's tools?
5. What are the organization's file format export options for exporting organization data out of the cloud? What are the expenses associated with this process?
6. Is the cloud provider or a third party providing e-discovery services to the organization?
   a. What specific e-discovery services by the cloud provider are included in the contract?
   b. Will the cloud provider or third party provide training on the e-discovery tools offered?
   c. What project management resources will be available for the e-discovery services?
   d. Have the e-discovery services of the cloud provider or third party been tested? If collection is one of the e-discovery services provided, is the collection method forensically sound?

   e. Can the organization modify the e-discovery protocol/process of the cloud service provider or third party as warranted?
   f. How will e-discovery of data in the cloud be handled during user migration?
   g. Does the cloud provider have forensic or litigation experts available to answer questions and/or sign affidavits regarding the e-discovery services provide in the cloud?
   h. Will the cloud provider and third-party employees sign chain of custody affidavits to demonstrate the integrity of the data when needed for litigation purposes?
   i. If requested, will the cloud provider be able to supply the organization with audit trails, exception reports, and transaction logs?
   j. What if any additional charges will be required for e-discovery services discussed above?
7. Does the contract require that the organization fund or otherwise support the cloud provider's response to a third party?
8. Is the contract clear that the cloud provider and all associated subcontractors shall not release any organization information and/or data without written organization approval or about circumstances when such approval is not needed?
   a. Is the contract clear that the cloud provider will notify the organization within a mutually agreed upon time frame when a request for organization information or data is received by the cloud provider or subcontractor? Who is the designated organization point of contact(s) for this notice?
9. If the organization desired to extract the data so that it can be loaded into a separate review platform, will product from the cloud review platform be transferable to a separate review database?
10. Will attorneys and staff have immediate access to review the data in the review platform if hosted by the cloud provider in the cloud?
    a. Is there 24/7 access to the review platform?
    b. Can approved, non-organization personnel (i.e., other organizations or contractors) access the review platform in the cloud?

Cybersecurity Questions

1. Does the contract include provisions to meet all requirements?
2. If authentication and digital signature are required, is HSPD-12 required as the standard?

3. Does the contract address how standards are applied by cloud providers?
4. What is the CSP's key escrow program for encrypted data and how are the terms and conditions of escrow applied to accessing encrypted data?
5. Is it clear that the organization's owns all network logs, archived data, or other information and access to this must not be restricted?
6. What requirements (clearances, etc.) apply to cloud providers' employees accessing data in a cloud environment?
7. What happens when material infringing on the intellectual property rights of the organization is located in a cloud system deployed by a cloud provider?
    a. What level of indemnity and supporting insurance and/or capital will be provided by the cloud provider?
    b. What access to cloud provider intellectual property rights will the organization need to address various issues, particularly audits?
8. What happens when data is stored or transported in non-bannered environments and devices, particularly if those environments also contain data not belonging to the organization?
9. What security guidelines apply to operations of various cloud components and how are they measured for compliance?
10. Was there an assessment by the organization or cloud provider of how server and telephony locations may impact access and security of the data?

Privacy Questions

1. When implementing a cloud solution, did the organization consider whether any personally identifiable information (PII) would be involved?
2. Did the organization consider whether any other categories of personal information, such as those protected by special privacy legislation and regulations like protected health information (PHI) under the Health Insurance Portability and Accountability Act (HIPAA) Privacy Rule, would be involved?
3. If there is PII at issue, did the organization assess whether the Privacy Act of 1974 applied to the PII in question?
    a. If so, did the organization ensure that the agreement included mandatory FAR language on operating Privacy Act systems of records?

4. If there is PII at issue, did the organization conduct a Privacy Impact Assessment?
5. If there is PII at issue, does the agreement provide instruction and requirements on what to do in the event of a breach or unintentional release of PII?
6. If there is PII at issue, did the organization make any arrangements to ensure that either organization staff created appropriate PII training guidelines or actually delivered PII training to the cloud providers?
7. If there is PII at issue, does the organization agreement provide instruction and requirements on what to do in the event of any request for disclosure, subpoena, or other judicial process seeking access to the records?
8. If there is PII at issue, does the organization agreement limit uses strictly to support the organization and prohibit uses for other purposes?
9. If there is PII at issue, does the organization agreement provide instruction and requirements on terminating storage and deleting data upon expiration of the agreement term and option extensions?
10. If there is PII at issue, does the organization agreement specify whether the data servers, including redundant servers, may be located outside the United States?

Record-Keeping Questions

1. Is the information that will be moved to the cloud-based system adequately scheduled?
2. Does the cloud provider allow the organization to destroy (truly delete) all copies or renditions of records from the cloud when appropriate?
3. Does the cloud provider allow the organization to implement records disposition policies across categories of records?
4. Is the cloud provider using non-propriety file formats so that the data will remain useful outside of the system in which it was created?
5. Is the cloud provider capable of retaining the integrity of the files for the duration in which the organization's records schedule contemplates them being kept?
6. Can the cloud provider migrate records to an organization's in-house servers on demand, in the event it is necessary to do so?

7. If the agreement is for infrastructure as a service, has the organization considered the kind of record material that may be lost if the cloud provider were to change?
8. Did the organization consider if there were special substantive categories of records, such as vital records, being moved to the cloud for which increased records management attention is needed?

Appendix G: Computer Use Policy

In consideration of being authorized by ______ (hereinafter referred to as "Company") to use and access Company computer and communications facilities and resources (hereinafter referred to as "Company facilities and resources"), I agree to comply with the conditions set forth in paragraphs (a) through (j) below

(a) Use of and access to Company facilities and resources is provided only for Company business. I will use or access Company facilities and resources only in ways that are cost-effective and in the Company's best interest. I will not attempt to use or access resources or data that I have not been authorized to use or access.

(b) When a user ID is assigned to me I will change the password so that it is not easily guessed. I will not share, write down, electronically store (without strong encryption), or otherwise disclose the password, authentication code, or any other device associated with any user ID assigned to me. I will take precautions to ensure that no other person makes use of any Company facilities and resources with any of my user IDs.

(c) All data stored on or originating from, and all communications transmitted or received using, Company facilities and resources are considered the property of the Company. Such data and communications are subject to monitoring or review by authorized personnel designated by Company Management. The term *private* as referred to in operating systems, application software, or electronic mail does not refer to personal privacy of an individual's data or mail. I also acknowledge that my use of or access to Company facilities and resources may be monitored at any time to ensure that such use or access is in compliance with these conditions.

(d) Company information in any form shall be safeguarded. I will not copy, or distribute to others, any Company sensitive information except as authorized. I will not upload, publish, transmit, or otherwise disclose any such information concerning the Company, its operations and activities, on or through non-Company networks without prior approval of authorized Company Management.

(e) I will respect and observe the customs, traditions, and laws of the ____ and other countries where ____ has computer assets. I will not use Company facilities and resources to access or attempted access any computer data or computer site, or send or knowingly receive any electronic transmission that contains political, religious, pornographic, indecent, abusive, defamatory, threatening, illegal, or culturally offensive materials. I will report any such material with the source of the site name of such material to the concerned organization.

(f) I will not use Company facilities and resources for unauthorized access to, interference with, or disruption of any software, data, hardware, or system available through Company facilities and resources. I will use standard Company procedures to check all downloaded files for viruses or destructive code prior to using the files on Company facilities and resources.

(g) I will not copy or download any material or any portion thereof protected by copyright without proper authorization from the copyright owner.

(h) I will not connect or use any channel of communication not authorized in compliance with Company policy and guidelines. For any situation in which I am uncertain of what behavior is expected of me in regard to using or accessing company facilities and resources, I will contact the concerned organization.

(i) I will not utilize unauthorized Internet access connections.

(j) I acknowledge that any violations of the above paragraphs (a) through (i) may result in disciplinary action including loss of access to Company facilities and resources, termination of my employment, my contract, or my employer's contract, legal action, or other measures, as appropriate.

ACKNOWLEDGMENT

I acknowledge that I have read and understood the Computer Use Policy as set forth above and I shall abide by them while using or accessing Company computer and communication facilities and resources.

Employee Name ____________ Signature ___________ Date _________

Appendix H: Benchmarking Data Collection Methods

Without proper information it is difficult, if not impossible, to initiate a proper benchmarking effort. Information gathered in this process—called data collection by planners and requirements elicitation by software developers—will enable the organization to develop valid measures against which it should be measured.

INTERVIEWING

The most common method of gathering information is by interviewing people. Interviewing can serve two purposes at the same time. The first is a fact-finding mission to discover what each person's goals and objectives are with respect to the project, and the second is to begin a communications process that enables one to set realistic expectations for the project.

There are a wide variety of stakeholders that can and should be interviewed. Stakeholders are those that have an interest in seeing this project successfully completed—that is, they have a "stake" in the project. Stakeholders include employees, management, clients, and benchmarking partners.

Employees

Interviews have some major obstacles to overcome. Interviewees may resist giving information out of fear, they may relate their perception of how things should be done rather than how they really do them, or they may have difficulty in expressing themselves. On the other hand, the analyst's own mind-set may also act as a filter too. Interviewers sometimes have to set aside their own technical orientation and make the best effort that they can to put themselves in the position that the interviewee is in. This requires that the analyst develop a certain amount of empathy.

An interview outline should contain the following information:

1. Name of interviewee
2. Name of interviewer
3. Date and time
4. Objectives of interview—that is, what areas you are going to explore and what data you are going to collect
5. General observations
6. Unresolved issues and topics not covered
7. Agenda—that is, introduction, questions, summary of major points, closing

Recommended guidelines for handling the employee interview process include the following:

1. Determine the process type to be analyzed (tactical, strategic, hybrid).
2. Make a list of departments involved in the process.
3. For each department, either request or develop an organization chart that shows the departmental breakdown along with the name, extension, and list of responsibilities of each employee.
4. Meet with the department head to request recommendations and then formulate a plan that details which employees are the best interview prospects. The "best" employees to interview are those (a) who are very experienced (i.e., senior) in performing their job function; (b) who may have come from a competing company and, thus, have a unique perspective; (c) who have had a variety of positions within the department or company.
5. Plan to meet with employees from all units of the department. In some cases, you may find that interviewing several employees at a time is more effective than dealing with a single employee as interviewing a group of employees permits them to bounce ideas off each other.
6. If there are many employees within a departmental unit it is not optimum to interview every one. It would be wrong to assume that the more people in a department, the higher the number of interviewees. Instead, sampling should be used. Sampling is used to (a) contain costs; (b) improve effectiveness; (c) speed up the data gathering process; and (d) reduce bias. Systems analysts often use a random sample. However, calculating a sample size based on population size and your desired confidence interval is more accurate. Rather than provide a formula and instructions on how to calculate

sample size I direct the reader to the sample size calculator that is located at http://www.surveysystem.com/sscalc.htm.

7. Carefully plan your interview sessions. Prepare your interview questions in advance. Be familiar with any technical vocabulary your interview subjects might use.
8. No meeting should last longer than an hour. A half hour is optimum. There is a point of diminishing returns with the interview process. Your interviewees are busy and usually easily distracted. Keep in mind that some of your interviewees may be doing this against their will.

Customers

Customers often have experiences with other vendors or suppliers and can offer insight into the processes that other companies use or that they have experienced.

Guidelines for interviewing customers include the following:

1. Work with the sales and/or marketing departments to select knowledgeable and cooperative customers.
2. Prepare an adequate sample size as discussed in the prior section.
3. Carefully plan your interview sessions. Prepare your interview questions in advance.

Companies and Consultants

Another source of potentially valuable information is from other companies in the industry and consultants who specialize in the process areas being examined. While consultants can be easily located and paid for their expert advice, it is wise to tread slowly when working with other companies who are current or potential competitors.

Guidelines for interviewing other companies include the following:

1. Work with senior management and marketing to create a list of potential companies to interview. This list should contain the names of trading partners, vendors (companies that your companies buys from), and competitors.
2. Attend industry trade shows to meet and mingle with competitor employees and listen to speeches made by competitive companies.

3. Attend trade association meetings; sit on policy and standards committees.

Suppliers

Suppliers of the products you are considering are also an important source of ideas. These suppliers know a great deal about how their products are been used in the processes you are examining.

Types of Questions

When interviewing anyone it is important to be aware of how to ask questions properly. Open-ended questions are the best for gaining the most information because they do not limit the individuals to predefined answers. Other benefits of using open-ended questions include putting the interviewee at ease, providing more detail, inducing spontaneity, and being far more interesting for the interviewee. Open-ended questions require more than a yes or no answer (Yate, 1997). An example of an open-ended question is "What types of problems do you see on a daily basis with the current process?" These questions allow individuals to elaborate on the topics and potentially uncover the hidden problems at hand that might not be discoverable with a question that requires a yes or no answer.

One disadvantage of open-ended questions is that they create lengthier interviews. Another disadvantage is that it is easy for the interview to get off track and it takes an interviewer with skill to maintain the interview in an efficient manner.

Closed-ended questions are, by far, the most common questions in interviewing. They are questions that have yes and no answers and are utilized to elicit definitive responses.

Past-performance questions can be useful to determine past experiences with similar problems and issues. An example of how a past-performance question is used is, "In your past job how did you deal with these processes?"

Reflexive questions are appropriate for closing a conversation or moving it forward to a new topic. Reflexive questions are created with a statement of confirmation and by adding a phrase such as *don't you? couldn't you?* or *wouldn't you?*

Mirror questions form a subtle form of probing and are useful in obtaining additional detail on a subject. After the interviewee makes a statement, pause and repeat their statement back with an additional or leading question: "So, when this problem occurs, you simply move on to more pressing issues?"

Often answers do not give the interviewer enough detail so one follows the question with additional questions to prod the interviewee to divulge more details on the subject. For example,

1. Can you give some more details on that?
2. What did you learn from that experience?

Another, more subtle, prodding technique can be used by merely sitting back and saying nothing. The silence will feel uncomfortable causing the interviewee to expand on his or her last statement.

QUESTIONNAIRES/SURVEYS

If there are large numbers of people to interview, one might start with a questionnaire and then follow up with certain individuals that present unusual ideas or issues in the questionnaires. Survey development and implementation is composed of the following tasks, according to Creative Research Systems, makers of a software solution for survey creation (surveysolutions.com):

1. Establish the goals of the project—What you want to learn.
2. Determine your sample—Whom you will interview.
3. Choose interviewing methodology—How you will interview.
4. Create your questionnaire—What you will ask.
5. Pre-test the questionnaire, if practical—Test the questions.
6. Conduct interviews and enter data—Ask the questions.
7. Analyze the data—Produce the reports.

Similar to interviews, questionnaires may contain closed-end or open-ended questions or a hybrid, which is a combination of the two.

Survey creation is quite an art form. Guidelines for creation of a survey include the following:

1. Provide an introduction to the survey. Explain why it's important they respond to it. Thank them for their time and effort.
2. Put all important questions first. It is rare that all questions will be responded to. Those filling out the survey often become tired or bored of the process.
3. Use plenty of white space. Use an appropriate sized font (e.g., Arial), font size (e.g., at least 12), and do skip lines.
4. Use nominal scales if you wish to classify things (e.g., What make is your computer? 1 = Dell, 2 = Gateway, 3 = IBM).
5. Use ordinal scales to imply rank (e.g., How helpful was this class? 3 = not helpful at all, 2 = moderately helpful, 1 = very helpful).
6. Use interval scales when you want to perform some mathematical calculations on the results (e.g., How useful was this class?).

Not useful at all				Very useful
1	2	3	4	5

Survey questions must be carefully worded. Ask yourself the following questions when reviewing each question:

1. Will the words be uniformly understood?

   In general, use words that are part of the commonly shared vocabulary of the customers. For example,
   a. (poor) Rate the proficiencies of the personnel.
   b. (better) Personnel are knowledgeable.
2. Do the questions contain abbreviations or unconventional phrases? Avoid these to the extent possible, unless they are understood by everyone and are the common way of referring to something. For example,
   a. (poor) Rate our walk-in desk.
   b. (better) Personnel at our front desk are friendly.
3. Are the questions too vague?
   Survey items should be clear and unambiguous. If they aren't, the outcome is difficult to interpret. Make sure you ask something that can truly be measured. For example:
   a. (poor) This library should change its procedures.
   b. (better) Did you receive the information you needed?

4. Are the questions too precise?
   Sometimes the attempt to avoid vagueness results in items being too precise and customers may be unable to answer them. For example:
   a. (poor) Each time I visit the library, the waiting line is long.
   b. (better) Generally, the waiting line in the library is long.
5. Are the questions biased?
   Biased questions influence the customer to respond in a manner that does not correctly reflect his/her opinion. For example:
   a. (poor) How much do you like our library?
   b. (better) Would you recommend our library to a friend?
6. Are the questions objectionable?
   Usually this problem can be overcome by asking the question in a less direct way. For example,
   a. (poor) Are you living with someone?
   b. (better) How many people, including yourself, are in your household?
7. Are the questions double-barreled?
   Two separate questions are sometimes combined into one. The customer is forced to give a single response and this, of course, would be ambiguous. For example,
   a. (poor) The library is attractive and well-maintained.
   b. (better) The library is attractive.
8. Are the answer choices mutually exclusive?
   The answer categories must be mutually exclusive and the respondent should not feel forced to choose more than one. For example,
   a. (poor) Scale range: 1, 2–5, 5–9, 9–13, 13 or over
   b. (better) Scale range: 0, 1–5, 6–10, 11–15, 16 or over
9. Are the answer choices mutually exhaustive?
   The response categories provided should be exhaustive. They should include all the possible responses that might be expected. For example:
   a. (poor) Scale range: 1–5, 6–10, 11–15, 16–20
   b. (better) Scale range: 0, 1–5, 6–10, 11–15, 16 or over

Tallying the responses will provide a "score" that assists in making a decision that requires the use of quantifiable information. When using interval scales keep in mind that not all questions will carry the same weight. Hence, it is a good idea to use a weighted average formula during calculation. To do this, assign a "weight" or level of importance to each question. For example, the question above might be assigned a weight of 5 on a scale of 1 to 5 meaning that this is a very important question. On the other hand a question such as: "Was the training center comfortable" might carry a weight of only 3. The weighted average is calculated by multiplying the weight by the score ($w \times s$) to get the final score. Thus the formula is $s_{new} = w \times s$.

There are several problems that might result in a poorly constructed questionnaire. Leniency is caused by respondents who grade non-subjectively—in other words, too easily. Central tendency occurs when respondents rate everything as average. The halo effect occurs when the respondent carries his good or bad impression from one question to the next.

There are several methods that can be used to successfully deploy a survey. The easiest and most accurate is to gather all respondents in a conference room and hand out the survey. For the most part, this is not realistic, so other approaches would be more appropriate. E-mail and traditional mail are two methodologies that work well although you often have to supply an incentive (e.g., prize) to get respondents to fill out those surveys on a timely basis. Web-based surveys (Internet and Intranet) are becoming increasingly popular as they enable the inclusion of demos, audio, and video. For example, a web-based survey on what type of user interface is preferable could have hyperlinks to demos or screen shots of the choices.

OBSERVATION

Observation is an important tool that can provide a wealth of information. There are several forms of observation: silent and directed. In silent observation, the analyst merely sits on the sidelines, pen and pad, and observes what is happening. If it is suitable, a tape recorder or video recorder can record what is being observed. However, this is not recommended if the net result will be several hours of random footage.

Silent observation is best used to capture the spontaneous nature of a particular process or procedure. For example,

1. When customers will be interacting with staff
2. During group meetings
3. On the manufacturing floor
4. In the field

Directed observation provides the analyst with a chance to micro-control a process or procedure so that it is broken down into its observable parts. At one accounting firm a tax system was being developed. The analysts requested that several senior tax accountants be coupled with a junior staff member. The group was given a problem as well as all of the manuals and materials they needed. The junior accountant sat at one end of the table with the pile of manuals and forms while the senior tax accountants sat at the other end. A tough tax problem was posed. The senior tax accountants were directed to think through the process and then direct the junior member to follow through on their directions to solve this problem. The catch was that the senior members could not walk over to the junior person nor touch any of the reference guides. This whole exercise had to be done verbally and using just their memories and expertise. The entire process was videotaped. The net result was that the analyst had a complete record of how to perform one of the critical functions of the new system.

PARTICIPATION

The flip side of observation is participation. Actually becoming a member of the staff, and thereby learning exactly what it is that the staff does so that it might be automated, is an invaluable experience.

DOCUMENTATION

It is logical to assume that there will be a wide variety of documentation available to the analyst. This includes, but is not limited to, the following:

1. Documentation from existing systems. This includes requirements and design specifications, program documentation, user manuals, and help files. This also includes whatever "wish" lists have been developed for the existing system.
2. Archival information
3. Policies and procedures manuals
4. Reports

5. Memos
6. Standards
7. E-mail
8. Minutes from meetings
9. Government and other regulatory guidelines and regulations
10. Industry or association manuals, guidelines, and standards (e.g., accountants are guided not only by in-house "rules and regulations" but by industry and other rules and regulations)

BRAINSTORMING

In a brainstorming session you gather together a group of people, create a stimulating and focused atmosphere, and let people come up with ideas without risk of being ridiculed. Even seemingly stupid ideas may turn out to be "golden."

FOCUS GROUPS

Focus groups are derived from marketing. These are structured sessions where a group of stakeholders are presented with a solution to a problem and then are closely questioned on their views about that solution.

REFERENCE

Yate, M. (1997). *Hiring the best* (4th ed.). Avon, MA: Adams Media Corporation.

Appendix I: Wireless Device Agreement

I, ______________________________, agree to the following terms and conditions in connection with the use of my own or the Organization's device while it is connected to the Organization's wireless network.

DEFINITIONS

All terms used in this agreement shall be defined as set forth in the Enterprise Access Control Security Policies and Standards dated MM/DD/YYYY.

SCOPE

This agreement applies both to (a) individuals who own devices (tablet, smartphone, etc.) connected to the Organization's wireless network and (b) individuals who use Organization-issued devices connected to the Organization's wireless network.

AGREEMENT

The individual noted on this form acknowledges and understands the following

1. The Organization retains, and when reasonable and in pursuit of legitimate needs for supervision, control, securing the environment, and criminal investigations will exercise, the right to inspect any user-owned or Organization-owned computer or device (tablet, smartphone, etc.) that is connected to Organization information

technology resources (ITRS), any data contained therein, and any data sent or received by the device. With respect to user-owned devices, the Organization will exercise this right only insofar as such data is related to the user's work with respect to the Organization or the security of Organization ITRs.

2. Use of Organization ITRS (including without limitation network and systems) constitutes the user's express consent for the Organization to monitor and/or inspect any data that he or she creates or receives, any messages they send or receive, and any websites that they access, insofar as such data, messages, or access relate to the user's work with respect to the Organization or the security of Organization ITRs.
3. Organization-owned devices are authorized for use only by the individual to whom they are issued. Unauthorized users are not permitted to use Organization-owned devices.
4. Users may not tamper with or alter any security controls configured for an Organization-owned device including but not limited to:
    a. Authentication (Logon)
    b. Authorization
    c. Cryptographic techniques
    d. Backups
    e. Malware protection
    f. Mobile device management
5. Users must not store Organization data classified as having high sensitivity on user-owned or Organization-owned devices connected to the Organization's wireless network or unless such data is encrypted and explicitly allowed by the CIO.
6. Users must report a lost or stolen user-owned or Organization-owned device that was connected to the Organization's wireless network immediately upon realization that the device is missing, by contacting Name of Person, Phone number.
7. Users of user-owned or Organization owned devices connected to the Organization's wireless network are required to comply with the ANF Acceptable User Policy at all times when using an Organization issued mobile device.

Signature ____

Date ____

Print Name ____

Title ____

I have received, reviewed, and understand the above Agreement.
Signature ____
Date ____

Appendix J: Mobile Device Management Vendors

Website	Product Name
http://www.absolute.com	Absolute Manage
http://www.air-watch.com/	AirWatch
http://www.amtelnet.com	Amtel MDM
http://www.appblade.com	AppBlade
http://www.apple.com/support/lionserver/profilemanager/	Apple Profile Manager
http://www.boxtone.com	BoxTone
http://www.jamfsoftware.com/solutions/mobile-device-management	Casper Suite
http://www.centrify.com/mobile	Centrify DirectControl for Mobile
http://www.dialogs.de/en_US/produkte/smartman.html	DIALOGS smartMan Device Management
http://www.endpointprotector.com	Endpoint Protector MDM
http://www.excitor.com	EXCITOR DME
http://www.fancyfon.com	FancyFon Mobility Center (FAMOC)
http://www.maas360.com/	Fiberlink MaaS360
http://www.filewave.com	FileWave
http://www.good.com	Good for Enterprise
http://www-142.ibm.com/software/products/us/en/ibmendpmanaformobidevi	IBM Endpoint Manager for Mobile Devices
http://www.landesk.com	LANDesk Mobility Manager
http://www.mcafee.com/us/products/enterprise-mobility-management.aspx	MacAfee EMM
http://www.meraki.com/products/systems-manager/	Meraki System Manager
http://www.mformation.com/enterprise-solutions	Mformation Enterprise Manager
http://www.mobileiron.com	MobileIron
http://www.mobiquant.com/	MobileNX Enterprise Suite
http://www.notifycorp.com/notifymdm/mdm_home/index.html	Notify Technology—NotifyMDM
http://www.nuvizz.com/mdm	nuVizz enterprise MDM
http://www.odysseysoftware.com/	Odyssey Software

Website	Product Name
http://www.pushmanager.com	PUSHMANAGER
http://robotcloud.net	Robot Cloud
http://www.simplemdm.com	SimpleMDM
http://www.sophos.com/en-us/products/mobile/sophos-mobile-control.aspx	Sophos Mobile Control
http://www.soti.net/Mobicontrol/	SOTI MobiControl
http://www.sybase.com/products/mobileenterprise/afaria	Sybase Afaria
http://go.symantec.com/mobile	Symantec Mobile Management
http://www.tangoe.com	Tangoe MDM
http://www.equinux.com/us/products/tarmac/	TARMAC
http://www.zenprise.com	Zenprise

Appendix K: Best Practices Security Checklist

BYOD and other mobile users will necessarily use their browsers to access various services located on the Internet. This checklist can be used to ascertain the level of security these service vendors provide.

GENERAL

	Vulnerability	Description Criteria	Documentation Criteria	Demonstration Criteria
1	Does the vendor have a documented and provable security policy for IT? List of items to be included 1. Statement of purpose 2. Organization structure 3. Physical security 4. Hiring & termination procedures 5. Data classification 6. Access control 7. Operating systems 8. Hardware & software 9. Internet use 10. E-mail 11. Technical support 12. Virus protection, firewall, VPN, remote access 13. Backups & disaster recovery 14. Intrusion detection & incident response 15. Personnel security 16. Software development 17. Outsourcing (off shore) 18. Help desk development	Does not have a policy or cannot describe policy = 0 Can describe policy = 1	Does not have a policy or policy is not documented or documented but does not include any of the noted items = 0 Documented & includes 1–9 of 18 items = 1 Documented & included 10 –18 items = 2	Does not have a policy or site cannot demonstrate policy = 0 Site can demonstrate policy but does not include any of the noted items = 1 Site can demonstrate policy & it includes 1–9 of 18 items = 2 Site can demonstrate policy & it includes 10–18 of 18 items = 3
	Score			

	Vulnerability	Description Criteria	Documentation Criteria	Demonstration Criteria
2	Is this policy reviewed and updated on a regular basis? Question to ask 1. How often is the policy updated?	Does not have a policy or cannot describe review & update process = 0 Can describe review & update process = 1	Does not have a policy or policy review & update is not documented = 0 Can provide documentation for review & update to be completed less frequently than yearly = 1 Can provide documentation for review & update to be completed yearly or more frequently = 2	Not Applicable
	Score			

	Vulnerability	Description Criteria	Documentation Criteria	Demonstration Criteria
3	Does the vendor have management buy-in to security?	Does not have a corporate security policy with management approval or cannot describe their corporate security policy = 0 Can describe their corporate security policy = 1	Does not have a corporate security policy with management approval or cannot provide documentation of their corporate security policy = 0 Can provide documentation of their corporate security policy = 2	Not Applicable
	Score			

ACCESS CONTROL

	Vulnerability	Description Criteria	Documentation Criteria	Demonstration Criteria
4	Is the application PKI enabled for the client?	Application is not PKI enabled for the client = 0 Can describe how their application uses PKI for their client = 1	Cannot provide documentation that describes application PKI enabled for the client = 0 Can provide documentation the application uses PKI = 2	Cannot demonstrate the application is PKI enabled = 0 Can demonstrate the application uses PKI = 2
	Score			

	Vulnerability	Description Criteria	Documentation Criteria	Demonstration Criteria
5	Is the application PKI enabled for the server and configured to require PKI for authentication?	Application is not PKI enabled for server & configured to require PKI for authentication = 0 Can describe how their application is PKI enabled for the server & configured to require PKI for authentication = 1	Application is not PKI enabled for server & configured to require PKI for authentication or cannot provide documentation = 0 Can provide documentation application is PKI enabled for the server & configured to require PKI for authentication = 2	Application is not PKI enabled for the server & configured to require PKI for authentication or cannot demonstrate = 0 Can demonstrate the application is PKI enabled for the server & configured to require PKI for authentication = 2
	Score			

	Vulnerability	Description Criteria	Documentation Criteria	Demonstration Criteria
6	Does the vendor have robust revocation checking?	Does not have robust revocation checking = 0 Does have robust revocation checking = 1	Do not have robust revocation checking or cannot provide documentation = 0 Can provide documentation = 2	Do not have robust revocation checking or cannot demonstrate = 0 Can demonstrate process = 3
	Score			

	Vulnerability	Description Criteria	Documentation Criteria	Demonstration Criteria
7	Is there a registration process for new users? Question to ask 1. Is the registration process provided to new users?	Does not have registration process for new users = 0 Does have registration process for new users = 1	Does not have registration process for new users or process is not documented = 0 Can provide documentation but it is not provided to new users = 1 Can provide documentation & it is provided to new users = 2	Does not have registration process for new users or cannot demonstrate registration process = 0 Can demonstrate new user registration process = 3
	Score			

	Vulnerability	Description Criteria	Documentation Criteria	Demonstration Criteria
8	Does the vendor have an access request form? List of Items to be included 1. *Type of request (Initial, Modification, Deactivation) 2. *System name 3. System location 4. *Date 5. *Name 6. Social Security number/ employee number 7. Organization 8. Phone number 9. *E-mail address 10. Job title 11. Physical address 12. *Citizenship 13. User agreement 14. *Justification for access/ need to know 15. *Type of access 16. *Supervisor approval	Does not have a form = 0 Can describe form = 1	Does not have a form or cannot provide form = 0 Can provide blank form & it contains all of the asterisked items = 1 Can provide blank form & it contains all of the asterisked items & all of the non-asterisked items = 2	Does not have a form or cannot provide form = 0 Can provide completed form & it contains all of the asterisked items = 1 Can provide completed form & it contains all of the asterisked items & 1–4 of the 7 non-asterisked items = 2 Can provide completed form & it contains all of the asterisked items & 5–7 of the 7 non-asterisked items = 3

17. *Security manager verification
18. *Verification of need to know

Score

	Vulnerability	Description Criteria	Documentation Criteria	Demonstration Criteria
9	Does the vendor have a role-based policy for user access? Questions to ask 1. Do administrators have an account for administrator work only & have an additional account for other purposes? 2. Are administrator privileges only granted to administrators & not to all users? 3. Are limits put on each user who has access to the application? 4. Are user privileges based on need-to-know? 5. Are permissions periodically reviewed to include superusers?	Does not have a role-based policy for user access or cannot describe their role-based policy = 0 Can describe their role-based policy for user access = 1	Does not have a role-based policy for user access or cannot provide documentation or can provide documentation but the documentation includes answers to only 1–2 of questions = 0 Can provide documentation & the documentation includes answers to 3–4 of questions = 1 Can provide documentation & the documentation includes answers to all of the 5 questions = 2	Does not have a role-based policy for user access or cannot demonstrate their policy = 0 Can demonstrate the answers to 1–2 of 5 questions = 1 Can demonstrate the answers to 3–4 of 5 questions = 2 Can demonstrate the answers to 5 of questions = 3
	Score			

	Vulnerability	Description Criteria	Documentation Criteria	Demonstration Criteria
10	Is there a process for checking for inactive and terminated users?	Does not have a process for checking for inactive & terminated users or cannot describe process = 0 Can describe their process for checking for inactive & terminated users = 1	Does not have a process for checking for inactive & terminated users or the process is not documented = 0 Can provide documentation for a manual process = 1 Can provide documentation for an automated process = 2	Does not have a process for checking for inactive & terminated users or the process cannot be demonstrated = 0 Can demonstrate manual process = 2 Can demonstrate automated process = 3
	Score			

	Vulnerability	Description Criteria	Documentation Criteria	Demonstration Criteria
11	What is the period for revocation of users (the length of the contract, one year or whichever comes first)? Question to ask 1. What is the length of the revocation period?	Does not have a period for revocation of users or cannot describe period of revocation = 0 Can describe period for revocation of users = 1	Does not have a period for revocation of users or cannot provide documentation = 0 Can provide documentation for revocation of users & the period is less frequently than the length of the contract or one year = 1 Can provide documentation for revocation of users & the period is the length of the contract, or one year or more frequently = 2	Does not have a period for revocation of users or cannot demonstrate that users are revoked = 0 Can demonstrate the revocation of users & the period is less frequently than the length of the contract or one year = 2 Can demonstrate the revocation of users & the period is the length of the contract, or one year or more frequently = 3
	Score			

	Vulnerability	Description Criteria	Documentation Criteria	Demonstration Criteria
12	Does the vendor have a strong password policy? List of items to be included 1. A minimum of nine characters 2. Includes at least one uppercase alphabetic character 3. Includes at least one lowercase alphabetic character 4. Includes at least one non-alphanumeric (special) character 5. Includes at least one numeric character 6. Expires after 60 days 7. Is different than the previous 10 passwords used 8. Is changeable by the administrator at any time 9. Is changeable by the associated user only once in a 24-hour period (for human user accounts)	Does not have a password policy or cannot describe policy = 0 Can describe their password policy = 1	Does not have a password policy or policy is not documented = 0 Can provide documentation for their policy & it includes 1–5 of listed items = 1 Can provide documentation for their policy & it includes 6–10 of listed items = 2	Does not have a password policy or cannot demonstrate their policy = 0 Can demonstrate their policy & it includes 1–4 of listed items = 1 Can demonstrate their policy & it includes 5–7 of listed items = 2 Can demonstrate their policy & it includes 8–10 of listed items = 3

	Vulnerability		Description Criteria	Documentation Criteria	Demonstration Criteria
	10. Is not changeable by users other than the administrator or the user with which the password is associated				
		Score			

	Vulnerability		Description Criteria	Documentation Criteria	Demonstration Criteria
13	Does the vendor permit the use of default accounts, default passwords, community strings, or other default access control mechanisms?		Uses default access control mechanisms or cannot describe the prohibition of these mechanisms = 0 Can describe how they do not use default access control mechanisms = 1	Uses default access control mechanisms or cannot provide documentation for prohibiting these mechanisms = 0 Can provide documentation that no default access control mechanisms are used = 2	Uses default access control mechanisms or cannot demonstrate that these are not in use = 0 Can demonstrate that no default access control mechanisms are used = 3
		Score			

	Vulnerability		Description Criteria	Documentation Criteria	Demonstration Criteria
14	Does the vendor permit the use of shared accounts?		Permits shared accounts or cannot describe how shared accounts are not permitted = 0 Can describe how shared accounts are not permitted = 1	Permits shared accounts or cannot provide documentation that prohibits shared accounts = 0 Can provide documentation that prohibits shared accounts = 2	Permits shared accounts or cannot demonstrate that no shared accounts are used = 0 Can demonstrate that no shared accounts are used = 3
		Score			

CONFIDENTIALITY

	Vulnerability	Description Criteria	Documentation Criteria	Demonstration Criteria
15	Does the vendor utilize appropriate file permissions on sensitive data? Question to ask 1. Are file permissions based on roles & need to know?	Does not have appropriate file permissions on sensitive data or cannot describe their file permissions on sensitive data = 0 Can describe their file permissions & they are appropriate for sensitive data = 1	Does not have appropriate file permissions on sensitive data or cannot provide documentation on sensitive data file permissions = 0 Can provide documentation that system file permissions are appropriate for sensitive data = 1 Can provide documentation that system file & application file permissions are appropriate for sensitive data = 2	Does not have appropriate file permissions on sensitive data or cannot demonstrate file permissions on sensitive data = 0 Can demonstrate that system file permissions are appropriate for sensitive data = 2 Can demonstrate that system file & application file permissions are appropriate for sensitive data = 3
	Score			

	Vulnerability	Description Criteria	Documentation Criteria	Demonstration Criteria
16	Are authentication credentials stored in an encrypted format?	Authentication credentials are not stored in encrypted format or cannot describe how encryption is used to store authentication credentials = 0 Can describe how authentication credentials are stored in encrypted format = 1	Authentication credentials are not stored in encrypted format or cannot provide documentation of the requirement = 0 Can provide documentation that authentication credentials are stored in encrypted format = 2	Authentication credentials are not stored in encrypted format or cannot demonstrate that authentication credentials are stored in encrypted format = 0 Can demonstrate that authentication credentials are stored in encrypted format = 3
	Score			

	Vulnerability		Description Criteria	Documentation Criteria	Demonstration Criteria
17	Is SSL used with sensitive web traffic?		Cannot describe how SSL is used = 0 Can describe how SSL is used with sensitive web traffic = 1	SSL is not used for sensitive web traffic = 0 Can provide documentation that SSL is used with unclassified, sensitive web traffic = 2	SSL is not used for sensitive web traffic or cannot demonstrate how it is used = 0 Can demonstrate that SSL is used with sensitive web traffic = 3
		Score			

	Vulnerability		Description Criteria	Documentation Criteria	Demonstration Criteria
18	Is SSL used to protect sensitive data and data in transit?		SSL is not used to protect sensitive data & data in transit or cannot describe how it is used = 0 Can describe how SSL is used to protect sensitive data & data in transit = 1	SSL is not used to protect sensitive data & data in transit or cannot provide documentation that states this requirement = 0 Can provide documentation that SSL is used to protect sensitive data & data in transit = 2	SSL is not used to protect sensitive data & data in transit or cannot demonstrate this requirement = 0 Can demonstrate that SSL is used to protect sensitive data & data in transit = 3
		Score			

	Vulnerability		Description Criteria	Documentation Criteria	Demonstration Criteria
19	Are the authentication credentials encrypted during transmission?		Authentication credentials are not encrypted during transmission or cannot describe how they are encrypted = 0 Can describe how authentication credentials are encrypted during transmission = 1	Authentication credentials are not encrypted during transmission or cannot provide documentation of this requirement = 0 Can provide documentation that authentication credentials are encrypted during transmission = 2	Authentication credentials are not encrypted during transmission or cannot demonstrate this requirement = 0 Can demonstrate that authentication credentials are encrypted during transmission = 3
		Score			

	Vulnerability		Description Criteria	Documentation Criteria	Demonstration Criteria
20	Does the vendor maintain separation of data to prevent disclosure of information?		Does not maintain separation of data or cannot describe how data will be separated = 0 Can describe how they will maintain separation of data = 1	Does not maintain separation of data or cannot provide documentation requiring separation of data = 0 Can provide documentation that vendor does maintain separation of data = 2	Does not maintain separation of data or cannot demonstrate the separation of data = 0 Can demonstrate that vendor does maintain separation of data = 3
		Score			

INTEGRITY

	Vulnerability		Description Criteria	Documentation Criteria	Demonstration Criteria
21	Does the vendor have a trust mark or site seal to validate users have reached the vendor site?		Does not have a trust mark or site seal or cannot describe their trust mark or site seal = 0 Has a trust mark or site seal = 1	Does not have a trust mark or site seal or this requirement is not documented = 0 Can provide documentation that vendor has a trust mark or site seal = 2	Does not have a trust mark or site seal or cannot show their trust meal or site seal = 0 Can show that vendor has a trust mark or site seal = 3
		Score			

	Vulnerability		Description Criteria	Documentation Criteria	Demonstration Criteria
22	Are the documents loaded to the vendor site scanned for viruses prior to posting?		Does not virus scan documents prior to posting or cannot describe their scanning process = 0 Can describe their process for virus scanning documents prior to posting = 1	Does not virus scan documents prior to posting or process is not documented = 0 Can provide documentation that vendor does virus scan documents prior to posting = 2	Does not virus scan documents prior to posting or cannot demonstrate scanning = 0 Can demonstrate that vendor does virus scan documents prior to posting = 3
		Score			

	Vulnerability		Description Criteria	Documentation Criteria	Demonstration Criteria
23	Are virus signatures updated at least every 14 days? Question to ask 1. Is the process manual or automated?		Virus signatures are not updated at least every 14 days or vendor cannot describe update process = 0 Can describe process used to update virus signatures at least every 14 days = 1	Virus signatures are not updated at least every 14 days or update process is not documented = 0 Can provide documentation that virus signatures are updated at least every 14 days using a manual process = 1 Can provide documentation that virus signatures are updated at least every 14 days using a automated process = 2	Virus signatures are not updated at least every 14 days or update process cannot be demonstrated = 0 Can demonstrate that virus signatures are updated at least every 14 days using a manual process = 2 Can demonstrate that virus signatures are updated at least every 14 days using a automated process = 3
		Score			

	Vulnerability	Description Criteria	Documentation Criteria	Demonstration Criteria
24	Does the vendor scan the server for viruses on a regular basis? Question to ask 1. How often does the vendor scan for viruses?	Does not scan for viruses on a regular basis or cannot describe scanning process = 0 Can describe scanning process & how frequently scanning is done = 1	Does not scan for viruses on a regular basis or cannot provide documentation of scanning process = 0 Can provide documentation that vendor scans for viruses less frequently than weekly = 1 Can provide documentation that vendor scans for viruses weekly or more frequently = 2	Does not scan for viruses on a regular basis or cannot demonstrate scanning = 0 Can demonstrate that vendor scans for viruses less frequently than weekly = 2 Can demonstrate that vendor scans for viruses weekly or more frequently = 3
	Score			

	Vulnerability	Description Criteria	Documentation Criteria	Demonstration Criteria
25	Does the vendor scan the server for spyware on a regular basis? Question to ask 1. How often does the vendor scan for spyware?	Does not scan for spyware on a regular basis or cannot describe scanning process = 0 Can describe process used for scanning for spyware & how frequently scanning is completed = 1	Does not scan for spyware on a regular basis or cannot provide documentation of process = 0 Can provide documentation that vendor scans for spyware less frequently than weekly = 1 Can provide documentation that vendor scans for spyware weekly or more frequently = 2	Does not scan for spyware on a regular basis or cannot demonstrate scanning process = 0 Can demonstrate that vendor scans for spyware less frequently than weekly = 2 Can demonstrate that vendor scans for spyware weekly or more frequently = 3
	Score			

	Vulnerability	Description Criteria	Documentation Criteria	Demonstration Criteria
26	Does the vendor scan the server for adware on a regular basis? Question to ask 1. How often does the vendor scan for adware?	Vendor does not scan for adware on a regular basis or cannot describe scanning process = 0 Vendor can describe process used to scan for adware & how frequently scanning is completed = 1	Vendor does not scan for adware on a regular basis or cannot provide documentation of scanning = 0 Can provide documentation that vendor scans for adware less frequently than weekly = 1 Can provide documentation that vendor scans for adware weekly or more frequently = 2	Vendor does not scan for adware on a regular basis or cannot demonstrate scanning process = 0 Can demonstrate that vendor scans for adware less frequently than weekly = 2 Can demonstrate that vendor scans for adware weekly or more frequently = 3
	Score			

AVAILABILITY

	Vulnerability	Description Criteria	Documentation Criteria	Demonstration Criteria
27	Does the vendor have a policy for backups? List of items to be Included 1. Schedule for regular backups 2. Backups to be stored off-site 3. Recovery plan 4. Clearly defined activities & responsibilities of individuals 5. Policy should be tested annually 6. Personnel trained annually 7. Backups should maintain separation of data	Does not have a policy for backups or cannot describe backup policy = 0 Vendor can describe policy for backups = 1	Does not have a policy for backups or cannot provide documentation of policy or policy does not include any of the items listed = 0 Can provide documentation that vendor has policy & it includes 1–3 of listed items = 1 Can provide documentation that vendor has policy & it includes 4–7 of listed items = 2	Does not have a policy for backups or cannot demonstrate backups = 0 Can demonstrate that vendor has policy and it includes 1–2 of listed items = 1 Can demonstrate that vendor has policy and it includes 3–4 of listed items = 2 Can demonstrate that vendor has policy and it includes 5–7 of listed items = 3
	Score			

	Vulnerability	Description Criteria	Documentation Criteria	Demonstration Criteria
28	Does the vendor have a documented, executable process for backups? Question to ask 1. Is the process manual or automated?	Does not have a backup process or cannot describe the process = 0 Can describe backup process = 1	Does not have a backup process or cannot provide documentation of their backup process = 0 Can provide documentation of the manual backup process = 1 Can provide documentation of the automated backup process = 2	Does not have a backup process or cannot demonstrate backup process = 0 Can demonstrate the manual backup process = 2 Can demonstrate the automated backup process = 3
	Score			

	Vulnerability	Description Criteria	Documentation Criteria	Demonstration Criteria
29	Does the backup process include operating system files? Question to ask 1. Is the process manual or automated?	Backup process does not include operating system files or cannot describe process = 0 Can describe backup process & it includes operating system files = 1	Backup process does not include operating system files or cannot provide documentation of process = 0 Can provide documentation of the manual backup process that includes operating system files = 1 Can provide documentation of the automated backup process that includes operating system files = 2	Backup process does not include operating system files or cannot demonstrate process = 0 Can demonstrate the manual backup process that includes operating system files = 2 Can demonstrate the automated backup process that includes operating system files = 3
	Score			

	Vulnerability	Description Criteria	Documentation Criteria	Demonstration Criteria
30	Does the backup process include user data? Question to ask 1. Is the process manual or automated?	Backup process does not include user data or cannot describe process = 0 Can describe backup process & it includes user data = 1	Backup process does not include user data or cannot provide documentation of process = 0 Can provide documentation of the manual backup process = 1 Can provide documentation of the automated backup process = 2	Backup process does not include user data or cannot demonstrate process = 0 Can demonstrate the manual backup process = 2 Can demonstrate the automated backup process = 3
	Score			

	Vulnerability		Description Criteria	Documentation Criteria	Demonstration Criteria
31	Is the backup process tested on a regular basis?		Backup process is not tested on a regular basis or cannot describe test of backup process = 0 Can describe backup process being tested on a regular basis = 1	Backup process is not tested on a regular basis or cannot provide documentation of testing backup process = 0 Can provide documentation that backup process is tested on a regular basis = 2	Backup process is not tested on a regular basis or cannot demonstrate that backup process has been tested on a regular basis = 0 Can demonstrate that backup process is tested on a regular basis = 3
		Score			

	Vulnerability		Description Criteria	Documentation Criteria	Demonstration Criteria
32	Are the results of the backup process verified?		Backup process results are not verified or cannot describe verification process = 0 Can describe verification of backup process = 1	Backup process results are not verified or cannot provide documentation of verification of backups = 0 Can provide documentation that backup process results are verified = 2	Backup process results are not verified or cannot demonstrate verification of backup process = 0 Can demonstrate that backup process results are verified = 3
		Score			

	Vulnerability		Description Criteria	Documentation Criteria	Demonstration Criteria
33	Are the backups stored off-site?		Backups are not stored off-site or cannot describe where backups are stored = 0 Can describe off-site storage of backups = 1	Backups are not stored off-site or cannot provide documentation that requires backups to be stored off-site = 0 Can provide documentation that backups are stored off-site = 2	Backups are not stored off-site or cannot demonstrate that backups are stored off-site = 0 Can demonstrate that backups are stored off-site = 3
		Score			

	Vulnerability		Description Criteria	Documentation Criteria	Demonstration Criteria
34	Does the vendor have a restore and recovery process? Things to consider 1. Restore & recovery node 2. High availability failover Question to ask 1. Is the process manual or automated?	Score	Does not have a restore & recovery process or cannot describe their process = 0 Can describe their restore & recovery process = 1	Does not have restore & recovery process or cannot provide documentation of this process = 0 Can provide documentation of manual restore & recovery process = 1 Can provide documentation of automated restore & recovery process = 2	Does not have a restore & recovery process or cannot demonstrate their process = 0 Can demonstrate manual restore & recovery process = 2 Can demonstrate automated restore & recovery process = 3

	Vulnerability		Description Criteria	Documentation Criteria	Demonstration Criteria
35	Is the restore and recovery process tested on a regular basis?	Score	Does not test their restore & recovery process or cannot describe testing their process = 0 Can describe testing of restore & recovery process = 1	Does not test their restore & recovery process or cannot provide documentation of this process = 0 Can provide documentation of the testing of restore & recovery process = 2	Does not test their restore & recovery process or cannot demonstrate this process = 0 Can demonstrate the testing of restore & recovery process = 3

	Vulnerability		Description Criteria	Documentation Criteria	Demonstration Criteria
36	Have the results of the recovery and restore process been verified?	Score	Results are not verified or cannot describe verification process = 0 Can describe verification of results = 1	Results are not verified or cannot provide documentation of verification process = 0 Can provide documentation that results have been verified = 2	Results are not verified or cannot demonstrate verification of results = 0 Can demonstrate that results have been verified = 3

	Vulnerability	Description Criteria	Documentation Criteria	Demonstration Criteria
37	Does the application support a maximum number of concurrent users based on contract requirements without impact to availability of application? Things to consider 1. Scalability	Application does not have maximum number of concurrent users or cannot describe maximum number of concurrent users = 0 Can describe that application does have a maximum number of concurrent users = 1	Application does not have maximum number of concurrent users or cannot provide documentation of this number = 0 Can provide documentation that application has maximum number of concurrent users but maximum number is not scalable = 1 Can provide documentation that application has maximum number of concurrent users & maximum number is scalable = 2	Application does not have maximum number of concurrent users or cannot demonstrate the maximum number of concurrent users = 0 Can demonstrate that application has maximum number of concurrent users but this maximum number is not scalable = 2 Can demonstrate that application has maximum number of concurrent users & this maximum number is scalable = 3
	Score			

	Vulnerability	Description Criteria	Documentation Criteria	Demonstration Criteria
38	Does the application limit the maximum number of concurrent sessions per user?	Application does not have a maximum number of concurrent sessions per user or cannot describe maximum number = 0 Can describe that application has maximum number of concurrent sessions per user = 1	Application does not have a maximum number of concurrent sessions per user or cannot provide documentation = 0 Can provide documentation that application has maximum number of concurrent sessions per user = 2	Application does not have a maximum number of concurrent sessions per user or cannot demonstrate the maximum number sessions = 0 Can demonstrate that application has maximum number of concurrent sessions per user = 3
	Score			

	Vulnerability	Description Criteria	Documentation Criteria	Demonstration Criteria
39	Does the vendor have an alternative power supply or uninterruptible power supply in support of the application and data transmissions?	Vendor does not have alternative or uninterruptible power supply or cannot describe alternative power supply = 0 Can describe their alternative or uninterruptible power supply = 1	Vendor does not have alternative or uninterruptible power supply or cannot provide documentation of power supply = 0 Can provide documentation of alternative or uninterruptible power supply = 2	Vendor does not have alternative or uninterruptible power supply or cannot demonstrate this power supply = 0 Can demonstrate alternative or uninterruptible power supply = 3
	Score			

	Vulnerability	Description Criteria	Documentation Criteria	Demonstration Criteria
40	Does the vendor provide the appropriate level of redundancy of all application components based on contract requirements?	Does not provide appropriate redundancy or cannot describe redundancy = 0 Can describe how they provide appropriate redundancy = 1	Does not provide appropriate redundancy or cannot provide documentation of redundancy = 0 Can provide documentation of appropriate redundancy = 2	Does not provide appropriate redundancy or cannot demonstrate redundancy = 0 Can demonstrate appropriate redundancy = 3
	Score			

	Vulnerability	Description Criteria	Documentation Criteria	Demonstration Criteria
41	Does the vendor utilize a system performance monitoring tool to analyze performance in real time?	Does not utilize system performance tool or cannot describe how they use this tool = 0 Can describe how they utilize a system performance tool = 1	Does not utilize system performance tool or cannot provide documentation of utilizing tool = 0 Can provide documentation of a system performance tool = 2	Does not utilize system performance tool or cannot demonstrate this tool = 0 Can demonstrate a system performance tool = 3
	Score			

NON-REPUDIATION

	Vulnerability	Description Criteria	Documentation Criteria	Demonstration Criteria
42	Does the vendor use cryptography to implement encryption, key exchange, digital signature, and hash?	Does not use cryptography or cannot describe how it used in their application = 0 Can describe how they use cryptography = 1	Does not use cryptography or cannot provide documentation of using cryptography in their application = 0 Can provide documentation of cryptography = 2	Does not use cryptography or cannot demonstrate use of cryptography = 0 Can demonstrate use of cryptography = 3
	Score			

	Vulnerability	Description Criteria	Documentation Criteria	Demonstration Criteria
43	Does the vendor perform auditing? List of items to be included 1. Operating system 2. Application 3. Web server 4. Web services 5. Network devices 6. Database 7. Wireless	Does not perform auditing or cannot describe how they perform auditing = 0 Can describe their auditing process = 1	Does not perform auditing or cannot provide documentation requiring auditing = 0 Can provide documentation of auditing & auditing includes 1–3 of listed items = 1 Can provide documentation auditing & auditing includes 4–7 of listed items = 2	Does not perform auditing or cannot demonstrate auditing = 0 Can demonstrate auditing & auditing includes 1–2 of listed items = 1 Can demonstrate auditing & auditing includes 3–4 of listed items = 2 Can demonstrate auditing & auditing includes 5–7 of listed items = 3
	Score			

	Vulnerability	Description Criteria	Documentation Criteria	Demonstration Criteria
44	Does the vendor audit both success and failure of logon attempts to the application?	Does not audit both success & failure of logon attempts to the application or cannot describe how they audit these events = 0 Can describe how they audit both success & failure of logon attempts to application = 1	Does not audit both success & failure of logon attempts to the application or cannot provide documentation of auditing both events = 0 Can provide documentation of auditing both success & failure of logon attempts to application = 2	Does not audit both success & failure of logon attempts to application or cannot demonstrate auditing of these events = 0 Can demonstrate of auditing both success & failure of logon attempts to application = 3
	Score			

	Vulnerability		Description Criteria	Documentation Criteria	Demonstration Criteria
45	Does the vendor have a policy for reviewing audit logs? Things to consider 1. Frequency of review (daily, weekly)		Does not have policy for reviewing audit logs or cannot describe their policy = 0 Can describe their policy for reviewing audit logs = 1	Does not have policy for reviewing audit logs or cannot provide documentation of policy = 0 Can provide copy of policy for reviewing audit logs & reviews are completed less frequently than daily = 1 Can provide copy of policy for reviewing audit logs & reviews are completed daily or more frequently = 2	Does not have policy for reviewing audit logs or cannot demonstrate policy = 0 Can demonstrate reviewing logs & reviews are done less frequently than weekly = 1 Can demonstrate reviewing logs & reviews are completed weekly or more frequently but less frequently than daily = 2 Can demonstrate reviewing logs & reviews are completed daily or more frequently = 3
		Score			

	Vulnerability		Description Criteria	Documentation Criteria	Demonstration Criteria
46	What events does the vendor log? List of items to be included 1. Audit all failures 2. Successful logon attempt 3. Failure of logon attempt 4. Permission changes 5. Unsuccessful file access 6. Creating users & objects 7. Deletion & modification of system files 8. Registry key/kernal changes		Does not audit or vendor's auditing does not include any of the listed items or cannot describe what events are audited = 0 Can describe events audited = 1	Does not audit or vendor's auditing does not include any of the listed items or cannot provide documentation of events in log = 0 Can provide documentation for auditing & it includes auditing 1–4 of items = 1 Can provide copy of policy for auditing & it includes auditing 5–8 of items = 2	Does not audit or vendor's auditing does not include any listed items or cannot demonstrate events in log = 0 Can show audit log & log contains 1–2 of listed items = 1 Can show audit log & log contains 3–4 of listed items = 2 Can show audit log & log contains 5–8 of listed items = 3
		Score			

	Vulnerability	Description Criteria	Documentation Criteria	Demonstration Criteria
47	What events does the application log? List of items to be included 1. Startup & shutdown 2. Authentication 3. Authorization/ permission granting 4. Actions by trusted users 5. Process invocation 6. Controlled access to data by individually authenticated user 7. Unsuccessful data access attempt 8. Data deletion 9. Data transfer 10. Application configuration change 11. Application of confidentiality or integrity labels to data 12. Override or modification of data labels or markings 13. Output to removable media 14. Output to a printer	Application does not audit or cannot describe what application is logging = 0 Can describe what application audit = 1	Application does not audit or cannot provide documentation for application auditing = 0 Can provide documentation for application auditing & it includes auditing 1–7 of listed items = 1 Can provide documentation for application auditing & it includes auditing 8–14 of listed items = 2	Application does not audit or cannot demonstrate what application is logging = 0 Can show application audit log & log contains 1–5 of listed items = 1 Can show application audit log & log contains 6–10 of listed items = 2 Can show application audit log & log contains 11–14 of listed items = 3
	Score			

PROTECTION

	Vulnerability	Description Criteria	Documentation Criteria	Demonstration Criteria
48	Does the vendor follow some type of guidance to secure the vendor computing and network infrastructure?	Follows no guidance for securing their computing & network infrastructure or cannot describe what guidance they follow = 0 Follows guidance for securing their computing & network infrastructure & can describe what that guidance is = 1	Follows no guidance for securing their computing & network infrastructure or cannot provide documentation of guidance = 0 Can provide copy of guidance but it does not include defense in depth = 1 Can provide copy of guidance & it includes defense in depth = 2	Follows no guidance for securing their computing & network infrastructure or cannot demonstrate guidance = 0 Can demonstrate their security guidance but it does not include defense in depth = 2 Can demonstrate their security guidance & it includes defense in depth = 3
	Score			

	Vulnerability	Description Criteria	Documentation Criteria	Demonstration Criteria
49	Does the vendor employ a firewall?	Does not employ firewall or cannot describe their firewall = 0 Does employ firewall & can describe their firewall = 1	Does not employ firewall or cannot provide documentation of employing firewall = 0 Can provide documentation of employment of firewall = 2	Does not employ firewall or cannot demonstrate employment of firewall = 0 Can demonstrate employment of firewall = 3
	Score			

	Vulnerability	Description Criteria	Documentation Criteria	Demonstration Criteria
50	Are the firewall ACLs set to deny by default, allow by exception?	Does not have firewall ACLs set to deny by default, allow by exception or cannot describe their firewall ACLs = 0 Has firewall ACLs set to deny by default, allow by exception & can describe their ACLs = 1	Does not have firewall ACLs set to deny by default, allow by exception or cannot provide documentation of firewall ACLs = 0 Can provide documentation of firewall ACLs but they are not set to deny by default, allow by exception = 1 Can provide documentation of firewall ACLs & they are set to deny by default, allow by exception = 2	Does not have firewall ACLs set to deny by default, allow by exception or cannot demonstrate their firewall ACLs = 0 Can demonstrate firewall ACLs but they are not set to deny by default, allow by exception = 2 Can demonstrate firewall ACLs & they are set to deny by default, allow by exception = 3
	Score			

	Vulnerability	Description Criteria	Documentation Criteria	Demonstration Criteria
51	Does the vendor deploy and monitor network intrusion detection tools?	Does not deploy & monitor network intrusion detection tools = 0 Vendor does deploy & monitor network intrusion detection tools = 1	Does not deploy & monitor network intrusion detection tools = 0 Can provide documentation for deploying & monitoring network intrusion detection tools = 2	Does not deploy & monitor network intrusion detection tools = 0 Can demonstrate that network intrusion detection tools have been deployed & are monitored = 3
	Score			

	Vulnerability	Description Criteria	Documentation Criteria	Demonstration Criteria
52	Does the vendor deploy and monitor host-based intrusion detection tools?	Does not deploy & monitor host-based intrusion detection tools or cannot describe their use of HIDs = 0 Can describe their use of host-based intrusion detection tools = 1	Does not deploy & monitor host-based intrusion detection tools or cannot provide documentation of deployment & monitoring = 0 Can provide documentation for deploying & monitoring host-based intrusion detection tools = 2	Does not deploy & monitor host-based intrusion detection tools or cannot demonstrate their HIDs = 0 Can demonstrate that host-based intrusion detection tools have been deployed & are monitored = 3
	Score			

	Vulnerability	Description Criteria	Documentation Criteria	Demonstration Criteria
53	Does the vendor have strong two-factor authentication for management/ admin traffic? Things to consider 1. Something you have 2. Something you are 3. Something you know	Does not have strong two-factor authentication for management/ admin traffic or cannot describe their two-factor authentication = 0 Can describe their strong two-factor authentication for management/ admin traffic = 1	Does not have strong two-factor authentication for management/ admin traffic or cannot provide documentation of their strong two-factor authentication = 0 Can provide documentation for strong two-factor authentication for management/ admin traffic = 2	Does not have strong two-factor authentication for management/ admin traffic or cannot demonstrate two-factor authentication = 0 Can demonstrate strong two-factor authentication for management/ admin traffic = 3
	Score			

	Vulnerability	Description Criteria	Documentation Criteria	Demonstration Criteria
54	Does the vendor have a patch management process?	Does not have patch management process or cannot describe their process = 0 Can describe their patch management process = 1	Does not have patch management process or cannot provide documentation for patch management process = 0 Can provide documentation for patch management process = 2	Does not have patch management process or cannot demonstrate patch management process = 0 Can demonstrate patch management process = 3
	Score			

	Vulnerability	Description Criteria	Documentation Criteria	Demonstration Criteria
55	What is the vendor's patch management process? Question to ask 1. Does the vendor subscribe to the application vendor hardware/software notification sites for the latest patch notifications? 2. Is there a schedule for applying patches? 3. Are patches tested before applying to productions? 4. Is the severity of the vulnerability considered during determination of the timeliness of applying the patch?	Does not have patch management process or cannot describe their patch management process = 0 Vendor can describe their patch management process = 1	Does not have patch management process or cannot provide documentation of their patch management process = 0 Can provide documentation of their patch management process & it addresses 1–2 of questions = 1 Can provide documentation of their patch management process & it addresses 3–4 of questions = 2	Does not have a patch management process or cannot demonstrate their patch management process = 0 Can demonstrate their patch management process & it addresses 1–2 of questions = 2 Can demonstrate their patch management process & it addresses 3–4 of questions = 3
	Score			

	Vulnerability	Description Criteria	Documentation Criteria	Demonstration Criteria
56	Does the vendor have a verification process for ensuring patches have been applied?	Does not have verification process or cannot describe their verification process = 0 Can describe their verification process = 1	Does not have verification process or cannot provide documentation of verification process = 0 Can provide documentation that requires verification that patches have been applied = 2	Does not have verification process or cannot demonstrate patches have been applied = 0 Can demonstrate patches have been applied = 3
	Score			

	Vulnerability	Description Criteria	Documentation Criteria	Demonstration Criteria
57	Does the vendor perform security self-assessments on a regular basis? Question to ask 1. How often does the vendor perform self-assessments?	Does not perform self-assessments or cannot describe self-assessment process = 0 Does perform self-assessments = 1	Does not perform self-assessments or cannot provide documentation of self-assessment requirement = 0 Can provide documentation requiring self-assessments to be performed less frequently than monthly = 1 Can provide documentation requiring self-assessments to be performed monthly or more frequently = 2	Does not perform self-assessments or cannot demonstrate their self-assessment process = 0 Can demonstrate self-assessments are performed & they are completed less frequently than monthly = 2 Can demonstrate self-assessments are performed & they are completed monthly or more frequently = 3
	Score			

	Vulnerability	Description Criteria	Documentation Criteria	Demonstration Criteria
58	Are self-assessment results reviewed on a regular basis?	Does not review self-assessment results or cannot describe review or self-assessment results = 0 Can describe review self-assessment results = 1	Does not review self-assessment results or cannot provide documentation of review of results = 0 Can provide documentation that requires review of self-assessment results = 2	Does not review self-assessment results or cannot demonstrate review of self-assessment results = 0 Can demonstrate review of self-assessment results = 3
	Score			

	Vulnerability	Description Criteria	Documentation Criteria	Demonstration Criteria
59	Does the vendor require sanitation of equipment and media prior to disposal?	Does not require sanitation of equipment & media prior to disposal or cannot describe sanitation process = 0 Can describe the sanitation of equipment & media prior to disposal = 1	Does not require sanitation of equipment & media prior to disposal or cannot provide documentation of sanitation = 0 Can provide documentation of sanitation of equipment & media prior to disposal = 2	Does not require sanitation of equipment & media prior to disposal or cannot demonstrate sanitation = 0 Can demonstrate sanitation of equipment & media prior to disposal = 3
	Score			

	Vulnerability	Description Criteria	Documentation Criteria	Demonstration Criteria
60	Does the vendor's security policy and process contain guidance for maintaining and monitoring a baseline configuration?	Does not have guidance for baseline configuration or cannot describe their baseline configuration = 0 Can describe their guidance for baseline configuration = 1	Does not have guidance for baseline configuration or cannot provide documentation of guidance = 0 Can provide documentation of baseline configuration = 2	Does not have guidance for baseline configuration or cannot demonstrate baseline configurations = 0 Can demonstrate baseline configuration = 3
	Score			

	Vulnerability	Description Criteria	Documentation Criteria	Demonstration Criteria
61	Does the vendor have a process in place to routinely verify baseline configuration?	Does not have process for routinely verifying baseline configuration or cannot describe process = 0 Can describe process for routinely verifying baseline configuration = 1	Does not have process for routinely verifying baseline configuration or cannot provide process documentation = 0 Can provide process documentation that requires routine verification of baseline configuration = 2	Does not have process for routinely verifying baseline configuration or cannot demonstrate the process = 0 Can demonstrate process for verifying baseline configuration = 3
	Score			

	Vulnerability	Description Criteria	Documentation Criteria	Demonstration Criteria
62	Does the vendor employ a baseline configuration tool?	Does not employ baseline configuration tool or cannot describe their baseline configuration tool = 0 Can describe employment of baseline configuration tool = 1	Does not employ baseline configuration tool or cannot provide documentation of employment of a baseline configuration tool = 0 Can provide documentation that requires using a baseline configuration tool = 2	Does not employ baseline configuration tool or cannot demonstrate employment of baseline configuration tool = 0 Can demonstrate using a baseline configuration tool = 3
	Score			

DETECTION

	Vulnerability	Description Criteria	Documentation Criteria	Demonstration Criteria
63	Does the vendor's security policy contain guidance for regularly scheduled routine security audits performed by an external party? List of items to be included 1. Operating systems 2. Web servers 3. Browser 4. Web services 5. Database 6. Network sensors 7. Firewalls 8. Applications 9. Wireless	Does not contain guidance for regularly scheduled routine security audits performed by an external party or cannot describe policy = 0 Can describe security policy & it contain guidance for regularly scheduled routine security audits performed by an external party = 1	Does not contain guidance for regularly scheduled routine security audits performed by external party or cannot provide documentation of policy = 0 Can provide a copy of security policy that requires routine security audits performed by external party but policy does not include all of listed items = 1 Can provide a copy of security policy that requires routine security audits performed by external party & policy does include all of listed items = 2	Does not contain guidance for regularly scheduled routine security audits performed by external party or cannot demonstrate policy = 0 Can demonstrate security policy that requires routine security audits performed by external party but policy includes only operating systems = 1 Can demonstrate security policy that requires routine security audits performed by external party but policy includes operating systems but not all of listed items = 2 Can demonstrate security policy that requires routine security audits performed by external party & policy includes all of listed items = 3
	Score			

	Vulnerability	Description Criteria	Documentation Criteria	Demonstration Criteria
64	Does the vendor perform verification of their perimeter router policies? Question to ask 1. How often does the vendor perform verification of their perimeter router policies?	Does not perform verification of their perimeter router policies or cannot describe verification process = 0 Can describe verification of their perimeter router policies = 1	Does not perform verification of their perimeter router policies or cannot provide documentation of verification = 0 Can provide documentation that requires performing verification of perimeter router policies less frequently than monthly = 1 Can provide documentation that requires performing verification of perimeter router policies monthly or more frequently than monthly = 2	Does not perform verification of their perimeter router policies or cannot demonstrate verification = 0 Can demonstrate verification of their perimeter router policies & verification is done less frequently than quarterly = 1 Can demonstrate verification of their perimeter router policies & verification is done quarterly or less frequently than monthly = 2 Can demonstrate verification of their perimeter router policies & verification is done monthly or more frequently than monthly = 3
	Score			

	Vulnerability	Description Criteria	Documentation Criteria	Demonstration Criteria
65	Is the vendor firewall or network sensor configured to alert for unauthorized access attempts and privilege escalation?	Firewall/network sensor is not configured to alert or cannot describe how firewall/ network sensor is configured to alert = 0 Can describe how firewall/network sensor is configured to alert for unauthorized access attempts & privilege escalation = 1	Firewall/network sensor is not configured to alert or cannot provide documentation on how firewall/ network sensor is configured to alert = 0 Can provide documentation on how firewall/ network sensor is configured to alert = 2	Firewall/network sensor is not configured to alert or cannot demonstrate how firewall/network sensor is configured to alert = 0 Can demonstrate how firewall/network sensor is configured to alert = 3
	Score			

	Vulnerability		Description Criteria	Documentation Criteria	Demonstration Criteria
66	Does the vendor routinely check that no new ports, protocols, or services are activated without approval by the configuration management board?		Does not routinely check that no PPS are activated without approval or cannot describe checking process = 0 Can describe process for routinely checking that no new PPS are activated without approval = 1	Does not routinely check that no PPS are activated without approval or cannot provide documentation of checking process = 0 Can provide documentation for routinely checking that no new PPS are activated without approval = 2	Does not routinely check that no PPS are activated without approval or cannot demonstration of checking process = 0 Can demonstrate checking that no new PPS are activated without approval = 3
		Score			

	Vulnerability		Description Criteria	Documentation Criteria	Demonstration Criteria
67	Does the vendor comply with ports, protocols, and services guidance?		Does not comply with the guidance or cannot describe how they do comply = 0 Can describe how they comply with the guidance = 1	Does not comply with the guidance or cannot provide documentation on how they do comply = 0 Can provide documentation on how they do comply = 2	Does not comply with the guidance or cannot demonstrate how they do comply = 0 Can demonstrate on how they do comply = 3
		Score			

	Vulnerability	Description Criteria	Documentation Criteria	Demonstration Criteria
68	Does the vendor's security policy require routine review of HIDs, NIDs, and firewall rules for accuracy, efficiency, and their ability to withstand new attacks? Question to ask 1. How often are reviews completed?	Does not require routine review of HIDs, NIDs & firewall rules or cannot describe policy with this requirement = 0 Can describe how they routine review HIDs, NIDs & firewall rules = 1	Does not require routine review of HIDs, NIDs & firewall rules or cannot provide policy with this requirement = 0 Can provide documentation on how they routine review HIDs, NIDs & firewall rules but review is performed less frequently than monthly = 1 Can provide documentation on how they routine review HIDs, NIDs & firewall rules but review is performed monthly or more frequently than monthly = 2	Does not require routine review of HIDs, NIDs & firewall rules or cannot demonstrate the policy with this requirement = 0 Can demonstrate how they routinely review HIDs, NIDs & firewall rules but review occurs less frequently than quarterly = 1 Can demonstrate how they routinely review HIDs, NIDs & firewall rules but review occurs quarterly or more frequently than quarterly but less frequently than monthly = 2 Can demonstrate how they routinely review HIDs, NIDs & firewall rules but review occurs monthly or more frequently than monthly = 3
	Score			

REACTION

	Vulnerability	Description Criteria	Documentation Criteria	Demonstration Criteria
69	Does the vendor have a documented Incident Response Program?	Does not have documented Incident Response Program or cannot describe Incident Response Program = 0 Can describe Incident Response Program = 1	Does not have documented Incident Response Program or cannot provide documentation of Incident Response Program = 0 Can provide documentation of the Incident Response Program = 2	Does not have documented Incident Response Program or cannot demonstrate the Incident Response Program = 0 Can demonstrate Incident Response Program = 3
	Score			

	Vulnerability	Description Criteria	Documentation Criteria	Demonstration Criteria
70	Does the vendor have a documented Incident Response policy? List of items to be included 1. Statement of management commitment 2. Purpose & objectives of policy 3. Scope of policy 4. Definition of computer incident & their consequences 5. Organizational structure 6. Roles, responsibilities & level of authority 7. Prioritization or severity rating of incident 8. Performance measures 9. Methods of secure communication 10. Reporting & contract forms	Does not have documented Incident Response policy or cannot describe Incident Response policy = 0 Can describe Incident Response policy = 1	Does not have documented Incident Response policy or Incident Response policy does not include any of listed items or cannot provide Incident Response policy = 0 Can provide Incident Response policy & it includes 1–5 of listed items = 1 Can provide Incident Response policy & it includes 6–10 of listed items = 2	Does not have documented Incident Response policy or Incident Response policy does not include any of listed items or cannot demonstrate Incident Response policy = 0 Can demonstrate Incident Response policy & it includes 1–3 of listed items = 1 Can demonstrate Incident Response policy & it includes 4–7 of listed items = 2 Can demonstrate Incident Response policy & it includes 8–10 of listed items = 3
	Score			

	Vulnerability	Description Criteria	Documentation Criteria	Demonstration Criteria
71	Does the vendor have documented Incident Response procedures? List of items to be included 1. Standard operating procedures (SOP) 2. Identification of incident 3. Reporting of incident 4. Actions to be taken 5. Containment of incident 6. Eradication of incident 7. Recovery of incident 8. Contact information a. Internal parties b. External parties 9. List of threats to guard against & respond to 10. Incident reporting forms (internal) 11. Incident reporting forms (external) 12. Equipment list 13. Checklists	Does not have documented Incident Response procedures or cannot describe Incident Response procedures = 0 Can describe Incident Response procedures = 1	Does not have documented Incident Response procedures or cannot provide documentation of Incident Response procedures = 0 Can provide Incident Response procedures & it includes 1–7 of listed items = 1 Can provide Incident Response procedures & it includes 8–15 of listed items = 2	Does not have documented Incident Response procedures or cannot demonstrate Incident Response procedures = 0 Can demonstrate Incident Response procedure & it includes 1–5 of listed items = 1 Can demonstrate Incident Response procedure & it includes 6–10 of listed items = 2 Can demonstrate Incident Response procedure & it includes 11–15 of listed items = 3
	Score			

	Vulnerability	Description Criteria	Documentation Criteria	Demonstration Criteria
72	Are the Incident Response procedures published in hard copy?	Are not published in hard copy or cannot describe requirement for publishing in hard copy = 0 Can describe requirement for Incident Response procedures to be published in hard copy = 1	Are not published in hard copy or cannot provide documentation of requirement for publishing in hard copy = 0 Can provide hard copy of the Incident Response procedures = 2	Are not published in hard copy or cannot demonstrate publishing in hard copy = 0 Can demonstrate publishing hard copy of Incident Response procedures = 3
	Score			

	Vulnerability	Description Criteria	Documentation Criteria	Demonstration Criteria
73	Are the Incident Response procedures published on the Intranet or some shared media?	Are not published on Intranet or some shared media or cannot describe requirement for publishing on Intranet or some shared media = 0 Are published on Intranet or some shared media = 1	Are not published on Intranet or some shared media or cannot provide documentation of requirement for publishing on Intranet or some shared media = 0 Can provide documentation of requirement for publishing on Intranet or some shared media = 2	Are not published on Intranet or some shared media or cannot demonstrate that procedures are published on Intranet or some shared media = 0 Can demonstrate that procedures are published on Intranet or some shared media = 3
	Score			

	Vulnerability	Description Criteria	Documentation Criteria	Demonstration Criteria
74	Is the Incident Response policy reviewed and updated on a regular basis? Question to ask 1. How often is the review updated?	Is not reviewed & updated or cannot describe process for reviewing & updating policy = 0 Can describe how policy is reviewed & updated = 1	Is not reviewed & updated or cannot describe process for reviewing & updating policy = 0 Can describe process for reviewing & updating policy & process performed less frequently than yearly = 1 Can describe process for reviewing & updating policy & process performed yearly or more frequently than yearly = 2	Is not reviewed & updated or cannot demonstrate process for reviewing & updating policy = 0 Can demonstrate process for reviewing & updating policy & process has been performed less frequently than yearly = 2 Can demonstrate process for reviewing & updating policy & process has been performed yearly or more frequently than yearly = 3
	Score			

	Vulnerability	Description Criteria	Documentation Criteria	Demonstration Criteria
75	Is initial Incident Response training provided to user community?	Is not provided to users or cannot describe the requirement for providing initial training to user = 0 Can describe their requirement for providing initial Incident Response training to user = 1	Is not provided to users or cannot provide documentation of providing initial training to user = 0 Can provide documentation of providing initial Incident Response training to user = 2	Is not provided to users or cannot demonstrate providing initial training to user = 0 Can demonstrate providing initial Incident Response training to user = 3
	Score			

	Vulnerability	Description Criteria	Documentation Criteria	Demonstration Criteria
76	Is refresher Incident Response training provided periodically to user community? Question to ask 1. How often is training provided?	Is not provided to users or cannot describe requirement for providing refresher training to user = 0 Can describe requirement for providing refresher Incident Response training to user = 1	Is not provided to users or cannot provide documentation of providing refresher training to user = 0 Can provide documentation of providing refresher Incident Response training to user & training is provided less frequently than yearly = 1 Can provide documentation of providing refresher Incident Response training to user & training is provided yearly or more frequently than yearly – 2	Is not provided to users or cannot demonstrate providing refresher training to user = 0 Can demonstrate providing refresher Incident Response training to user & training is provided less frequently than yearly = 2 Can demonstrate providing refresher Incident Response training to user & training is provided yearly or more frequently than yearly = 3
	Score			

	Vulnerability	Description Criteria	Documentation Criteria	Demonstration Criteria
77	Is there an Incident Response reporting mechanism in place? List of Items to be included 1. Who discovered the incident 2. How incident was recognized 3. Nature of incident 4. When did the incident occur 5. When was the incident detected 6. What is the impact to clients 7. Who was involved 8. What evidence was recovered 9. Where did the incident occur 10. Affected computer information 11. Why it happened 12. How it occurred 13. Team activities 14. Who was notified a. Internal b. External 15. Resolution	Does not have Incident Response reporting mechanism or cannot describe Incident Response reporting mechanism = 0 Can describe Incident Response reporting mechanism = 1	Does not have Incident Response reporting mechanism or cannot provide documentation of Incident Response reporting mechanism = 0 Can provide documentation of Incident Response reporting mechanism & it includes 1–8 of listed items = 1 Can provide documentation of Incident Response reporting mechanism & it includes 9–16 of listed items = 2	Does not have Incident Response reporting mechanism or cannot demonstrate Incident Response reporting mechanism = 0 Can demonstrate reporting mechanism & it includes 1–6 of listed items = 1 Can demonstrate reporting mechanism & it includes 7–11 of listed items = 2 Can demonstrate reporting mechanism & it includes 12–16 of listed items = 3
	Score			

	Vulnerability	Description Criteria	Documentation Criteria	Demonstration Criteria
78	Is the Incident Response reporting mechanism on a computer database, paper, or both?	Is not on database, paper, or both or cannot describe their requirement for reporting mechanism to be on database, paper, or both = 0 Can describe their requirement for reporting mechanism to be on database, paper, or both = 1	Is not on database, paper, or both or cannot provide documentation of their requirement for reporting mechanism to be on database, paper, or both = 0 Can provide documentation of reporting mechanism to be on paper only = 1 Can provide documentation of requirement for reporting mechanism to be on paper & database = 2	Is not provided to users or cannot demonstrate providing initial training to user = 0 Can demonstrate reporting mechanism to be on paper only = 1 Can demonstrate reporting mechanism to be on database only = 2 Can demonstrate reporting mechanism to be on paper & database = 3
	Score			

	Vulnerability	Description Criteria	Documentation Criteria	Demonstration Criteria
79	Are the Incident Response reports sent to management on a regular basis? Question to ask 1. How often are reports sent to management?	Are not sent to management on regular basis or cannot describe how reports are sent to management on regular basis = 0 Can describe how reports are sent to management on regular basis = 1	Are not sent to management on regular basis or cannot provide documentation of requirement for reports to be sent to management on regular basis = 0 Can provide documentation of requirement for reports to be sent to management on regular basis & reports are sent less frequently than monthly = 1 Can provide documentation of requirement for reports to be sent to management on regular basis & reports are sent monthly or more frequently than monthly = 2	Are not sent to management on regular basis or cannot demonstrate requirement for reports to be sent to management on regular basis = 0 Can demonstrate requirement for reports to be sent to management on regular basis & reports are sent yearly or less frequently than yearly = 1 Can demonstrate requirement for reports to be sent to management on regular basis & reports are sent quarterly or less frequently than quarterly but more frequently than yearly = 2 Can demonstrate requirement for reports to be sent to management on regular basis & reports are sent monthly or less frequently than monthly but more frequently than quarterly = 3
	Score			

	Vulnerability	Description Criteria	Documentation Criteria	Demonstration Criteria
80	Are the Incident Response procedures tested periodically through exercises or simulations? Question to ask 1. How often are the procedures tested?	Are not tested periodically or cannot describe how procedures are tested periodically = 0 Can describe how procedures are tested periodically = 1	Are not tested periodically or cannot provide documentation on how procedures are tested periodically = 0 Can provide documentation on how procedures are tested periodically & procedures are tested less frequently than monthly = 1 Can provide documentation on how procedures are tested periodically & procedures are tested monthly or more frequently than monthly = 2	Are not tested periodically or cannot demonstrate how procedures are tested periodically = 0 Can demonstrate how procedures are tested periodically & procedures are tested & procedures are tested yearly or less frequently than yearly = 1 Can demonstrate how procedures are tested & procedures are tested quarterly or less frequently than quarterly but more frequently than yearly = 2 Can demonstrate how procedures are tested & procedures are tested monthly or less frequently than monthly but more frequently than quarterly = 3
	Score			

	Vulnerability	Description Criteria	Documentation Criteria	Demonstration Criteria
81	Does the Incident Response Team include members from all key functional areas? List of items to be included 1. Senior management 2. Human resources/ personnel 3. Information technology/ information security 4. Technical staff members 5. Budget or finance	Does not have members from all key functional areas or cannot describe who is on the Incident Response Team = 0 Can describe who is on the Incident Response Team = 1	Does not have members from all key functional areas or cannot provide documentation for who is on team = 0 Can provide documentation of who is on the Incident Response Team & it includes 1–3 of the listed items = 1 Can provide documentation of who is on the Incident Response Team & it includes 4–5 of the listed items = 2	Does not have members from all key functional areas or cannot demonstrate who is on team = 0 Can demonstrate who is on the Incident Response Team & it includes 1–2 of the listed items = 1 Can demonstrate who is on the Incident Response Team & it includes 3–4 of the listed items = 2 Can demonstrate who is on the Incident Response Team & it includes 5 of the listed items = 3
	Score			

CONFIGURATION MANAGEMENT

	Vulnerability	Description Criteria	Documentation Criteria	Demonstration Criteria
82	Does the configuration management plan include hardware, operating system, utility software, communication, network device changes, application and facilities?	Does not exist or it does not include all of the items or cannot describe the configuration management plan = 0 Can describe the configuration management plan & it includes all of the items = 1	Does not exist or it does not include all of the items or cannot provide documentation of the configuration management plan = 0 Can provide documentation of the configuration management plan = 2	Does not exist or it does not include all of the items or cannot demonstrate the configuration management plan = 0 Can demonstrate the configuration management plan = 3
	Score			

	Vulnerability	Description Criteria	Documentation Criteria	Demonstration Criteria
83	Does the configuration management plan contain the necessary items? List of items to be included 1. Identify the configuration change 2. Contain an approval process 3. Review the configuration change 4. Schedule the configuration change 5. Track the implementation of the configuration change 6. Track system impact of the configuration change	Does not have configuration management plan or cannot describe configuration management plan = 0 Can describe configuration management plan = 1	Does not have configuration management plan or cannot provide documentation of configuration management plan = 0 Can provide documentation of configuration management plan & it includes 1–5 of listed items = 1 Can provide documentation of configuration management plan & it includes 6–11 of listed items = 2	Does not have configuration management plan or cannot demonstrate plan = 0 Can demonstrate configuration management plan & it includes 1–4 of listed items = 1 Can demonstrate configuration management plan & it includes 5–8 of listed items = 2 Can demonstrate configuration management plan & it includes 9–11 of listed items = 3

	Vulnerability	Description Criteria	Documentation Criteria	Demonstration Criteria
	7. Record & report configuration change to the appropriate party 8. Back out plan if the configuration change does not work as planned 9. Provide for minutes of the meeting 10. Emergency change procedures 11. List of team members from key functional areas			
	Score			

	Vulnerability	Description Criteria	Documentation Criteria	Demonstration Criteria
84	Is the configuration management process automated or manual?	Does not have configuration management process or cannot describe configuration management process = 0 Can describe configuration management process = 1	Does not have configuration management process or cannot provide documentation of configuration management process = 0 Can provide documentation of configuration management process & process is manual = 1 Can provide documentation of configuration management process & process is automated = 2	Does not have configuration management process or cannot demonstrate configuration management process = 0 Can demonstrate configuration management process & process is manual = 2 Can demonstrate configuration management process & process is automated = 3
	Score			

VULNERABILITY MANAGEMENT

	Vulnerability	Description Criteria	Documentation Criteria	Demonstration Criteria
85	Does the vendor's security policy contain guidance for regularly scheduled internal vulnerability audits? Question to ask 1. How often are vulnerability audits performed?	Does not require regularly scheduled internal vulnerability audits or cannot describe the requirement = 0 Can describe the requirement for regularly scheduled vulnerability audits = 1	Does not require regularly scheduled internal vulnerability audits or cannot describe the requirement = 0 Can provide documentation that requires regularly scheduled internal vulnerability audits & audits are performed less frequently than monthly = 1 Can provide documentation that requires regularly scheduled internal vulnerability audits & audits are performed monthly or more frequently than monthly = 2	Does not require regularly scheduled internal vulnerability audits or cannot describe the requirement = 0 Can demonstrate requirement for regularly scheduled vulnerability audits & audits are performed yearly or less frequently than yearly = 1 Can demonstrate requirement for regularly scheduled vulnerability audits & audits are performed quarterly or less frequently than quarterly but more frequently than yearly = 2 Can demonstrate requirement for regularly scheduled vulnerability audits & audits are performed monthly or less frequently than monthly but more frequently than quarterly = 3
	Score			

	Vulnerability	Description Criteria	Documentation Criteria	Demonstration Criteria
86	Does the vendor utilize a network vulnerability scanner? Question to ask 1. How often is the network scanned?	Does not utilize network vulnerability scanner or cannot describe how their scanner is used = 0 Can describe how their scanner is used = 1	Does not utilize network vulnerability scanner or cannot provide documentation of how their scanner is used = 0 Can provide documentation of how their scanner is used & scans are performed less frequently than monthly = 1 Can provide documentation of how their scanner is used & scans are performed monthly or more frequently than monthly = 2	Does not utilize network vulnerability scanner or cannot demonstrate how their scanner is used = 0 Can demonstrate how their scanner is used & scans are performed yearly or less frequently than yearly = 1 Can demonstrate how their scanner is used & scans are performed quarterly or less frequently than quarterly but more frequently than yearly = 2 Can demonstrate how their scanner is used & scans are performed monthly or less frequently than monthly but more frequently than quarterly = 3
	Score			

	Vulnerability	Description Criteria	Documentation Criteria	Demonstration Criteria
87	Are the results of the network vulnerability scans sent to management on a regular basis?	Are not sent to management or cannot describe the requirement for network vulnerability scan results to be sent to management = 0 Can describe the requirement for network vulnerability scan results to be sent to management = 1	Are not sent to management or cannot provide documentation of the requirement for network vulnerability scan results to be sent to management = 0 Can provide documentation of the requirement for network vulnerability scan results to be sent to management = 2	Are not sent to management or cannot demonstrate the requirement for network vulnerability scan results to be sent to management = 0 Can demonstrate network vulnerability scan results to be sent to management = 3
	Score			

	Vulnerability	Description Criteria	Documentation Criteria	Demonstration Criteria
88	Is there a process in place to regularly correct discovered vulnerabilities and configuration discrepancies?	Does not have process to correct discovered vulnerabilities & configuration discrepancies or cannot describe the process to correct discovered vulnerabilities & configuration discrepancies = 0 Can describe process to correct discovered vulnerabilities & configuration discrepancies = 1	Does not have process to correct discovered vulnerabilities & configuration discrepancies or cannot provide documentation of process to correct discovered vulnerabilities & configuration discrepancies = 0 Can provide documentation of process to correct discovered vulnerabilities & configuration discrepancies = 2	Does not have process to correct discovered vulnerabilities & configuration discrepancies or cannot demonstrate process to correct discovered vulnerabilities & configuration discrepancies = 0 Can demonstrate process to correct discovered vulnerabilities & configuration discrepancies = 3
	Score			

	Vulnerability	Description Criteria	Documentation Criteria	Demonstration Criteria
89	Does the vendor have a verification process for ensuring vulnerabilities and configuration discrepancies have been corrected?	Does not have process for ensuring vulnerabilities & configuration discrepancies have been corrected or cannot describe correction process = 0 Can describe the vulnerability & configuration discrepancy correction process = 1	Does not have process for ensuring vulnerabilities & configuration discrepancies have been corrected or cannot provide documentation of correction process = 0 Can provide documentation of the correction process = 2	Does not have process for ensuring vulnerabilities & configuration discrepancies have been corrected or cannot demonstrate correction process = 0 Can demonstrate corrections have been made = 3
	Score			

	Vulnerability	Description Criteria	Documentation Criteria	Demonstration Criteria
90	Does the vendor routinely run a port scanning tool to ensure no new or unexpected ports, protocols, or services are discovered? Question to ask 1. How often are ports scanned?	Does not utilize port scanner to ensure no new or unexpected PPS are discovered or cannot describe how their scanner is used = 0 Can describe how their scanner is used = 1	Does not utilize port scanner to ensure no new or unexpected PPS are discovered or cannot provide documentation of requirement to use a port scanner = 0 Can provide documentation of requirement to use port scanner & scans are performed less frequently than monthly = 1 Can provide documentation of requirement to use port scanner & scans are performed monthly or more frequently than monthly = 2	Does not utilize port scanner to ensure no new or unexpected PPS are discovered or cannot demonstrate how their scanner is used = 0 Can demonstrate how their scanner is used & scans are performed yearly or less frequently than yearly = 1 Can demonstrate how their scanner is used & scans are performed quarterly or less frequently than quarterly but more frequently than yearly = 2 Can demonstrate how their scanner is used & scans are performed monthly or less frequently than monthly but more frequently than quarterly = 3
	Score			

	Vulnerability		Description Criteria	Documentation Criteria	Demonstration Criteria
91	Is the vendor's application compliant with the Ports, Protocols, and Services CAL?		Is not compliant with the CAL or cannot describe how they are compliant = 0 Can describe how they are compliant with the PPS CAL = 1	Is not compliant with PPS CAL or cannot describe how they are compliant = 0 Can provide documentation of compliancy with the PPS CAL = 2	Is not compliant with PPS CAL or cannot describe how they are compliant = 0 Can demonstrate they are compliant with the PPS CAL = 3
		Score			

	Vulnerability		Description Criteria	Documentation Criteria	Demonstration Criteria
92	Are the results of the port scans sent to management on a regular basis?		Are not sent to management or cannot describe requirement for ports scan results to be sent to management = 0 Can describe requirement for port scan results to be sent to management = 1	Are not sent to management or cannot provide documentation of the requirement for port scan results to be sent to management = 0 Can provide documentation of the requirement for port scan results to be sent to management = 2	Are not sent to management or cannot demonstrate requirement for port scan results to be sent to management = 0 Can demonstrate port scan results to be sent to management = 3
		Score			

	Vulnerability		Description Criteria	Documentation Criteria	Demonstration Criteria
93	What ports, protocols, and services are necessary for access to the application from outside the local enclave?		List of ports, protocols and services is not available = 0 List of ports, protocols and services is available = 1	Ports, protocols, and services not documented = 0 Ports, protocols and services are documented = 2	Cannot demonstrate security aspects of access from outside the local enclave = 0 Can demonstrate security aspects of access from outside the local enclave = 2
		Score			

	Vulnerability	Description Criteria	Documentation Criteria	Demonstration Criteria
94	Does the vendor routinely run a web-scanning tool to check for new web vulnerabilities?	Does not utilize web scanner to check for new web vulnerabilities or cannot describe how their web scanner is used = 0 Can describe how their web scanner is used = 1	Does not utilize web scanner to check for new web vulnerabilities or cannot provide documentation of requirement to scan web = 0 Can provide documentation of requirement to scan web & scans are performed less frequently than monthly = 1 Can provide documentation of requirement to scan web & scans are performed monthly or more frequently than monthly = 2	Does not utilize web scanner to check for new web vulnerabilities or cannot demonstrate how their web scanner is used = 0 Can demonstrate how their web scanner is used & scans are performed yearly or less frequently than yearly = 1 Can demonstrate how their web scanner is used & scans are performed quarterly or less frequently than quarterly but more frequently than yearly = 2 Can demonstrate how their web scanner is used & scans are performed monthly or less frequently than monthly but more frequently than quarterly = 3
	Score			

	Vulnerability	Description Criteria	Documentation Criteria	Demonstration Criteria
95	Are the results of the web scans sent to management on a regular basis?	Are not sent to management or cannot describe requirement for web scan results to be sent to management = 0 Can describe the requirement for web scan results to be sent to management = 1	Are not sent to management or cannot provide documentation of requirement for web scan results to be sent to management = 0 Can provide documentation of requirement for web scan results to be sent to management = 2	Are not sent to management or cannot demonstrate requirement for web scan results to be sent to management = 0 Can demonstrate web scan results are sent to management = 3
	Score			

	Vulnerability	Description Criteria	Documentation Criteria	Demonstration Criteria
96	Does the vendor routinely run a password checking tool?	Does not utilize password checking tool or cannot describe how their password checking tool works = 0 Can describe how their password checking tool works = 3	Does not utilize password checking tool or cannot provide documentation of requirement for tool = 0 Can provide documentation of requirement for password checking tool & it is run monthly or more frequently than monthly or they are using PKI = 3	Does not utilize password checking tool or cannot demonstrate how their password checking tool works = 0 Can demonstrate how their password checking tool works & it is run monthly or more frequently than monthly or they are using PKI = 3
	Score			

	Vulnerability	Description Criteria	Documentation Criteria	Demonstration Criteria
97	Are the results of the password checking tool sent to management on a regular basis?	Are not sent to management or cannot describe requirement for password checking results to be sent to management = 0 Can describe requirement for password checking results to be sent to management = 1	Are not sent to management or cannot provide documentation of requirement for password checking results to be sent to management = 0 Can provide documentation of requirement for password checking results to be sent to management = 2	Are not sent to management or cannot demonstrate requirement for password checking results to be sent to management = 0 Can demonstrate password checking results are sent to management = 3
	Score			

	Vulnerability	Description Criteria	Documentation Criteria	Demonstration Criteria
98	Does the vendor subscribe to the applicable vendor's security notification sites for the latest security vulnerabilities' notifications?	Does not subscribe to security notification sites or cannot describe requirement for subscribing to security notification sites = 0 Can describe requirement for subscribing to security notification sites = 1	Does not subscribe to security notification sites or cannot provide documentation of requirement for subscribing to security notification sites = 0 Can provide documentation of requirement for subscribing to security notification sites = 2	Does not subscribe to security notification sites or cannot demonstrate they have subscribed to security notification sites = 0 Can demonstrate they have subscribed to security notification sites = 3
	Score			

PERSONNEL SECURITY

	Vulnerability	Description Criteria	Documentation Criteria	Demonstration Criteria
99	Does the vendor have a documented requirement for a background security investigation? Question to ask 1. What type of background security investigation is required?	Does not have requirement for background security investigation or cannot describe their background security investigation = 0 Can describe their background security investigation = 1	Does not have requirement for background security investigation or cannot provide documentation of requirement for background security investigation = 0 Can provide documentation of the requirement for background security investigation = 1	Does not have background security investigation or cannot demonstrate background security investigation has been done = 0 Can demonstrate background security investigation has been done = 1
	Score			

	Vulnerability	Description Criteria	Documentation Criteria	Demonstration Criteria
100	Does the vendor perform background security investigations on a regular basis? Question to ask 1. How frequently are background investigations performed?	Does not have background security investigation or cannot describe their background security investigation = 0 Can describe their background security investigation = 1	Does not have background security investigation or cannot provide copy of background security investigation = 0 Can provide documentation of background security investigation & investigation is performed less frequently than every 5 years = 1 Can provide documentation of background security investigation & investigation is performed every 5 years or more frequently than every 5 years = 2	Does not have background security investigation or cannot demonstrate background investigation has been done = 0 Can demonstrate security investigation has been done & investigation is performed less frequently than every 5 years = 2 Can demonstrate security investigation has been done & investigation is performed every 5 years or more frequently than every 5 years = 3
	Score			

	Vulnerability		Description Criteria	Documentation Criteria	Demonstration Criteria
101	Can the vendor prove they perform background security investigations? Thing to consider 1. Is having a clearance a requirement in the Statement of Work?		Cannot prove they do background investigations = 0 Can prove they do background investigations = 2	NA	NA
		Score			

	Vulnerability		Description Criteria	Documentation Criteria	Demonstration Criteria
102	Does the vendor's background security investigation include pertinent areas? List of items to be included 1. Does the hiring process restrict hiring a convicted felon? 2. Does the investigation cover participation or membership of subversive activities or groups? 3. Does the investigation research the credit background of the potential employee? 4. Does the hiring process require a drug screening test?		Does not require background security investigation or they cannot describe their background investigation = 0 Can describe their background investigation = 1	Does not require background security investigation or they cannot provide documentation of their background investigation = 0 Can provide documentation of their background investigation & it includes 1–2 of listed items = 1 Can provide documentation of their background investigation & it includes 3–4 of listed items = 2	Does not require background security investigation or they cannot demonstrate their background investigation = 0 Can demonstrate their background investigation & it includes 1–2 of listed items = 1 Can demonstrate their background investigation & it includes 3 of listed items = 2 Can demonstrate their background investigation & it includes 4 of listed items = 3
		Score			

	Vulnerability	Description Criteria	Documentation Criteria	Demonstration Criteria
103	Are vendor personnel subject to a background check? List of items to be included 1. System administrators 2. Help desk 3. Administrative personnel 4. Management 5. Janitorial staff	Are not subject to background check or cannot describe their background check = 0 Can describe their background check = 1	Are not subject to background check or cannot provide documentation of their background check = 0 Can provide documentation of their background check & system administrators & help desk are subject to background check = 1 Can provide documentation of their background check & all 5 of listed items are subject to background check = 2	Are not subject to background check or cannot demonstrate their background check = 0 Can demonstrate their background check & system administrators & help desk are subject to background check = 1 Can demonstrate their background check & system administrators, help desk & management are subject to background check = 2 Can demonstrate their background check & all 5 of listed items are subject to background check = 3
	Score			

	Vulnerability	Description Criteria	Documentation Criteria	Demonstration Criteria
104	Does the personnel assigned to doing background checks have a security clearance?	Do not have security clearance or vendor cannot describe requirement for these personnel to have clearance = 0 Can describe requirement for these personnel to have clearance = 1	Do not have security clearance or vendor cannot provide documentation of requirement for these personnel to have clearance = 0 Can provide documentation of requirement for these personnel to have clearance = 2	Do not have security clearance or vendor cannot demonstrate requirement for these personnel to have clearance = 0 Can demonstrate these personnel to have clearance = 3
	Score			

PHYSICAL SECURITY

	Vulnerability		Description Criteria	Documentation Criteria	Demonstration Criteria
105	Does the vendor have a documented requirement for a background security investigation? Question to ask 1. What type of background security investigation is required?		Does not have requirement for background security investigation or cannot describe their background security investigation = 0 Can describe their background security investigation = 1	Does not have requirement for background security investigation or cannot provide documentation of requirement for background security investigation = 0 Can provide documentation of the requirement for background security investigation = 1	Does not have background security investigation or cannot demonstrate background security investigation has been done = 0 Can demonstrate background security investigation has been done = 1
		Score			

	Vulnerability		Description Criteria	Documentation Criteria	Demonstration Criteria
106	Does the vendor perform background security investigations on a regular basis? Question to ask 1. How frequently are background investigation performed?		Does not have background security investigation or cannot describe their background security investigation = 0 Can describe their background security investigation = 1	Does not have background security investigation or cannot provide copy of background security investigation = 0 Can provide documentation of background security investigation & investigation is performed less frequently than every 5 years = 1 Can provide documentation of background security investigation & investigation is performed every 5 years or more frequently than every 5 years = 2	Does not have background security investigation or cannot demonstrate background investigation has been done = 0 Can demonstrate security investigation has been done & investigation is performed less frequently than every 5 years = 2 Can demonstrate security investigation has been done & investigation is performed every 5 years or more frequently than every 5 years = 3
		Score			

	Vulnerability	Description Criteria	Documentation Criteria	Demonstration Criteria
107	Can the vendor prove they perform background security investigations? Thing to consider 1. Is having a clearance a requirement in the Statement of Work?	Cannot prove they do background investigations = 0 Can prove they do background investigations = 2	NA	NA
	Score			

	Vulnerability	Description Criteria	Documentation Criteria	Demonstration Criteria
108	Does the vendor's background security investigation include pertinent areas? List of items to be included 1. Does the hiring process restrict hiring a convicted felon? 2. Does the investigation cover participation or membership of subversive activities or groups? 3. Does the investigation research the credit background of the potential employee? 4. Does the hiring process require a drug screening test?	Does not require background security investigation or they cannot describe their background investigation = 0 Can describe their background investigation = 1	Does not require background security investigation or they cannot provide documentation of their background investigation = 0 Can provide documentation of their background investigation & it includes 1–2 of listed items = 1 Can provide documentation of their background investigation & it includes 3–4 of listed items = 2	Does not require background security investigation or they cannot demonstrate their background investigation = 0 Can demonstrate their background investigation & it includes 1–2 of listed items = 1 Can demonstrate their background investigation & it includes 3 of listed items = 2 Can demonstrate their background investigation & it includes 4 of listed items = 3
	Score			

	Vulnerability		Description Criteria	Documentation Criteria	Demonstration Criteria
109	Are vendor personnel subject to a background check? List of items to be included 1. System administrators 2. Help desk 3. Administrative personnel 4. Management 5. Janitorial staff		Are not subject to background check or cannot describe their background check = 0 Can describe their background check = 1	Are not subject to background check or cannot provide documentation of their background check = 0 Can provide documentation of their background check & system administrators & help desk are subject to background check = 1 Can provide documentation of their background check & all 5 of listed items are subject to background check = 2	Are not subject to background check or cannot demonstrate their background check = 0 Can demonstrate their background check & system administrators & help desk are subject to background check = 1 Can demonstrate their background check & system administrators, help desk & management are subject to background check = 2 Can demonstrate their background check & all 5 of listed items are subject to background check = 3
		Score			

	Vulnerability		Description Criteria	Documentation Criteria	Demonstration Criteria
110	Does the personnel assigned to doing background checks have a security clearance?		Do not have security clearance or vendor cannot describe requirement for these personnel to have clearance = 0 Can describe requirement for these personnel to have clearance = 1	Do not have security clearance or vendor cannot provide documentation of requirement for these personnel to have clearance = 0 Can provide documentation of requirement for these personnel to have clearance = 2	Do not have security clearance or vendor cannot demonstrate requirement for these personnel to have clearance = 0 Can demonstrate these personnel to have clearance = 3
		Score			

SECURITY AWARENESS AND TRAINING

	Vulnerability	Description Criteria	Documentation Criteria	Demonstration Criteria
111	Do employees receive general security training? Questions to ask 1. Are training materials made available? 2. Is initial & annual training given & documented?	Does not have general security training or cannot describe their general security training = 0 Can describe their general security training = 1	Does not have general security training or cannot provide documentation of their general security training = 0 Can provide documentation of their general security training but it is only training material made available = 1 Can provide documentation of their general security training & it includes initial & annual training & the training is documented = 2	Does not have general security training or cannot demonstrate their general security training = 0 Can demonstrate their general security training but it is only training material made available = 2 Can demonstrate their general security training & it includes initial & annual training & the training is documented = 3
	Score			

	Vulnerability	Description Criteria	Documentation Criteria	Demonstration Criteria
112	Do privileged users receive additional security training specific to their duties? Questions to ask 1. Are privileged users given additional training? 2. Do system administrators, security personnel & other privileged users required to be certified?	Do not receive additional security training or cannot describe privileged users' additional training = 0 Can describe privileged users' additional training = 1	Do not receive additional security training or cannot provide documentation of privileged users' additional training = 0 Can provide documentation of privileged users' additional training = 1 Can provide documentation of system administrators, security personnel & privileged users' additional training = 2	Does not have general security training or cannot demonstrate their general security training = 0 Can demonstrate privileged users' additional training = 2 Can demonstrate system administrators, security personnel & privileged users' additional training = 3
	Score			

Index

N

Q

R

S

T

U